INITIATED

"Init *ed* is breathtaking—gorgeously written, fierce, political, personal and deeply inspiring. I love this book."

—MICHELLE TEA, author of *Modern Tarot*

" world desperately in need of re-enchantment, *Initiated* provides ore than its fair share. It is a battle cry, a blueprint, and most of all love letter to the traditions of witchcraft, the benefits of co-creat and interdependence, and our innate ability to manifest our colle ve power as women and humans."

—LEAH DIETERICH, author of *The Vanishing Twins*

"As ch as witches are warriors, we are also guardians—of a history, lture, and practice that's been erased and persecuted for mille ia. Recently, I've been hoping for a visibility that cannot divo witchcraft from its insurrectionary origins, its lineage of liber on, its blood memory that connects us to its feminist fire. As I *ated* luminously testifies, Amanda Yates Garcia is the kind of w ior *and* guardian witches need: subversive and scholarly, empow d and devoted, a magician and a firebrand."

—JOHANNA HEDVA, author of *On Hell*

"To ad *Initiated* is to undergo your own. Somewhere between a memoir and a grimoire, this book invites the reader to reflect on their own cycles of life and death as well as their own relationship to the witch. All in a way that's uplifting, engaging, feminist as fuck, and so unapologetically fierce." —GABRIELA HERSTIK, author of *Inner Witch: A Modern Guide to the Ancient Craft*

"I see Amanda Yates Garcia realizing a kind of magic choreography here: reaching back through millennia; dragging forth darkness by the handful; recalling ancient women misremembered, denied, hounded, and destroyed; holding the pain of misogyny and changing it with intention, into light."

—GRACE KRILANOVICH, author of *The Orange Eats Creeps*

"With oppressive regimes and violence against the planet and our people at our every turn, Amanda Yates Garcia's *Initiated* peers within the abyss, creating magic and meaning despite—and as a reaction toward—the darkness. In these pages, a battle cry. A mythic celebration of inner power. And a meditation on healing and justice." —LISA MARIE BASILE, author of *Wordcraft Witchery* and *Light Magic for Dark Times*

"*Initiated* is a page-turning word orgasm of flowering language. It's a reexamination of patriarchal hierarchy, embracing fierce feminine energy that crackles with the transformative excitement of giving birth to one's self, standing in our own power, and releasing old narratives that have held us back."

—NIKKI DARLING, author of *Fade Into You*

"*Initiated* is a stunning act of generosity from a fearless and wise spirit guide. Amanda Yates Garcia has cracked open her life—the brutal lessons, the romantic entanglements, the yearning to be a force of love—to empower all of us to write our own magic myth into the sky." —MARGARET WAPPLER, author of *Neon Green*

INITIATED

Memoir of a Witch

AMANDA YATES GARCIA

sphere

SPHERE

First published in the United States in 2019 by Grand Central Publishing
First published in Great Britain in 2019 by Sphere

1 3 5 7 9 10 8 6 4 2

A CIP catalogue record for this book is available from the British Library.

ISBN 978-0-7515-7455-5

Printed and bound in Great Britain by Clays Ltd, Elcograf S.p.A

Papers used by Sphere are from well-managed forests and other responsible sources.

FSC
www.fsc.org

MIX
Paper from
responsible sources
FSC® C104740

Sphere
An imprint of
Little, Brown Book Group
Carmelite House
50 Victoria Embankment
London EC4Y 0DZ

An Hachette UK Company
www.hachette.co.uk

www.littlebrown.co.uk

*For my mother, for the Mother, for all my
witch sisters, brothers, and cousins across the world,
for all our ancestors going back in deep time:
healers, seers, lovers, artists, oracles, inventors, wise ones...
I see you, I love you, I honor you.*

Caveats

ℭ   ℭ   ℭ

This book is an alchemical mixture of memoir, mythology, manifesto, theory, visions, and dreams. As in dreams, sometimes it was necessary to bend time, make grand leaps between events. I had to keep some stories in my Book of Shadows, to be told another time. Sometimes mythological figures that may be familiar to you surface here in unorthodox forms. All this is to be expected in a book written by a witch. As unconventional, unorthodox, and alchemical as these stories may be, they are also true.

For behold, I have been with you from the beginning and I am That which is attained at the end of desire.

> Doreen Valiente, as adapted by Starhawk,
> "The Charge of the Star Goddess"

Now, I—woman am going to blow up the Law: an explosion henceforth possible and ineluctable; let it be done, right now, in language.

> Hélène Cixous, "The Laugh of the Medusa"

Prologue

ᚳ   ᚳ   ᚳ

when you are in your trouble
and turn from death
this is what to do
find the meeting place:
intersectionality
under stars
way to gnosis
saying this is the place
this is indeed the place
with many layers
lie down here...

Anne Waldman, *Trickster Feminism*

Search for the three stars that make up the belt of Orion. I squinted through the starlight, tracing my finger along a line of instructions I'd written in my Book of Shadows, the place where witches inscribe their favorite spells. Alone at a crossroads deep in the Mojave Desert, it was to the constellation of Orion that I was to address my invocation. Into the night I chanted,

"AŌTH ABRAŌTH BASYM ISAK SABAŌTH IAŌ." Hot wind seared up from the borderlands near Mexico. My candles in their safety glass sputtered and died. I clamped down on the pages of my notebook lest they vanish into the spectral scrub surrounding me on all sides.

I was in the desert to perform the Headless Rite, an arcane piece of ceremonial magic where you declare yourself divine. You call down the goddess Isis to enter you; you speak in her voice: *I am the one who makes the lightning flash and the thunder roll; I am the one whose sweat falls upon the earth as rain so that life can begin.* I was there because I didn't want to, because I could not, play by the rules of the status quo anymore. I was done. Done capitulating. The Headless Rite was to be the last in a series of magical initiations I saw myself as having begun at birth.

Barefoot and virtually naked, the sheer cotton dress I used during my solitary rituals snapped around my legs like wolves in the dark. I stood inside a towering cove of red rocks, each a million years old and warm to the touch, still radiating the sun's heat at midnight. Spiny fields of jumping cactus, luminous in the starlight, formed a sea around me, waiting to leap out and pierce my bare legs with their thorns. It was dangerous land. Rattlesnakes, coyotes skulking through the creosote brambles. But I was mostly worried about the desert dwellers: macho, meth-addled young men in their monster trucks, out there somewhere guzzling 40s, howling their bloodlust into the desert void.

Like most women and femmes, witches are familiar with the demons of patriarchy. They follow us everywhere. Even out in the desert wilderness, we can't be alone in our rites. The shadow of

2

violence falls unbidden, and for many of us, just the threat of it, the lifetime of warnings to be careful, the accumulation of micro and macro assaults, are enough to keep us home, "safe" under the protective aegis of the patriarchal father gods. Every time I saw headlights advancing along the horizon or heard the low growl of a motorcycle bounce off the canyon walls, I fought the urge to run and hide. But I would not be chased from my magic by bad boy bros who thought they owned the world. I was there on principle. I was there out of a commitment to create the kind of world I wanted to live in. A world where witches raise power in the desert. A world where a woman could chant hymns to the Goddess miles away from civilization without worrying that she might be attacked. So I chanted my incantations and spattered my libations into the red earth. And tried not to think about how I'd never had to test my magic against men who, should they appear, I felt sure would have guns.

I've always made it a policy to do things that scare me.

An initiation is a beginning, a rite of passage, a ceremony that signals an advance of some kind, into adulthood or a new form of knowledge. During my ceremonial initiation into witchcraft on my thirteenth birthday, my mother and I sat with a skein of red cord binding my wrist to hers inside a circle of mothers and daughters from our community. Called the Rite of Roses for the rose wands our mothers brushed against our dewy young cheeks, this was the ceremony for the adolescent witches of my coven as we dedicated our lives to the Goddess, and to each other. Lit by the glow of red candles, bouquets of roses festooned with ferns and puffs of baby's breath perfumed our living room. Women and girls warmed the room like coals; we were there to celebrate our blood, that life force that passes through our veins, throbbing its way back to the beginning of all life on earth, carrying us forward into the unknown future we must create for ourselves. That night, we chanted the names of our matrilineal ancestors, beginning as far back into the historical mist as we could reach. When we finally spoke my mother's name, and then mine, we used a pair of scissors as an athame—a ceremonial knife—to cut the red umbilicus that bound us together. I was now my own woman, a free agent. To celebrate, we took a walk through an overgrown suburban park, the full moon transmuting my girlfriends and me into silhouettes as we skipped ahead, giggling, through the weeds. It was an initiation in name only; I was still just a girl. And my life was about to explode.

Since then I've learned that more than any formal initiation ceremony given to you by an authority, your true initiation process is the one Life creates just for you. Your life initiates you to the work that only you can do. You don't need to be born to a witch mother or receive an initiation from a high priestess to become a witch; you just need to pay attention to the lessons the Goddess is teaching you through your own experiences, and then rise up and take action.

Furthermore, witchcraft isn't just for women. It's for men, and trans folx, and fairy creatures and animal spirits and anything in between. You don't need to menstruate or have a uterus to be a witch. You can find your power in being whoever you are. However, throughout this book, I refer to witches as "she," because that's my pronoun, and also because this book is a love letter to

4

the femmes of the world. If you're not a femme, this book is still for you. Any lover of the Goddess is welcome here, and even those who are just "questioning."

In his book *Rites and Symbols of Initiation*, anthropologist Mircea Eliade says that puberty initiations usually begin with an act of rupture. The child is separated from her mother. Persephone is dragged down to Hades. A brutal process. Yet in Ancient Greece, the Eleusinian Mysteries were rites of initiation almost everyone chose to perform. Initiates were sworn to secrecy, killed if they ever spoke or wrote of their experience. In the fourth century CE, Christian invaders came from the north. They tore down the temple at Eleusis, ground the remains into dust, and built their churches on the rubble. Hardly any record remains of the Eleusinian mysteries. But we do know they were in honor of Demeter, Goddess of the Harvest, and Persephone, her maiden daughter who was abducted to hell by the Lord of the Underworld, where she was forced to be his "bride."

Ready or not, our traumas drag us into the underworld, initiating us, often unwillingly, into the mysteries of sex and death and, eventually, hopefully, if we're lucky—rebirth. The latter only if somehow, by our wiles, we manage to escape the underworld labyrinth. And if we don't, if we fail to master our initiations, we stay there, trapped, undead shades, our bones crushed beneath the temples of the oppressor.

Left to their own devices, most teenage girls are natural witches, and I was no exception. I played fortune-telling games with folded

5

paper and contacted spirits with Ouija boards. I let the spirit of the Lover possess me as I made out with my friends. At slumber parties we used rhythmic chants to lift each other to the ceiling with our pinky fingers. We wore mood rings and ankhs and vials of blood around our necks. The world was once an enchanted place for me and my little coven of teenage witches. But even though my mother was a witch, even though I was initiated into witchcraft before I even completed my first year of high school, it never occurred to me that I could *be* a witch. That witchcraft could be my profession. And in our world, unless you have a trust fund, you have to have a profession. You have to work. It's a moral imperative. And by the accounts of virtually every adult in my life, that meant you had to be miserable. Eight hours a day, sometimes more, five days a week, sometimes more, until you retired, sick and exhausted. That was what my elementary school education was training me to do and what the world expected of me. And by the time I'd skidded into my thirties, I'd tried almost every job a young woman could think of, and each one was miserable in its own special way. Yet, through it all, I resisted the imperatives of capitalist patriarchy. My goal was to avoid playing by the rules of a status quo that had actively sought to disempower me, keep me small, and utilize my labor to amass ungoddessly resources for itself. You might say that I wanted to witch the system. But every time I thought I'd found a way to escape, I always seemed to find myself back in the same place: the underworld.

By the time I was in the desert conducting the Headless Rite, it was deep summer, I'd been supporting myself as a witch for several years, and I felt more liberated and empowered than ever. In the months after my desert rite, every time I tuned in, I heard the Goddess asking me to come out of the broom closet in a big way, to stake a claim for us witches. She told me that now was not the time when the wild womxn of the world could afford to stand on decorum. It was time that we activated. It was time that we sought to inspire others. Even if we worried that we'd be laughed at or get death threats. Even if we were afraid it would be a waste of our time, that we'd lose, be judged, or get it wrong. By Her grace, I found myself holding rituals at art museums, interviewed by the *LA Times*, arguing politics with conservative pundits on Fox News. Mixed in with the threats of rape and beheading that I received after these appearances were hundreds of emails from people thanking me for pointing their path toward witchcraft. In the lectures I gave on witchcraft at universities, students, especially the young women, would line up, eyes hungry and shining as they gripped their binders, asking for ways they could start practicing at home. Witchcraft is an act of healing and an act of resistance. Declaring oneself a witch, practicing magic, has everything to do with claiming authority and power for oneself. Life itself initiates each of us according to our own peculiar stories. Our stories lead us toward our purpose in this world. Each initiation strips something away and gives us a gift. If we want to meet our full form, we are obligated to give that gift to the world.

I write this book because I know you, dear witches, I see you, wherever you are, pulling like a demon horse against the bridle this patriarchal world has put on you. We are allies; we are each other's guardians. And just as I hope for this book to help you, your presence—just the knowledge that you exist—helps me to keep going myself, to flesh out my world, to make it sacred. I see you, surrounded by stones, a pleasure-seeking beast with *resistance* tattooed across your chest. I see you, face turned up to the moon, fists full of desert flowers. You, untamable creature, barefoot and slipping into trances. Weaving the voices of the wilderness into your songs. The seeds that drip from your fingers will regenerate the earth. All acts of love and pleasure are your rituals. You are an initiate of the Goddess of Love, even if you don't know it yet. Take heart, dear witch, because by the end of this book, you will.

Chapter 1

c c c

FAMILIARS

For many people, ordinary life itself is already a more or less unconscious process of initiation through the fire trial...

Rudolf Steiner, *How to Know Higher Worlds*

My mother's body resisted letting me come into this world; she knew the brutal way witches are treated here. One thousand years ago, my mother would have leaned into the arms of her midwives, chanting hymns to Hecate and baptizing me in a bath of mugwort tea. Ten thousand years ago, I'd have sprung into being from a peat bog, guarded by stags, under the silver light of a waning moon. As it was, I came into the world at a teaching hospital near Sacramento, under a glare of fluorescent lights, flocked by a panic of medical students still reeking of last night's kegger. They were unprepared for such a difficult birth.

Only twenty-three years old, but already well acquainted with the corrupting influence of the material world, my mother's body wanted to keep me inside where I'd be safe. Her cervix wouldn't dilate. But I insisted on making it here. I insisted on freedom. I kicked and clawed from her watery world like a reptile, until my umbilical cord tangled around my neck. I was turned the wrong way around. When my mother's water broke, it was black; I was more Goth at birth than I ever was in my teenage years. My mother remembers being rushed on a gurney down the halls of the hospital. Flashing lights, a tube in her arm. The lightning zigzag monitoring my heart rate sagged to a flat line. One minute, two minutes, three minutes, five; my heart was still. The Goddess of the netherworld had claimed me for her own.

I died before I was born. I saw the face of the Goddess. Witches have many goddesses and Hecate is primary among them. As Guardian of the Crossroads, Hecate is a sorceress; she knows the secrets of the herbs and can speak to the dead. As Queen of Witches, she is a traveler between the worlds. She leaps through hell, a black dog by her side. She soars into the future, into the past, into the body and beyond riding on the black wings of a crow. It was Hecate I saw in my mother's womb as I was struggling to breathe. Near-death experiences pull you into witchcraft. The Goddess pulls you under, and there you see Her face, and you know you are not alone in this world. You are a child of nature, and She will never leave you.

My mother had seen Hecate too, on Mother's Day, five years before I was born, when she was eighteen years old. She was inner-tubing with her friends on the American River. At some point she slipped, caught in the boiling froth, the rapids pulling her downriver, away from her friends who called out and reached for her to no avail. Trapped beneath a stone, she struggled upward for breath, panicked and hit her elbow on a rock, then gasped. Water flooded her lungs. Everything started moving in slow motion. Green light called her through a long spiraling tunnel. When she emerged, the Goddess was all around her. She could see 360 degrees in all directions, the face of the Goddess: Earth! Bright and shining. Drifting peacefully in the atmosphere of our world, my mother was still herself, but expanded somehow. Soon she noticed a group of people below gathered around a pale and lifeless woman, beside whom a man crouched, pounding on the woman's ribs. My mother didn't care. The world around her shone, a breathing, living planet awash with light. Still, she descended, closer and closer, until she was nose to nose with the lifeless body beneath her. Then she felt a yank. Jerked back into her body as if by rope, her first feeling was outrage that she'd been forced to return. She didn't want to be back in the human realm of violence and treachery. But come back she must; she had more work to do in this world.

When I was born, after my mother awoke, she thought I was dead. Alone in the hospital room, her belly had been hacked open and sewn shut with black wires. Finally, the nurse appeared and dropped me in her arms. People tell her there is no way this could've happened, but my mother swears when I first opened my eyes, I smiled. Having already died before I was born, I was grateful just to be in this strange and beautiful world, to enter conversation with its beauty through the rituals of witchcraft.

My mother says that during my birth, my father was at the bar across the street turning a violent shade of drunk. My father counters that he was in the waiting room of the hospital, crying and terrified we'd both died. Either way, six months after I was born, my mother hatched a plan to leave him. She spirited us away from the foggy vineyard farmhouse they were renting in Northern California and brought me to a tiny wooden bungalow on the Central Coast in San Luis Obispo. One of my first memories is of my mother standing above a cauldron of bubbling water in our tiny apartment, singing blessings over our Kraft macaroni and cheese.

Witchcraft has always existed. The term comes from the Old English word *wicce*, pronounced "witch": a wise woman. She practices oracular arts and sings incantations; she knows the secrets of herb craft and can talk to spirits. The word *wit* and *witch* share the same root: "to know, to understand, to be a person of intelligence." Etymologically, the word *witch* refers to a kind of Northern European shamanness. That's the root of the word, though witchcraft is practiced throughout the world, by folks of all genders. You don't have to have Northern European ancestry to identify as a witch. In Spanish witchcraft is called *brujeria*; in African American folk magic, it's called *conjure*. In Italian, a witch is a *strega*. In Mandarin Chinese, a witch is a *wūpó*. Witches exist throughout space and time. Witchcraft brings together the magical people throughout the world for the shared goals of justice, liberation, and celebration of the life force of the earth.

The witch gene has traveled through my lineage. Eileen, meaning hazelnut, fruit of the Celtic tree of wisdom, is the middle name of each firstborn daughter in my family going back generations, back to the old country. My mother practiced witchcraft before she even knew that's what she was doing. Women in Northern Europe probably stopped calling themselves witches around the same time you could have your tongue ripped out for saying you were one. So instead, my mother called herself an activist when I was a child. Years later, she told me that she saw activism and witchcraft as two parts of the same practice: devotion to the Goddess. From an early age, she always wanted to protect women and children. Claimed by the goddess Demeter even before I, her eldest child, was born, my mother identified with the mother archetype.

In her early twenties, during Vietnam, my mother joined Mothers for Peace, to protest the war. Then, when the war was over and the activists turned their attention to preventing the destruction of the earth, she joined the Mothers in that work too. When I was about five years old, I remember she took me to a protest at Diablo Canyon, a nuclear power plant looming over the cliffs lining the Pacific Ocean, built on an active fault line. The Mothers dragged a brass bed to the beach with a muslin canopy. In the bed, a skull-faced capitalist in a top hat and tuxedo ravished his bride, a naïve woman in white, representing the people of Central California who were in bed with their doom. My mother didn't know her then, but Starhawk (grandmother of Reclaiming, a contemporary witch movement, whose book *The Spiral Dance* launched the rebirth of Goddess culture) was at that protest, and many others like it. Later, they would meet each other, but even then, they were working in service of the same Goddess, the earth herself.

People encouraged my mother to spank me. I was too wild, they said. When it was nap time, they'd find me dancing in the yard.

I wanted to be out running in the grass, making proud crowns of juniper, singing my elaborate incantations in honor of the sun and moon and the light on the leaves. Despite the fact that the school administration called my mother in more than once, I refused to wear anything but my purple unicorn shirt every day for over a year. In department stores, I'd hide in the sacred circles of the clothes racks, wrapping myself in sequined scarves and whispering oracles to startled shoppers as they passed by with their carts.

I talked back to adults. A receptionist at my school told my mother I was the rudest child she'd ever met. She didn't mention that she'd brought it on herself; she'd embarrassed my friend for having wet her pants, and she told us to shut up when she heard me comforting her about it, so I told the receptionist she should lead by example and shut up herself. Through it all, my mother refused to hit me. The world I was born into was brutal enough, she said. She'd been beaten by her own father. And, too, one of my childhood playmates was murdered by her stepfather, ketchup shoved down her throat, then thrown against the wall for refusing to eat her pancakes. Even as a child, I knew I needed to find a place where the "Law of the Father" could not reach me.

Children don't just *believe* in magic; they live it. Early child psychologists like Bruno Bettelheim were convinced that children are by nature animists. Children see the sun, the moon, the rivers, the animals, the trees, and the stones as alive and full of intelligence. Everything that moves is alive, and everything moves. Atoms buzz, the planets spin. Nothing is still. Every bit of the universe vibrates with Spirit.

14

René Descartes, exemplar of Western philosophy and fore-father of "the Enlightenment," is most remembered for his axiom *cogito, ergo sum.* "I think, therefore I exist." But, he argued, the existence of anything else must necessarily be doubted. The earth might be a trick. Your lover might not really be there. Other beings could all be a mirage, but you, dear individual thinking man, you exist for sure. On a roll, Descartes also said that animals are basically organic machines that cannot think or feel pain. It's pointless to feel compassion for them, he said. And from his argument, so celebrated within the canon of Western philosophy, evolve things like chattel slavery, factory farms, and the slash and burn of the Amazon. For Descartes, only humans—white male land-owning humans in particular—have minds and souls, and thus, only they have rights to consideration. But even in the seventeenth century, children knew that the world was speaking, calling out for love.

"Just because we don't understand what the animals are saying doesn't mean they're not saying anything," I remember telling my mother as a child as we were driving through the eucalyptus groves of San Luis, watching the hawks circle through the lazy sunshine. "We're just not listening right." But both Descartes and Bettelheim would have disagreed with me. Recognizing the intelligence of nature is just a temporary coping mechanism children and "primitive people" employ until they can be civilized into solving their problems through "reason" alone.

On the surface, the Enlightened Man's reason seems stronger than the magic of children, or even the magic of the witches and wizards and indigenous shamans of the world. But the

Enlightened Man finds his power by imposing kyriarchy (a word for the master/slave, oppressor/oppressed dynamic), and kyriarchy is slowly asphyxiating our species and all life on the planet. Kyriarchy is like a virus; it kills the organism that sustains it. Even as a child, I wasn't going to give the Enlightened Man all the applause, gold ribbons, and Christmas bonuses with which he awarded himself such a regular and hearty congratulations.

Bettelheim might argue that I only want to persist in my belief in magic now as an adult because as a child I was forced to abandon my magical thinking too early. In his book *The Uses of Enchantment*, he says:

> Many young people who today suddenly seek escape in drug-induced dreams, apprentice themselves to some guru, believe in astrology, engage in practicing "black magic," or who in some other fashion escape from reality into daydreams about magic experiences which are to change their life for the better, were prematurely pressed to view reality in an adult way.

Bettelheim may be right. As someone who loves astrology and magic of all shades, I know the kyriarchy tried to force me to abandon my magical thinking way too soon. But he was wrong when in the same book he argued that once a child was successfully convinced that life could be mastered in "realistic ways," she would let go of her childish magical thinking. What was the *realistic way* Bettelheim spoke of? The realistic way is that we capitulate. We're supposed to ignore that Western civilization was built upon the enslavement of people of color and the destruction of the natural world. We're supposed to ignore all of that and get good jobs as doctors and lawyers and bankers, or if we can't do that, at least try and marry one. We're supposed to ignore that the ice-caps are melting and the planet is heating and the bellies of the fish are filled with plastic. Buy more stuff. Be more *reasonable*. Bettelheim says: "By his own social, scientific, and technological progress, man [can free] himself from his fears and threats to his existence." But when we're encouraged to be rational, often we're really being encouraged to be more individualistic. We're being encouraged to see ourselves as separate and in competition with others. But magic is about connection, collaboration, magic is a process of bringing things together. Ultimately, magic is about love.

As is true of so many witches, I was born delighted with the world, seeing the radiant, interdependent spirit of stone and leaf and animal-kind. But, as is also true of nearly every witch I know, my childhood was less about learning to recognize my agency within that web of interdependence than being forced to concede that the power and freedom I saw as my sacred birthright was not recognized by the rest of my species. I wanted to play in the enchanted garden of the Goddess, to marvel at the way things grow, to encounter Her creatures, to dance in the fields and sing at Her altars. But the disenchanted world and its minions were always getting in the way.

Even Disney, a company that broadcasts its allegiance to enchantment, schooled me on the disenchantment of the world early on. I would always start bawling when Bambi's mother, explaining to her little fawn why they had to hide, laments, "Man has entered the forest." Soon, Bambi's mother would be shot dead and the forest would be on fire. Fawns learn early that "Man" is always interfering with the way the forest creatures want to experience the world.

In my first experiences at elementary school, "Man" demanded I be put on Ritalin. "Man" didn't want me to free the hamster from his prison; he wanted me to sit still at my desk under the glare of fluorescent lights, with both feet on the floor, looking my teacher straight in the eye. *Recite your multiplication tables,* "Man" demanded. *Repeat after me: George Washington never told a lie. Now…watch the* Challenger *explode.* From an early age, I saw that "Man" was perfectly happy to order you around, criticize you, put rules on you or withhold things from you, but if you resisted, you were branded rude, rebellious, and ungrateful. "Man" thinks you should smile more. "Man" diagnosed me as dyslexic and put me in all the remedial academic groups because "Man" was concerned I wouldn't be able to meet his demand for academic excellence. "Man" didn't care that I had better things to do.

"Man" made sure the school lawn was buzzed to a respectable length for competitive games, but he didn't see the ladybug queen-dom flourishing in the sour grass around the edges of the field. Yellow flowers with translucent green stems that, when chewed, would make the faces of my beautiful baby-witch friends pucker with joy. My childhood witch companions offered me solace in a hostile world. For instance, Vanessa, the petite earth-colored Austrian with a passion for altered states of consciousness, taught me to take too-hot baths, then swoon down on the bathroom floor to press our naked cheeks against a mercy of cold tiles. Or Leia the Generous, with wide Russian cheekbones, who gave me her rabbit talisman when I left mine at the creek. She and I spent countless hours sheltering in dark coves of pine, calling the fairies with thimbles full of tea and sour apple candy. We'd dress up in costumes, swathing ourselves in cloaks like the Nordic Völva, the wandering Scandinavian priestesses. We'd chase orbs through the woods and pound our staffs on the granite boulders in the hills behind her house, commanding the rains to come. I also loved Hanna, skinny and blond with a raspy voice. We shared a total animistic conviction that our stuffed animals held picnics the moment we left the room, complete with balloons, ribbons, songs, and carnivals. Hanna had all her animals in a circle around her when a stranger broke into her house in the middle of the day and raped her grandmother in the next room. My childhood friends and I lived in an enchanted world, but "Man" was always lurking, rapacious and sinister outside our windows.

For the first four years of my life, my mother and I were alone together. We lived in a little white house on Peach Street, in San Luis Obispo, with a gray tabby cat named Spencer and a little porch with vines growing up the lattice. A single mother, my mother worked hard to support us. When she wasn't working, she'd read me *D'Aulaires' Book of Greek Myths*. A book that schooled me: for thousands of years the gods of patriarchy have been hungry to devour their children. But still, I loved the stories and was seduced, naming the fish in my fish tank after the gods. Zeus, the guppy with the thunderous red tail, was true to his name. He'd eat all his guppy babies if I didn't swaddle them away in a separate tank. Iris, my rainbow neon tetra, was named after the messenger goddess; she shimmered between the water ferns and sunken temple leaves.

Night was different. I had nightmares. I'd sleepwalk. My mother would find me outside, wandering down the street in my nightgown. We live on haunted land, in a haunted world. Conquistadors and colonizers spilt the native people's blood; dark deeds haunt the lineage of many white American families. As a child, I was always sensitive to the ghosts of the land, of my lineage, of the oppressors and the oppressed. On the most haunted nights, I'd crawl into bed with my mother. She'd sing me lullabies and tell me stories about magical worlds with a little character named Amanda, who made friends with dragons and could slide down rainbows with Iris the messenger goddess.

As predicted by Bettelheim, when I was in control of my imagination, I felt safe. The danger happened when I felt like I was at the mercy of the libidinous, roiling imagination of our disenchanted civilization. Humanity's rejected monsters lurked around every corner. Every night before I went to sleep, my mother would perform a banishing ritual in my room, clapping her hands and banging pots and demanding all the evil spirits lurking there leave at once. "By the powers of the Goddess within me, I command all corrupt spirits to leave this place!" *Bang!* These were on the nights that she wasn't working at the Olde Port Inn as a cocktail waitress.

Days, she worked at Easy Ad; sometimes she'd take me to work with her when she'd make phone calls all day, selling ad space to local businesses. In subtle apology for having no other option but to bring her child to work, she'd parade me in like a young page bearing offerings of donuts in a pink cardboard box: maple crullers, old-fashioneds, thick waxy chocolate with a confetti of rainbow sprinkles.

Aunt Mickey ran a daycare center. Often if my mother was working, I'd be there, even though I hated it. There was a horrible teenage boy—I don't know if he was a cousin or just another kid at daycare—who would always threaten to flush my best friend, a little girl too young even to walk, down the toilet. He'd take her in there and laugh and flush while I pounded, weeping, on the door.

My mother remembers hearing my screams down the phone wires. One day at Aunt Mickey's, at around age two, I went to investigate the kitchen. I wanted to wrestle the thick black cords slithering around the counters, vines that wanted climbing. In the '70s, some coffeepots plugged straight into the wall. I was always a climber, an adventurer, into everything. My mother doesn't remember which of her Easy Ad coworkers drove her to the hospital. She just remembers the sound of my screams down the hospital hall, vibrating the room as if I were a Titan trying to escape a tiny steel cage. The coffee had scalded 80 percent of my body, blistering my toddler skin so that it crackled and oozed like pork rind.

The call to witchcraft often begins with trauma or illness. To navigate the underworld, you need to go there many times. A person who's been to the underworld can be of special service to those trying to escape its clutches. For months, I had to go to the

21

hospital every day to have my scabs peeled off so they wouldn't scar. It took three nurses and my mother to hold me down for the doctor; I was too young for anesthetic. My mother thinks the experience gave me an unconscious mistrust of her. She says if she had to do it again, she'd leave the room even if it took five nurses to hold me down. Years later, when I was beginning grade school, my mother would have to take detours so we wouldn't drive by the hospital on the way. If I glimpsed its imposing cement walls, I'd scream and claw at the seat belt, trying to throw myself from the moving car in an effort to get away.

Soon after the burn, I started to get asthma. My lungs would constrict until my lips turned blue, until you could see my heart begging for blood and oxygen from across the room. I would wheeze and wheeze, my ribs pinned by a steel corset, drawn into a rhythmic trance of pure survival. Everything would disappear, the world would turn black and fade away, all that existed was the silken string of my breath and I would hold fast to it like an astronaut lest I be sucked into the void.

From that void crept my first familiar.

When my father was called up for the National Guard, sometimes he'd come down from Northern California and stay in the army barracks at Camp San Luis. I remember orderly rows of long wooden buildings, whitewashed with green trim. Spartan rooms with nothing in them but metal cots, wool blankets pulled tight across starched white sheets, heavy wooden trunks at the base of each one. No room for anything personal, the sameness and regularity of the space frightened me.

My father went for a meeting with his commander, leaving me in the dark barracks, overhead fans ratcheting, pale sunlight infiltrating through industrial metal screens. No living troops were there on base; it was just me alone with the warrior spirits. The residual hum of march and step; *yes, sir; no, sir.* The regular rhythm of rifle fire.

When my father came back, he found me sitting cross-legged on a bed, perfectly still, incanting a low, guttural song. "Who are you singing to?" he asked me. I told him I was singing to my guardian, the crocodile Wheezer, who grinned out from beneath the bed, eager to snap out and protect me with supernatural speed.

Years later, when I grew up and learned more about animal familiars, it struck me that my first one took as its name one of my most painful torments: *Wheezer.* Asthma constricted my lungs so that every breath I took during an attack would cause me to wheeze. Asthma prevented me from taking action in the world. Christmas, Disneyland, birthday parties, any event that got my child-heart racing would invariably lead to my having an asthma attack and having to stay home, or with me languishing blue-lipped on the sidelines as my friends built sandcastles and frolicked in the ocean.

That my familiar introduced himself by the name of my wound tells me something. Through my wounds I can find my strength and my power. I can touch ancient places. My wounds may not come to me of my own volition, but they appear like bullet holes in the wall guarding my internal garden of Eden. I am not grateful for my wounds, but I am grateful for the power that has come seeping into my world through them.

Wheezer is fierce. I stand atop him like a surfboard. Crocodiles connect us to the primordial. Memory holders, they're stones that swim. The crocodile is an embodiment of the ancient, explosive power resting just beneath the surface of consciousness. In ancient Egypt, Sobek the Rager was one of the deities who took the form of a crocodile; according to *The Book of Symbols*, he was a personification of the "pharaoh's capacity to obliterate the enemies of the kingdom." Wheezer, too, was a rager, coming to me in the knowledge that my kingdom did in fact have enemies. *Man has entered the forest.* But always my rager, Wheezer sits at my feet, a languorous lizard with an explosive power coiled tightly at his core.

Your experience of the world changes when you imagine a crocodile by your side. Half asleep yet weary, head on your lap, one powerful little elbow crooked possessively over your thigh. Wheezer came to me for the first time in the army barracks. Our war-loving culture likes to pretend the army is mostly adventure and explosions, but really most of it is bureaucratic drudgery: photocopying documents in triplicate, waiting on the chain of command, bleaching the latrines. In that most disenchanted of places, Wheezer brought me orchids. Rising from the swamp mist, Wheezer brought me skeins of Spanish moss, the screaming of panthers and the snap of turtles, the glowing orbs of will-o'-the-wisp.

There's a famous pundit, a patriarch of the Incels, who sneers and says, as if it's an insult, that witches come from the swamp. In a way, he's right—witchcraft *is* born of the swamp. We witches come from the dark lagoon, bubbling and sulfurous. Black leathery eggs hatching underneath. At the base of this swamp is the decay of history, the primordial, of everything that was ever known. Our knowledge is held not in a computer chip but in the living, thinking organism of the planet, in the bodies of plants and animals and stones and roots and rain. When "Man," colonizer and castle-dweller, enters the swamp, he dies. But the swamp teems with life. A watery world, navigable only by boat, the shores of the swamp are constantly shifting with the tides. Our swamp represents the unconscious, the lizard brain, the root system that expands infinitely beneath the surface of the water. It's the undifferentiated place from which all forms emerge. To have a crocodile with you means you are empowered by this place of mystery, this dangerous territory, hinterland and underworld, wild and untamable; you are one of the beasts that lives there.

Why does the call to witchcraft demand a trip to the underworld? Why does it so often come with trauma, with illness, with strife? Because like shamans, witches are healers. To be a witch/shaman, you must visit the underworld. You must be humbled. You must recognize the limits of your power and confront the mystery, that there are forces that you can't see and don't understand, forces that have no beginning and no end. You emerged from those forces, a crocodile from the riverbank, and to them you will return, slipping back into currents dark and cold as outer space.

Today, I still call Wheezer to my side when I do my rituals. I raise my left hand and draw a path for him to come to me from the primordial realms. I whistle his signal, then tap my thigh until he comes to rest, coiling around my feet, hissing at all those who might seek to do me harm.

For witches, the portholes of the imagination do not slam shut at puberty. The animal spirits and guardians that came to us in our childhood are with us throughout our lifetimes. Even when we forget them, they wait, water sheening off their backs in blankets of light, watching for our return.

Our power doesn't come from denying the inherent spirit of the natural world, or in turning away from the Imagination. Our power as witches comes from our skill at weaving reason and magic together. We can work in collaborative concert with the world around us and the worlds beyond. Our spirit guardians and familiars are still here with us, waiting for us to call upon them, to reclaim the inspirited world that is our birthright.

Chapter 2

c c c

THE LANGUAGE OF THE BIRDS

1. SET CONFLICT RESOLUTION GROUND RULES
Recognize whose lands these are on which we stand.
Ask the deer, turtle, and the crane.
Make sure the spirits of these lands are respected and
Treated with goodwill.
The land is a being who remembers everything.
You will have to answer to your children,
and their children, and theirs...

Joy Harjo, *Conflict Resolution for Holy Beings*

"One for sorrow, two for joy, three for a girl, four for a boy." My new stepsister and I would read the augurs from the crows we spied out the back window of my father's red Plymouth Valiant. Long trips, twisting through the back roads of gold country in a car held together with bailing wire and duct tape. We didn't know that augury was the tongue of occult initiates, those who could understand "the language of the birds." The seers of ancient Rome determined when to launch ships and inaugurate their leaders based on the direction of crows in flight. The Yorùbá people

27

of southwest Nigeria wear beaded headdresses, strung with veils and crowned in birds who symbolize their ancestors, the grandmothers, whispering in their ears, giving their leaders guidance. One-eyed Odin, the Nordic god, master of ecstasy, poet, diviner, and traveler between the worlds, had two crow familiars, Hugin and Munin, cackling the news of the world into his ears and bringing him wisdom and the stories of the battlefield. Birds speak the messages of the gods. My sister and I watched the birds, and said our rhymes, but we didn't know what sorrow meant yet; we were only five years old.

My stepsister was new to me. We met when my mother sent me up to Northern California to live with my father for half a year; she was entering a relationship and didn't want me to become attached to the new man if it didn't work out. And since my father had been begging her for more access to me, there I was, in the little vineyard town of Lodi, California. My great-great-grandfather had built our little bungalow on Eureka Avenue with his own hands, and then died falling off the roof. Eureka is what the gold miners cried when they found gold. *Eureka!* Meaning, "I have found it!"

I'd met my sister on the first day of kindergarten and loved her at first sight. Her hair was so thick and sandy she couldn't fit a rubber band around it. She had thick glasses to match her hair, and buckteeth to match my own. By nature, my new sister was obedient, but when a little boy with permanent Kool-Aid stains on his top lip criticized the way I colored outside the lines, she rolled her eyes and said, "She's being *creative*." She sighed in exasperation at his stupidity; I decided to love her forever.

We introduced her single mother to my single father on a trip to the roller rink. There beneath the disco ball glitter, serenaded by the clack of fat pink wheels on leather skates and Juice Newton's "Queen of Hearts" playing on repeat, a romance ensued. Their love pact was signed in my blood. I streaked it across the waxed wooden floor before I even made it one time around the rink. Showing off how I could snap my fingers and skate at the same time, my stunt ended in the hospital with five wire stitches across my chin. As omens go, it wasn't a good one. And in fact, my father and new stepmother divorced ten years later.

But initially we lived in idyll. My father would write me and my sister songs about our alter egos, "the Weasel sisters," on his old acoustic guitar and sing them to us while we ate tuna sandwiches and fed rolled up balls of Wonder Bread to ducks at the lake. They'd hiss and squawk at us and my sister and I would squeal and clamber up onto the picnic tables. And even though my father laughed uproariously as we ran in terror from the monster-sized geese and the obscene red things hanging off their bills, I adored him. He'd take us to visit my aunt's ranch up in the foothills with the garter snakes and the horny toads and her whole coterie of stray dogs and new kittens. We'd watch *Star Trek* and get frozen yogurt at Honey Bear, or spend nights at the Pizza Garden chatting with Ray, the wizened old bartender who'd give us root beer–flavored Dum Dums while we played pilot on the red plastic buttons on the jukebox. Together as a family, we went panning for gold in the local creeks, mostly turning up pyrite, or "fool's gold," in our little pie pans, jiggling them in the water and watching their bright flecks shiver in the sunlight. Pyrite was common and brittle, worth nothing to most people since it couldn't be bent and shaped into jewelry, but it was fun to see it shivering in our pans. Most of the gold had been stripped from the hills long ago. But our most celebrated treasures were the obsidian arrowheads cast off by the Miwoks. I once even found one in our backyard. Sharp stone tools speaking of expert hands, speaking of a deeper history of the land and the people who've lived since here long before we arrived. People whom my own ancestral lineage had tricked, coerced, or killed. To find these relics, all one had to do was scratch the surface of the earth, and there they were, barely hidden beneath the imported grapevines.

Lodi smelled of Cheerios from the General Mills factory on the outskirts of town: a smell of earnest, wholesome childhood, forti-fied with vitamins and minerals. On the weekends, my dad would take me and my new sister fishing for perch, or exploring the sta-lactites and stalagmites at the Moaning Caverns, or camping at Big Trees where we would walk in a reverent hush beneath the mil-lenarian redwood trees towering hundreds of feet above us. We'd do the "Blind Walk," feeling the fibrous bark and sniffing at the pine needles, sharp as pins, and listening for the feet of the chip-munks as they shimmied through the branches. Unless my father was angry and cussing about all the foreigners visiting the park and the way they threw diapers on the ground, or the doofus way we'd tie the ropes on the rowboat, or how we couldn't follow simple directions pulling the kayak from the back of the truck. When-ever we showed up at the river, my sister and I would silently pray there wouldn't be any kids swimming in it already. We'd show up in our bathing suits and flip-flops, my father in his gym shorts, sports socks pulled up to his knees and his baseball cap high on his head. We'd have to hold him back from shouting at the "nancy boys" *drifting* in their inner tubes instead of rushing the rapids like "real men"—which is what *he* would have done as a child.

My father was determined to be a good dad, to do better than his father had done by him. But he was haunted by patriarchy, too, the rigid set of rules that dictates what men do and what they have a right to: everything. He knew as the patriarch he was supposed to have the power, but like the perch we tried and usually failed to catch, he had power but never felt like he could get a tight enough grip on it; the power to command us was always slipping through his hands. If only everybody would just fall into line— the neighbor's yapping dogs, his children, his wife—everything would just be so much better for everyone. But try as he might, he could never get everyone to submit to his authority and just be done with it. Our submission was never permanent. He'd herd us along at the mall, but we wanted to go into stores while he wanted us all to march in a straight line like soldiers. A subscriber to the *Tightwad Gazette* monthly newsletter, once every couple of weeks he'd splurge and take us out to the Sizzler all-you-can-eat buffet. A generous act for someone so concerned with saving coin, but we'd have to eat at least three plates to make it worth his money. I was a garbage disposal and would gladly eat five plates if he wanted, but my sister had trouble even finishing one, and so we'd all have to sit there, waiting, while she slowly pushed the food around and tried to sneak scraps of it to the floor while no one was looking; then she'd get a swat for making a mess. My father longed for a

31

return to the 1950s, when white teenagers picked the grapes in his town and women weren't constantly complaining about what men did wrong. "I want 'never kissed anyone's ass' to be written on my tombstone," my father says. But he forgets that no one likes kissing ass. No one has ever truly accepted anyone else's dominance. Patriarchs invented weapons *because* someone was always challenging their authority, not because anyone was naturally docile. People, animals, nature always struggle toward freedom.

My new sister and I loved to be alone together, without adults around to tell us what to do and how to do it. We had fantasies about tying up the adults around us so they couldn't lash out, then giving them a piece of our mind and throwing them in a volcano. She and I would kick our feet over the front porch, listening to the boats droning at the nearby lake, nipping the tips off the honeysuckle vines, drenching our tongues with their nectar. We'd scrunch rose blossoms with our child-damp palms and mix them with hose water to make love potions with a sweet, old-timey scent. Happy Dog, our patient little Queensland heeler, was our favorite doll. We dressed her in felt capes and pretended they were princess clothes. Happy would supervise us, panting in her finery, while Kristin and I spent all afternoon making mud pies, squishing the brown muck between our fingers, then hiding in the laundry hanging on the line, blaming the mess on our alter egos, fairies named Sparkle or Glitter or Shine.

I was around five years old when the Gorgon appeared. It was right around the same time we came under assault of our cousin, molested by our cousin, who was just a year or two shy of his eighteenth birthday. Aside from his abuse, I have little recollection of him. He had a damp upper lip and a nervous smile, like he was always laughing along with a joke that was on him. One of the only other memories I have is in the car, my dad driving us on a camping trip, my cousin pressing his slack ass to the window so he could fart out of it and not stink up the car for the rest of us. He was considerate like that. When he was molesting me, he would always ask me if I liked it, if it felt good. "No," I'd cry, and try to pull away. But his questions were rhetorical. He gripped my arm and didn't care about my answer. He did what he wanted and kept going. Pulling me out to the old trailer down the hill when we played hide-and-seek, he always demanded we partner up, then promised me chocolate bars that I didn't want for my "good behavior." And if I told anyone, *He'd kill me. He'd slit my throat. He'd kill my parents. I'd get in trouble, or he'd get in trouble, or we both would. I'd be punished. He'd go to prison and it would be my fault. It was my fault anyhow; I brought it on myself,* etc., etc. The usual. Abusers never accept any blame; they try to get everyone else to take it, especially children. He'd abuse me with my parents in the next room, with me crying and saying no and him laughing. With my sister looking on helpless. My nos meant nothing to him; my preferences meant nothing. My safety, my happiness. My boundaries. Nothing. Nothing.

No was supposed to be a magic word. You were supposed to "say NO, and GO, and TELL someone." But my magic *no* meant nothing and had no effect. And if I told someone, my cousin convinced me that it was I who would be punished for committing such shameful acts. Shameful acts in the crawl space with the kittens beneath the bed. Or "playing doctor" at his insistence on my bunk bed. He'd abuse us when my father and stepmother would have him over to babysit us. As a baby witch, I was defiant. Difficult. But my sister was less so. My defiance annoyed my teachers and frustrated my parents, but throughout my life it has saved me a thousand times.

My cousin would take my laudably compliant sister into my parents' bedroom while I banged helplessly on the door, jiggling the antique glass handle, demanding he let her go. I sat on the edge of the bathtub across the hall and concocted an escape plan as I listened to my sister crying and begging him to stop. "No, no, no, please no...," she incanted. My plan was to get him to let her use the bathroom. Then we'd lock the bathroom door and hoist ourselves up over the back of the toilet, slither through the little window above, then escape into the night. Run to Lodi Lake, hide in the blackberry brambles with the opossums and the raccoons, coyote pups and fairy creatures. After a lengthy shouting campaign, I did eventually convince him that my sister genuinely needed to pee, but he didn't let her out as I anticipated. He told her she could just hold it, or she could go in his mouth. *Would she like that?*

We hear the terms *rape, molestation, sexual assault* every day now. When I asked my grandmother how she didn't know that my mother was being raped by my grandfather, my grandmother said that she didn't know that such a thing existed. It wasn't so long ago that rape was just something that happened on Grecian urns or to drunk girls wandering alone through the woods at night. Now we know that this kind of assault happens all the time: at home, in churches, in doctor's offices, at film studios. But in the way we speak of it, abuse happens so fast, it seems like we should be able to get over it just as quickly. *She was molested.* It only takes three words to say it, a few seconds of speech, but it can take a lifetime to heal. Sometimes you never heal; sometimes the wound persists for generations. Each time we speak of someone's trauma, there's an event with a million details and a lifetime of messy repercussions that goes with it, which she, who received the trauma like a cursed trousseau chained to her raw and bloody ankle, drags around with her in perpetuity.

Creating a boundary is one of the most common practices in witchcraft. Spells always begin by casting a circle. The circle is a space only love can enter, a place between the worlds where the practicing witch, a historic target of assault, is protected and safe. Using her ceremonial knife to trace its perimeter, the witch walks three times *deosil*—with the direction of the sun—to create a circle around her. She calls upon the Guardians of the material world to enter this sacred space and protect her: "spirits of fire, air, water, and earth, be here with us!" She calls upon the strength of her own spirit and the Goddess of all Life. Into her circle she calls her animal guides, her familiars. Here she cultivates her power. She dances and makes it grow. She practices taking that sacred space with her out into the world. She practices keeping her space clear and safe. No wonder witchcraft is attractive to those whose boundaries have been violated by invaders. No wonder the witch is such a threat to patriarchy. Unless it constructs them itself—walls between countries, velvet cords outside the VIP room—the kyriarchy doesn't honor boundaries. Witches consecrate our spaces, our bodies, and our planet as sacred. One of the central practices of the witch is to say she has boundaries no "Man" can cross. Her body is a sacred space that cannot be violated.

A well-known axiom of witchcraft is called the Threefold Law: what you do comes back to you three times over. Actions have consequences. But even a brief study of history demonstrates that though all events have consequences, it's rarely the aggressor who has to face the worst of them. When your body is used as a receptacle for pain and abuse as a child, one of the most destructive consequences is that later you feel programmed to tolerate pain and expect transgression. You expect your boundaries to mean nothing. So when your already weakened boundaries *are* eventually transgressed, you blame yourself. You feel like any reference to your abuse is just an excuse you're making to avoid facing the consequences of your own actions and failures. But this mind-fuck is deliberate. Thousands of years of systemic abuse is no accident. It's just another way to convince you to hold pain that doesn't belong to you, to Bibbidi-Bobbidi-Boo you into becoming the bottom rat.

The Threefold Law of witchcraft is less a description of a universal truth and more a statement of intention: a commitment to living AS IF your actions will come back to you. A commitment to holding your own pain and transmuting it into something that leaves the world better than you found it. A witch is an agent;

with her community, she takes responsibility for her own pain, her own experience, we take responsibility together. Witches use magic to compost suffering into something nourishing, something that brings the world around us to life. Of course, this intention is an ideal; not even the most powerful witches I know are able to behave according to the Threefold Law all the time. One isn't born knowing how to do this work, but if we show up with courage, sometimes our guides and teachers emerge from unexpected places.

My sister and I lay in our bunk beds, crickets chanting through clumps of freshly cut grass outside our window, the air damp with twilight. At the time, we looked like twins, roasted dark brown, bound with white tan lines as if our bathing suits had been made out of duct tape. We went to bed still wet from the bath, our hair dripping and sun bleached white with streaks of chlorine green. Long after the horns of *Star Trek* boldly faded with my father's snores on the other side of the living room wall, we were exhausted from a day racing our bikes around the block and making balloon puppets at the library. As most children do, my sister and I insisted the closet door be all the way closed before we went to sleep. But for several nights, we'd been noticing the door was open come morning.

Late that night, the door of the closet clicked open, preceded by a hiss. "Kristin, Kristin," I whispered up to my sister from the bottom bunk. Inside the closet's black porthole stood a shade, a woman with blazing red eyes and a crown of writhing snakes. She raised her hand. A benediction? A greeting? A curse? She claimed me that night. Medusa, snake-headed monster of Greek mythology, the Lady of the Shadows, dark guardian and avatar of the Queen of the Underworld. I lay gasping, immobilized, like the catfish my father threw still living into our vegetable garden, where they would rot and become fertilizer. Eventually, the Medusa faded. Maybe it was a dream. But in the morning, my sister said she had seen her too.

Real or imagined, the spirits that come to us in our childhood mean something. Medusa came for a reason. Throughout my youth, she was to be my guide through the underworld. For many of us witch heroines, the first time we enter the underworld, it isn't by choice. We're made into monsters there in its caves, vilified and lonely. Medusa was my guardian, my monster, my guide, but it took me fifteen years to recognize that in the venom of her crown of snakes is powerful medicine.

Growing up, because my mother had experienced severe abuse at the hands of her father, because my sister and I had been abused, because so many of the other girls I knew had, because my father had often referred to his own traumas—beatings at the hands of his chief of police father, his mother locking herself in the bathroom threatening suicide. Looking back, I was told that even our cousin, source of one of my many early traumas, had also been abused, because history is awash with it, because my country was founded on it, I grew up believing that abuse happened to everyone. Trauma is ordinary. Trauma is inescapable.

The Greek root of the word *trauma* refers to a hurt or a wound, but also to a defeat. The hero Perseus beheads the Medusa, the

38

snake-headed female monster from Greek mythology, slitting her throat with his adamantine sword. The victor stands over his spoils, brandishing the Medusa's head, her crown of snakes his new weapon. The Medusa is traumatized: tricked, slain, defeated. But the eyes on her decapitated head still blink. The snakes in her hair still writhe. The Medusa still lives, only, her mind is separated from her body. After the Medusa's decapitation, her body and head are taken in different directions. Her head remains in captivity, attached to the shield of Athena, the Goddess of War, used as a weapon against advancing armies. Her body is left to rot where it falls. But even though I was terrified of the Medusa when she appeared, I could feel her power in me, rising, rising. I had a premonition that we would wander the world together, decapitated and blind, moving by feel, arms stretched out, uncertain which direction would take us back to ourselves and which would just lead to further punishment.

Soon after my first sighting of Medusa, my sister and I were playing in our front yard. In our fantastical play, I was a Native American protecting my vulnerable cowgirl sister with my magic. Barely in grade school, all I knew about history was that the Indians helped the Pilgrims at Thanksgiving and that it had something to do with the hand-shaped turkeys we would paint on construction paper and the wide-brimmed black felt hats with brass buckles. The Indians gave us corn, and in return we gave them blankets (infested with smallpox). My father hadn't yet taken us on the camping trip to Montana, to visit Little Big Horn, to see our ancestor: the man standing nearest to General

Custer when he finally met his consequences after a rampage of slaughter and betrayal across the indigenous territories of the Northwest.

Our game of cowgirls and Indians usually involved one or both of us having escaped from a despotic family situation, an evil husband, a murderous father, and we would take turns hiding and protecting each other by disguising ourselves as cows or other horned prairie beasts. That day, I stood in the bee clover, bowing and stomping a circular dance of protection; my sister was in the side yard. I heard a ruckus above my head, the slapping of silk wings in flight. A cawing protest, a battle cry. I stood there in my yard, alone, looking up. Barreling down from the ethers, a finch harassed a crow, a black asteroid in a stream of smoke and blood. The crow fell at my feet. It lay gasping, staring up at me, blinking and desperate as its life force drained out through its ebony maw, blood into the grass, marking my toes so that I would leave red footprints.

Chapter 3

LEAVING THE TEMPLE OF THE FATHER

I want to do what I want in a world that does not seem to want me to do what I want. I want to not have to fight.

Amy Fusselman, *Idiophone*

Having tasted the bitter fruit of the underworld, I returned from the north to find my mother engaged to Bela, a saturnine first-generation Hungarian she'd met at writers' group. Jet-black hair and thick mustache, tall and olive colored, he barely spoke, but he loved to write plays. He was living, but like trees or stones live, mostly he was silent. He was only a playwright by night, and sometimes weekends. The rest of the time he quantified carbon monoxide and other toxic particles for the Air Pollution Control District.

My soon-to-be stepfather hated being an engineer; he always said his parents made him do it. He rarely spoke, but when he did, that's what he'd say. His immigrant parents forced him to make the practical choice, and every day he would passively, bitterly resent them for it. And so to get back at them, he left them in rural Pennsylvania with the fireflies and their wooden house that smelled of potato-stuffed pierogies, left them with his sister, their daughter, a paltry substitute for a son. One of the only memories I have of Bela's sister is when she refused to sit in the back seat of the car with him, because otherwise their thighs would touch. Practically incest! Bela moved to California, where people go to find themselves. Mission accomplished: his name was Bela and he lived on Bela Avenue. And it turned out he was someone who wrote plays on the weekends and then suffered Sisyphean labors all week to please his parents two thousand miles away.

My mother had already moved our stuff over from our squat little apartment into Bela's house on Bela Avenue by the time I returned home from my father's. Bela's was a wooden house, wine-colored, that had a loquat tree in the front and an avocado tree in the back, and a deck that looked out over the field of my new elementary school. I was excited about the new school because its mascot was a panther and I loved big cats for their beauty and ferociousness. And my mother liked Bela because he was quiet and stable. He didn't beat her or rape me. He was kind to me, in fact. He had a good job and he was creative. He wrote radio plays for the local public access radio station and let me be in them. He even wrote roles just for me, to help me learn to read.

In the basement Bela had a woodshop where he'd tinker. He'd drill and sand and fiddle with wires while I hid in a box in the shadows and played with a paper towel holder, making it clippity clop. "Hey! There's a horse in here? Where is it?" He'd turn and look, and I'd giggle in my box, then do it again for hours. When I first came back from my dad's, Bela took me and my mother out to the Oktoberfest, where he bought us floppy hats. Mine had a transparent emerald-green visor that I liked to look through and reveal everyone's alien form. They ate bratwurst with sauerkraut and shared their tangy yellow mustard with me while I gnawed on my corn dog and ogled the busty beer maidens in their white dirndls and embroidered corsetry. On the way home, we stopped by the pet shop, and I got a whole cupful of neon tetras for my tank, new messengers to join with Iris, my old one. They flashed their blue stripes at me while I marveled at them. Breathing as shallow as I could and holding especially still, I pinned the cup between my knees and tried not to move the whole car ride home. But then, just as we'd prepared the water to put my new friends in the tank, I got too excited and knocked the cup into the carpet. I shook with tears as I clawed at the floor trying to rescue them in time, but they all died.

That night, I lay in my new bed, listening to the ghost fish whisper. The radio turned on by itself. I climbed out of bed and went to get into bed with my mother, like I used to do at our old apartment, but when I got there she brought me back to my room. "Bela doesn't want you to be in our bed, honey. He doesn't think it's right. But I'll lie with you here for a while, okay?" She cuddled me and told me stories just like always. But then when I went to sleep, my mother went back to her own bed. When she opened the door the next morning, she found me sleeping on the floor in front of her door, curled up in my tiger blanket for protection. She'd find me there often over the next few years. I wasn't allowed to touch their bed, even with a pinky. Bela didn't even like me to enter their room. When my brother was born a few years later, he slept in their bed all the time, while I slept on the floor outside their door, an exile.

* * *

When they first got together, my mother worked as a tour guide at Hearst Castle. I loved to go up there with her and swim in the pool lined with gold, surrounded by luminous marble statuary, the gods and heroes of ancient Rome. My mother and Bela got married at "the Castle," before the statue of the fierce lion goddess Sekhmet, healer and warrior, stolen from a treasury in Egypt. Sekhmet presided over the ceremony, fierce between two date palms, one fist open, one fist closed, the wind hurling golden orbs of grapefruit behind her. Her open palm symbolized times of peace and plenty; her closed fist brought flooding, famine, and destruction. According to myth, when Sekhmet closed her fist, the Nile would run red with blood, like the vein of iron that ran through the milky marble statue and through every witch's heart.

When I was nine, we moved from San Luis Obispo to Santa Barbara, where Bela would make more money and our house would be more expensive, though not much better, and my classmates would become snobbier, and—my parents told me with a pregnant pause—I would get a pool. When we went searching for homes, I liked one on the wrong side of Hollister Avenue; the girl's bedroom was painted lilac with a rainbow unicorn mural over the bed. I didn't care about the one with the pool, but to say so makes me sound ungrateful. I'm lucky that I had a roof over my head, much less my own bedroom (with or without a unicorn), which is far more than most of the people incarnating on earth right now have access to. Still, it's hard to be grateful for someone giving up their creative life so that you can have the luxury of a pool you didn't ask for, which they can then resent you for forever.

In fact, the Air Pollution Control District was just to be a temporary resting place for Bela. While he was working, my mother was to be at home, writing the Great American Novel. Once that sold, Bela would quit his job, and we would move to Cambria, on the pine coast of Central California, and live an aesthetic, Bohemian life amidst swirls of fog and mating monarch butterflies. We'd have well-behaved dogs and listen to coyotes and waves crashing and the tapping keys of the typewriter as we thumbed through worn copies of the *Utne Reader* off our patinaed coffee table.

But we never made it to the Cambrian age, the fantastical era of freedom and fulfillment, because we were trapped in our family legacy. Bela had always wanted to be a playwright, but he gave up the dream, thwarted by his immigrant parents' scrappy practicality. My biological father also wrote short stories when I was a child, and even a novel, but over the years he grew disconsolate when he couldn't get anyone to publish it, or even look at it really. He was offended by the form letters he got from publishers upon the return of his manuscript. "You can tell they didn't even read it," he'd spit in frustration.

My mother, too, all through my youth, sequestered herself in our little back study, pinching her eyebrows and sighing if I came in and interrupted her. She took thousands of pages of notes, crammed binders full of detailed outlines, for her epic historical trilogy about the fall of the ancient goddess cultures, which never materialized. I always had this horrible fear that I would never be able to complete my projects either, that my creative dreams would also end up as a series of miscarriages. Recently, my mother told me that when I was a teenager, she had a contract with Beacon Press to write a book about our tradition of witchcraft. *The Reluctant Pagan* was her title. I remembered her talking about it, but I didn't know she'd actually had a contract. Turns out she never finished the book. She never felt ready; she needed more time. Eventually she abandoned it altogether.

One purpose of magic is to help release us from our family's karmic bondage. There's a writing curse in my family, a curse I was determined eventually to break. Sprawling out across my lineages is a desire to tell stories, a ghostly mycelium, spawned in history, corded around the throats of my ancestors, preventing us from finishing our works, from speaking out, from being able to fully realize our aspirations. Something always got in the way: children, marriage, abuse, polio, lack of confidence. Our houses were filled with books, but somehow the books could never emerge through our own fingertips.

When I was eight years old, both of my parents, my mother and father, with their new spouses, had sons. Suddenly I had two new brothers on either side of the family, both of whom were far more interesting to my father and stepfather than I was. My stepfather now had a full-blooded child of his own. And my own father would wrap his arm around my brother's shoulder and chant, "My only son, my only son," so excited to finally have another male with whom he could "throw the football around." (Too bad for my father that my brother was practically born singing show tunes and was far more interested in ballet than ball games. My father still suffers over this, but I can promise the suffering he and the world have inflicted on my brother because of it is far, far worse.)

My mother knew I was now living in exile in my family home, a tolerated yet troublesome guest, and she didn't like it. But she didn't know how to change it. She had a new baby, no college degree, and her partner was stable and a good father to her son. She thought that if she was an extra good mother to me, if she led youth groups and made us heart-shaped pancakes on Valentine's Day, and led the PTA and Bluebirds, and sewed my Halloween costumes by hand, perhaps that would make up for the fact that my stepfather did not love me, nor even particularly want me around, and that my full-blood father was more concerned with his new family than me, his old one.

Despite my mother's best efforts, I struggled in school. Students were just starting to be diagnosed as dyslexic, and I was one of those students. Plunked into all of the most remedial groups, I was told constantly that I was *a slow learner* with an errant brain. And so the other kids would watch me walk the plank to my resource classes where I and all the other dummies would get stuck with all the most stunted math problems and boring books. *See Jane Run. See Amanda Pound Her Head on the Table in Frustration.* I'd run my finger along the well-worn tracks beneath the words, trying to sound them out. They'd get garbled in my mouth, fall out hard and heavy like stones: mute, stubborn, a runic language that had eons ago been lost to interpretation. I was lucky. I had a mother who had the time and inclination to sit with me at night, rearranging note cards to try and form sentences, to see if the scratch marks on the cards could somehow come to form a lattice of meaning. But they refused.

I loved when my mother read me *A Wrinkle in Time, The Phantom Tollbooth, Island of the Blue Dolphins, Where the Wild Things Are,* and *D'Aulaires' Book of Greek Myths.* I'd tear at the paper in the mythology book, trying to shred it open and let the stories out. I ached to read them myself, but the books were dense matter. I could grind my teeth in frustration and cry all I wanted, while the other children made fun of me and shunned me, but I couldn't pass through those pages to get to the other side where the meaning was.

In sixth grade I was still struggling, still in "resource" (like a poisoned well is a resource), but now convinced of my defectiveness. Just before I went to junior high, they had me reassessed with a woman assigned by the county, and to everyone's surprise, according to her tests I had one of the highest IQs of any child she'd ever tested. My thinking patterns and nonlinear abstract reasoning were highly unusual and inventive, and as a result, I must see the world in a different way than most people. But this time she meant different as a compliment. The dyslexic has the mind of an ancient astrologer. She sees stars spread out across the universe and assembles them into a lion, a ram, a water bearer. Her thoughts come together in a chorus, singing in a diversity of voices. A rose nebula bursts and she knows, *Now is when the king will fall.* Or, *Your fortunes will change come October.* In the primordial world, I imagine the non-neurotypical as the ones who found new paths, invented new uses, could conceive of a world outside of ordinary convention.

My sixth-grade teacher, Ms. Yokabaitus, put me in with the "Gifted and Talented Students" when I went into junior high. Overnight, I went from reading at a third-grade level to reading at a college level. I started reading Voltaire, W. Somerset Maugham, books like *Dangerous Liaisons* and *The Golden Bough* and *The Moon Under Her Feet* (about the priestesses in the temples of Inanna), and all the books on magic and witchcraft my mother had in her back library: Merlin Stone, Riane Eisler, Starhawk, Luisah Teish, Margot Adler, Scott Cunningham. Of all the things that have happened in my life, my learning to read is the thing that most convinces me of the efficacy of magic.

Once upon a time, meaning thumbed its nose at me from behind a locked door, but now as a witch I can read the clouds, read sticks fallen to the floor, read tarot cards and tea leaves, scrolls of Hermetic philosophy and postmodern theory. By transforming our perceptions, we transform our world. We tend to think of magic as hair-of-bat potions and anointed candles, when in reality magic is a shift in perception that allows us to open up new worlds, new possibilities for our lives. It wasn't that other people's beliefs changed me as a child; it was that suddenly, their encouragement made me believe in myself. That belief in myself changed me so profoundly it rewired my brain. Magic works.

Around the same time that I broke through to the meaning side of written language, my mother, with her writing and her imagination, was pulling more deeply into the territories of the Goddess. She was rediscovering her roots as a witch. But she always saw it as a practice of devotion. Witchcraft wasn't a means to become rich or attract a lover; it was a way to honor what was sacred in her life: to comfort the sick, empower the weak. It was a means of understanding the nature of reality. She wasn't interested in spells, though she had many books on them. I learned those later, on my own.

A passionate devotee of the sacred feminine, she taught me to read tarot cards. Piercing the earth of our potted philodendron with a stick of myrrh incense, we let the smoke curl around us until its stream shifted from a straight line to a diaphanous cloud and she knew we were ready to begin. On the carpet in the living room, she spread a paisley silk scarf on the floor. She kept her Motherpeace deck in a circular, lidded basket that she'd woven herself from pine needles. "Let yourself get still," she'd tell me, spreading the circular golden cards before us in an arc. I'd run my hand along the top and wait for the ones that felt hot on the center of my palm. Hasty with anticipation, I wanted to know how many I should choose. "Draw eleven, but take your time," she told me. She pointed to the places they should go. The significator was at the center; it revealed how Spirit saw me in my current situation. The other cards would fill in the story, telling of my hopes and fears, my future, my foundation. "What do you know that you've forgotten you know?" she'd ask as we gazed at the cryptic images, goddesses swathed in leopard skin reclining on a field of green, or priestesses leaping with gazelles and antelope before a red clay mountain, holding crystal wands aloft in their exultant hands.

On nights of the full moon, she gathered herbs from our garden—chamomile, lavender, mint, and mugwort—for the tea she'd provide her coven later that night: mothers, scientists, academics, businesswomen, leaders in our community. They'd sit in the dark, gazing into their scrying mirrors, bowls stained black with soot, then filled with salt water. The point was to see "beyond the veil," to look into the black mirror and past it, into the unfathomable, into "the mystery" as they called it, the realm of Hecate, keeper of all secrets, of everything known and unknown. They sat before an altar swathed in silks, bedecked with pentacles and sheaves of wheat, shells and chalices of wine. My mother's moon coven was in the Northern Californian tradition of Reclaiming. Their practice was one of reclaiming their bodies, their imaginations, and their power. Rewilding them. Rewilding everything. Rewilding the world. Incense hovering in our living room, they'd cackle into the night, chanting to the Triple Goddess:

> *Horned maiden huntress, Artemis, Artemis,*
> *New moon, come to us.*
> *Silver shining wheel of radiance, radiance,*
> *Mother, come to us.*
> *Honored queen of wisdom, Hecate, Hecate,*
> *Old one, come to us.*

My mother was gaining in her power and her voice, leading spiral dances with hundreds of people, where they'd look into each other's eyes and spiral into the center of a labyrinth chalked onto the plaza in Alice Keck Park and back out again. She always placed the old and infirm at the center of the spiral, so they could know how central they were to our community. She wrote a play called *Demeter's Daughter* and performed it at our local Unitarian

Universalist congregation. Too young to have a larger role, I played a river nymph, witness to Persephone's abduction. Draped in shimmering blue organza, I kneeled on the linoleum floor in the auditorium and bashfully directed the mourning goddess Demeter toward the gash in the earth, a black line of construction paper, into which I'd seen Hades drag her daughter.

In the evenings, my mother began leading Cakes for the Queen of Heaven workshops, classes in women's spirituality. Women from our community were constantly calling my mother for guidance, stopping her in the supermarket, on the street. It took us forever to go to the post office, as someone always recognized her. Sometimes, if I was alone, they'd stop me. "You're Amanda, Lucinda's daughter, aren't you?" When I responded that I was, they'd go moonish and passionate, saying, "I love your mother. She's so powerful; she's helped me so much."

Often, my mother would attend the bedside of the dying. She was paid sometimes, for croning or menarche ceremonies, or helping mothers heal from empty nests. But most of her labor was unpaid. Like many women and nurturers, she supported so many, but there was no way she could have supported herself financially through her labors, despite the endless hours she devoted to them. Though I was attracted to witchcraft and had an affinity, even a longing to serve as a priestess as my mother did, most of the time I didn't ask her to show me how. I had always longed for freedom, whereas my mother's spiritual life was full of obligations and responsibilities. My mother practiced magic, but her life was still hard. How could that be?

* * *

When I turned fourteen or fifteen, my evil grandfather started writing my mother letters. He was hiding out somewhere in Florida, molesting his new daughter and forcing her cancer-ridden mother to eat their TV dinners in another room so she wouldn't contaminate their meal. I never met this man. Everything I know about him, I learned through stories. I'd come into my mother's study to find her face blanched white as she studied the letters. I'd hover in the doorway and watch her reading; with every page, she seemed to shrink. These letters to my mother dangled the carrot of a father's love before her. He'd always loved her; couldn't she see that? If she could not see that, if she could not admit that he never abused her, that it was all in her mind, then, he told her, she needed to be careful. For me, for my brother. We would be in danger.

My mother was working then, at a small publishing company for tourist books, and was proud of the copy she was writing on Yosemite and the Statue of Liberty. When I latch-keyed my way home from school, hungry for turkey Hot Pockets and afternoons of *Oprah* and *Phil Donahue*, under no circumstances was I allowed to open the door. If someone knocked, I was to hide in a cupboard. If I saw any strange men lurking on the street, I was to run the other way. *Never get into the car. It would be better to die in the street, shot in the back, than to get in that car,* my mother told me. Whether or not they have a psychopathic grandfather, it's a warning many girls receive. If you get in that car, it's a fate worse than death.

No matter what abuse her father hammered upon her as a child, my mother would always resist. I knew this because (a) my grandmother told me, and (b) like most traumatized people, my mother

53

constantly talked about it without realizing that she did. From what I understand, the main goal of my grandfather was to get my mother to give in. To concede his right to do whatever he wanted to his family, to her, to the world that was his oyster. But my mother would never concede. She always resisted, regardless of what beating or sexual abuse he inflicted on her. That was the witch in her. The resister. As the eldest, she would protect her brothers and sisters from her father's malevolence. That was the witch in her too. But every time she resisted as a child, it cost her. Every hurt, every wound, pushed the witch in her further and further into the hinterlands, the dark woods of her psyche. The swamps. Inaccessible to the mundane traumas around her. Until my mother came out the other side and started to take refuge in ordinariness.

As a child, she always wanted that: to feel normal, to feel ordinary. Her family was constantly chased out of town when she was a kid, for the flashlight games her father would play at the windows with the little girls next door, and for what he would do to them at the playgrounds. To my mother, ordinary meant safe; her family was not normal or ordinary and it caused her so much pain. But then I was born and I was not normal or ordinary. I was a resister too. A witch from birth. Changing the lines in the fifth-grade school play because they weren't feminist enough, I whirled across the stage and said, "I want to *be* an astronaut when I grow up," instead of "I want to *marry* an astronaut," as my teacher had commanded. My mother beamed at me from the audience with tears in her eyes. But even though she loved and celebrated the fact that I was such a resister, and so full of spit and pride and wildness, she would often lament the fact that I didn't seem to want to *behave*.

By her early thirties, the witch in my mother had gone dormant. She was exhausted. Her struggles first with her father, then with my father, then as a single mother, then again to keep her marriage with my stepfather together had sucked her oceans dry. And for a while she thought if she could just be that perfect woman, wife, mother, daughter, be beautiful and kind and not complain, then things might get easier for her. But then, when things did get easier and her life stabilized, like a plant in your garden some call medicine and others call a weed, the witch in her came flowering back.

Witchcraft, as my mother saw it, was an aspect of women's history. She saw her witch work as part of the same project as her work preventing child abuse, preventing abuse of all kinds. Even as a teenager, she was a student board member of Planned Parenthood. Abortion rights and women's rights to their own bodies were as much a part of her spiritual belief system as prayers or invocations to the Goddess. Working on behalf of women, children, and the vulnerable people of the world *was* a prayer in itself.

But around the same time my mother's father reinvaded her life, her marriage to my stepfather was growing increasingly strained. We never knew who my stepfather voted for, what his true beliefs were about anything. If we talked about politics, he would always play the devil's advocate for either side and never reveal where he stood. Perhaps he stood nowhere. He was a ghost. He had no exact location in space. Their relationship was passionless; they never had sex. He told my mother they should stay in the marriage because of my brother. But he also told her that he could never love her, that she repulsed him. She should take a lover, he said. Then, when my brother was grown, they could separate.

But then, when my mother did take a lover, my stepfather was furious. My mother was a dirty whore. She was a fat slut. In a near suicidal depression, my mother the witch would sit in front of that luxurious pool they'd both sacrificed so much for and contemplate drowning herself in it. Her lover left her. Her marriage failed. She was broke. I'd already long since started going off the rails. Late-night rides clinging to a stranger's back as we stormed the San Gabriel Mountains on his motorcycle; LSD flashbacks while performing *The Glass Menagerie* in the high school play. I was sixteen then, had tested out of high school and started going to the community college. Testing my mother's nerves by spending nights, sometimes several nights in a row, away from home. I had always been in competition with my mother's pain. She had so much of it and she held it so close; it was so dear to her, a huge part of her identity. She talked about it all the time. She was so abused; she'd suffered so much. My suffering with my cousin was small in comparison. "I haven't told you all of it," she'd tell me. "I haven't told you everything." But even when I was a kid, I remember knowing a lot. I knew her father forced her to give him blow jobs, to teach her "what men liked." I don't know how I knew that. She says she never told me. But somehow I did know, either through some kind of sympathetic cognition, or because, without realizing it, she regularly shared her trauma with me. I felt like for my pain to be taken seriously it had to be worse or at least commensurate with hers. She'd always told me that she was forced to move out of

56

her parents' house at sixteen years old. And even then, her father pursued her, broke into her house, slashed her sheets. It was horrifying, but sometimes her suffering seemed to be the maypole she danced around; it was so central to her life and sense of herself. Wiccan priestess and journalist Margot Adler says, "The witch is woman as martyr; she is persecuted by the ignorant; she is the woman who lives outside society and outside society's definitions of woman." Because my mother had moved out at sixteen, I was determined to move out at sixteen too. And I did it, a week before my seventeenth birthday, sliding into a youth hostel on State Street in Santa Barbara, sharing a room with a homeless woman with a wet cough who liked to listen to white noise on the radio. My mother protested that she hadn't wanted to move out but was forced to by the circumstances of her family. I *did* want to move out. I was born wanting to be free. I always felt like I wanted to determine the course of my own life. But really, whether or not I wanted it, I didn't have much choice. My family home had fallen apart. My mother was moving back to San Luis Obispo to try and claw her way back toward survival, and I, as a spooky intruder in the house of my stepfather, had long since worn out my welcome.

Chapter 4

c c c

BLOOD RITES

In the form of a raven she emerged from her fairy-mound and perched on a standing-stone, singing of her Mysteries: "I have a secret that you shall learn. The grasses wave. The flowers glow golden. The goddesses three low like kine. The raven Morrigan herself is wild for blood."

Barbara Walker, quoting Norma Lorre Goodrich,
The Woman's Encyclopedia of Myths and Secrets

It was a golden summer. When I wasn't at school or at work, I'd spend my days at the Espresso Roma Cafe on State Street, with other local youths who'd sit around scribbling in unlined notebooks, smoking clove cigarettes, and writing short stories in the style of John Fante and Jack Kerouac. Within the Roma's brick walls, beneath graphic nudes painted by a local skateboard artist, I met and fell in love with a barista, Darshak. He'd slip by my table, dropping off free mochas and lattes and occasionally one of their half-baked chocolate croissants. Darshak loved to blast John Coltrane and Minor Threat from the café stereo; we'd listen to it and shout through the din about the stories we were reading in the English class we took together at City College. A few months after we started dating, Darshak and I moved in together, into a small bungalow shaped like a houseboat in a 1930s garden apartment complex called the Magnolia.

The eponymous magnolia tree towered three stories above our little garden village of Craftsman cottages, its waxy white blooms intoxicating us with the scent of youth and beauty. Raccoons prowled the grass in our garden like sea beasts on an ancient map, and our little bungalow sailed through blue-green waves of bamboo and morning glory. Darshak and I would spend our afternoons typing stories on his prize possession: an aged Royal typewriter. He in his ribbed white undershirts, khakis, and Converse, me in my Doc Martens, vintage slips, and plum velvet jacket lined in pink satin culled from a thrift store on State Street. We'd read our stories to each other sitting on blankets in the garden, eating seeded baguettes from Our Daily Bread slathered with tangy goat cheese and cheap black caviar we thought was the height of decadence.

Originally from Trinidad, Darshak would make me goat curry when I got home from school. His long brown fingers deftly chopped the carrots and onions into a vat of sizzling ghee as we listened to John Coltrane's *A Love Supreme* on vinyl and I'd read him our favorite excerpts from Salinger's *For Esmé—With Love and Squalor*. He'd reach out to hold my hand as we rode our bikes down Olive Street, our tires squishing through the fat fallen fruit as we rode toward the beach. When he left for work, he'd leave me notes on the tins of leftovers in the fridge, reminding me to warm up my food because he knew of my habit of eating cold beans from a can like my conservative father.

Late at night, we'd study and write each other love notes at Hot Spots, the all-night café. It was so close to the ocean you could hear the waves pounding even over the blare of music the baristas would entertain themselves with at four o'clock in the morning. Morrissey's lamentation on behalf of teenagers everywhere: *Please, please, please, let me, let me, let me get what I want. Lord knows it would be the first time.* Sometimes we'd make predawn pilgrimages up into the mountains, to the burned-out grotto of Knapp's Castle, watching the stars be gulped up by the milky blue morning. We hoped friendly aliens would come whisk us away to the land of milk and honey; we didn't realize we were already there.

We had it pretty good for a while, with Darshak "practicing the fine art of espresso" at the Roma, and me in my shifting array of bookstore and café jobs, studying philosophy and art history at community college, assembling our zines for free when our punk rock friend Jaime worked the late shift at Kinko's. "God is dead," my zines said, quoting my Nietzsche from class, "How are we to exist?" At that moment, we seemed to exist fairly easily without a god. When I moved out of my parents' house, I also moved away from the witchcraft and goddess worship I'd grown up with. I wanted to distance myself from my mother, who at that point just seemed miserable. I saw her goddess as a sad wish that could never be fulfilled. I was searching for a way to make sense of life. I wanted to find the delta where imagination and adventure, reason and security converged. A place where I could drink from those combined waters and become an agent for myself, not at the mercy of the gods, goddesses, or anyone else.

Rather than model myself after the PTA moms and divorcées that came to my mother's moon groups, it seemed preferable to align myself with Jean-Paul Sartre, Friedrich Nietzsche, and Albert Camus. They could exist in a state of questioning and still be celebrated by our culture. The women of my mother's moon group were second-generation feminists fighting for their rights for equal pay, birth control, and freedom from sexual violence. But they were still caught up in misguided racial politics and a middle-class life that seemed bloodless and depressing to me. Looking back, it's hard for me to believe it, but then, I wanted to be on the men's team. The team that had all the power and the best ideas. The team that created *Madame Bovary* and the Sistine Chapel. In Philosophy 101 class, there had been *one chapter* in our book devoted to all the female philosophers throughout history; it was called "The Philosophy of Care."[1] Women, when they could pull themselves away from obsessing about their lovers and milking their breasts in sticky rivulets all over their offspring, made philosophies about caring for things. Nurturing! Pfet! Disgusting. Clearly, nowhere near as important as the Socratic method, Cartesian logic, or the epistemologies of Immanuel Kant.

I started going around declaring that what was exceptional about humans was our ability to reason and telling my mother that there was no evidence there ever was a matriarchy. I wanted

---

1   For some reason Ayn Rand wasn't included in that chapter, despite her possession of a womb.

to be at the table with Sartre. But the philosophers I studied at school were all white men; if I imagined myself sitting around a dinner table with them, I knew I would be perceived not as an equal, or even a student, but as an amusing novelty. A mistress or a servant or a wife who'd eventually be banished to the ladies' sitting room. I hadn't yet found the allies I would later discover in the other exiles: Simone de Beauvoir, Simone Weil, James Baldwin, Hélène Cixous, Audre Lorde.

Simultaneous to my sojourns into continental philosophy, I took a somewhat guilty pleasure in hanging out at Paradise Found, a New Age bookstore on Anapamu Street, across from the library. Tinkling bells and singing bowls and crystal prisms catching the light. Fairy statues. What's alluring about the New Age is also what makes it vulnerable to criticism. New Age philosophy says that change can be instantaneous and easy and that we can get the things we want simply by embracing an abundance mentality or saying the right mantra. The larger social context of our desires is rarely taken into consideration. Everything in Paradise Found was personal; nothing was political. They had crystals and animal cards, messages channeled from gods and goddesses via Midwestern housewives, angels, and angelic beings with something important to say: there is a purpose to our lives, we are protected, everything is going according to a plan, and there are angelic watchers who will come to our rescue and prevent us from destroying ourselves.

While I did enjoy the idea of a host of angels guarding me who knew exactly how to help, I also wanted to live a life of bold intellectual adventure, recognizing the absurd and lonely human condition of perfect freedom. "I rebel, therefore I exist," said Albert Camus. "Yes!" said I. Not knowing how to reconcile my desire for rebellion with my desire to be safe and cared for, the main place I found solace was in dance class. In other words, it was in the body that I found my home. And it comforted me that Nietzsche himself said, "We should consider every day lost that we have not danced at least once." In dance, the questions of existence were worked out through the flesh, through weight and breath, music and movement. My dance teacher, Kay Fulton, a black woman in her forties with an exuberant smile and a passion for cowboy hats, was always dropping wisdom about allowing ourselves to be confident, to take up space. "Feel your feet on the earth. Let your body announce *I AM*," she coached us, and in doing so dismissed the Cartesians from my philosophy classes who favored the disembodied mind.

It was during all these investigations into adulthood that I received my first call to witchcraft on an evening I now refer to as my Blood Rite. Darshak and I were having sex on our futon. In general, our lovemaking was innocent, a bit fumbling, but performed with a rare affection. I traced my finger along the curve of his eyebrow; he'd bury his face in my neck so that I could feel the flutter of his long lashes. That night, our angular teenage forms pushed peaks into the blankets. After ten or so minutes of focused efforts, Darshak, giggling, asked me if I'd wet the bed. He asked because of the sloshy moist sound as we shifted our bodies.

We pulled back the covers and found that we were wet, knee to sternum, drenched with a warm, sticky substance, black in the dappled moonlight. Running into the bathroom, we turned on the lights and saw that it was blood. Somehow, immediately, blood was everywhere. Spattered on the walls, creating messy smears on the floor, running in rivulets down the shower curtain and onto the tile, running down his legs and mine, flooding the drain. We didn't know where it was coming from. I wasn't expecting my period, and they'd always been rather light anyway.

Turning on the shower, we looked down at Darshak's penis to see if he'd been cut. I thought I noticed a small scratch; Darshak grabbed the shower curtain as his knees gave way. He teetered and fell backward, and would've slammed his head against the tile had I not caught him in time. His face gaunt and drained a milky gray, I shouted his name. "Darshak, Darshak!" I thought he had died. I didn't know what to do. Without thinking, I jumped up and ran out the door, into the night garden, shouting for help. I banged on the door of our first neighbor and no one answered. I realized I was naked and covered in blood. I ran back into our bungalow to grab a towel, and I saw Darshak's eyes had fluttered open. He was okay. I climbed into the bathtub to try and pull him out and get him dry. But the blood was still gushing down my legs, big clumps of it globbing in the shower drain. Then it was my turn to faint.

Something had broken free in me. I wanted to return to the wild. Destroy civilization. Fuck women. Voracious appetites consumed me. I'd stopped eating. I didn't feel like I needed it. I could eat the sunlight. There was so much of it. I could gulp the air. I'd never be hungry. I didn't want to participate in the life assigned to me. Suddenly, I just couldn't anymore. After my Blood Rite, I awakened. I could feel the full rush and force of my power. I was like an arrow, shot through the air, wind rushing over sharp contours. Flying free. Until patriarchy raised its shield, and there my arrow lodged, right in the forehead of the Medusa.

Some kind of rupture had happened in my uterus, the part of my body that by cultural decree assigns me as female. I never found out why. My gynecologist said it could have been a miscarriage, but there was really no way to know. That this Blood Rite happened during sex is significant because sex is one way we are initiated into adulthood. This was an initiation related to sex, to sexuality, to partnership, to motherhood, but ultimately to my role as a woman. The womb itself is a threshold: go one way you are born; go the other and you become a sexual being, an "adult" capable of procreation.

Historically, panculturally, initiation rites around sexuality exist in order to educate children about the roles they will be expected to take on in their culture. These initiations teach young people their culture's creation myths; they teach them who in their civilization has power and who doesn't. Genital initiation rites might include circumcision, menstruation, loss of virginity, and so on; they're supposed to help children understand their place in the world, and to be able to perform what will be expected of them as adults. Unfortunately for many of us, our puberty rites often awaken us to the injustices of our culture. You grow breasts, and the puberty rites of America inform you that it is on the pleasing qualities of your breasts that you will be judged. But a call to witchcraft initiates us down a different path. When you are awakened to the culture of the witch, you are being called to a culture of interdependence and co-creation. There, your value is not contingent on your worth as a sexual amusement, reproducer of the workforce, or your ability to generate capital, but on what you contribute to the process of re-enchanting the world. Our call to witchcraft presents us with the things we need to heal, rise up, and seize our power. I would've been able to spare myself years of struggle and confusion if I had been able to recognize my call for what it was, a call to power, instead of just a time of crisis that left me begging for mercy as I was pounded to the floor.

Around the time of my Blood Rite, I reached into my little velvet pouch and drew the Hagalaz rune. Runes are the Norse divination tools from pre-Christian Scandinavia, often carved in stone or bone. I'd created mine out of clay at summer camp around age thirteen and had painted them with my menstrual blood. Clearly one of the most existential runes, Hagalaz would have been favored by Nietzsche; it is the rune of disruption, but also the rune of initiation. Something breaks, an opening appears, we walk through it.

Be aware, my *Book of Runes* told me,[2] that what operates in the Hagalaz rune does not come from the outside. "You are not at the mercy of the external world," it said. "Your own nature is creating what's happening, and you are not without power in this situation. The inner strength you have funded until now in your life is your support and guide at a time when everything you've taken for granted is being challenged."

I wasn't able to heed the wisdom of my runes. I was distracted, disoriented. Soon after the Blood Rite, colors were brighter. Red

---

2   From *The Book of Runes* by Ralph Blum.

curbs became brilliant electric slashes across the pavement. Everything seemed to have some sort of special significance I felt like I should understand but couldn't quite remember. The octagonal shape of the stop signs. The sound of the wind through the magnolia branches. Every little bit of stimuli crying, "Remember? Remember!" But remember what? I didn't know how to interpret the signs.

Crows began following me. For months, I could hear the whoosh of black wings above me as I came home from work or school. These dark guardians would appear at crossroads and watch me from electric power lines, shunting from telephone pole to treetop as they made their pursuit. Cocking and calling, peering at me with their black eyes, expectant and wanting a response. Sometimes they'd caw at me and I'd caw back. One time in particular the crow nearly jumped out of its skin with enthusiasm at my attention. Cawing and nodding and shifting from foot to foot, the crow addressed me and I tried to respond. My sense was that I was being hailed.

Crows circle above charnel grounds. They strut around carcasses with no respect for the dead, parading and guffawing, like knights at a table. Crows are the harbingers of initiation. Without death there can be no rebirth. Before you can be initiated into your new way of life, the old way, your old self, has to die.

The Morrígan are the Celtic triple goddesses who often appear in the form of a crow. Sometimes merging into a single being, the Morrígan are known as the Queen of Phantoms and are guardian spirits to those whom they wish to lead toward victory. Companions to many goddesses of the underworld, crows are carrion birds picking apart corpses in places where they bury them straight in the ground or let them rot on a pyre. Crows always appear near openings to the underworld. Persephone, the maiden goddess, was abducted into a palace of graves. Eventually, she also became phantom queen of that world, a goddess in her own right, parallel in power to her own mother, Demeter, Goddess of the Harvest. Maiden becomes mother becomes crone. Creator, preserver, destroyer.

Hecate completes the triad in yet another form of the triple Goddess. She is the crone, traveler between the worlds, between the above and the below, life and death. Hecate is the ancient goddess of magic and witchcraft, keeper of all knowledge and experience. She stands at the crossroads, flocked by her crow familiars. Crafty and intelligent, these birds make plans, use tools, and remain untamed, even in the depths of the city. Dropping their shining treasures in our yards, marking their territory, they call to each other across the trees. Sharp, crisp cries; guttural alerting croaks. Crows bring wisdom and warning. The crows had called me and I made an attempt to follow. They would feast and laugh around the carcass of my old life. They would cluck and cackle and circle overhead as the porthole to the underworld materialized before me and I took my first steps toward its hungry maw.

In an effort to ground, to stabilize, I started a regime every Wednesday getting free acupuncture in my ears at a nonprofit rehab clinic. I didn't drink or do drugs more than any ordinary teenager, but it was supposed to calm you down, and it would work, sometimes, for a little while. I scrambled to get some kind of low-cost mental health care through my community college, but there was a long waiting list. I clung to my dance classes in an effort to pull myself back into my body. I hadn't danced since I was a child, but soon I began to live for those classes. It got to the point where I was only happy when I was dancing. Shaking my shoulders and doing jazzy slides across the floor to War's "Low Rider": "Low rider knows every street, yeah...take a little trip, take a little trip and see."

Still the calls came in different forms, rushing louder and louder. Impossible to ignore. Someone was calling my name. A woman's voice. A female scream. A cry for help. The first time I heard the screaming, I was in our little houseboat apartment, reading. I put my book down and went out to search. I thought maybe a neighbor was in trouble, but I couldn't find the source. At first, I only heard the screams when I was alone at home, and sometimes it would be hours or days between occurrences. But eventually it happened when Darshak was home. I'd been telling him about it, asking him if he thought there was some abusive situation going on with our neighbors. But he never heard anything, even when we were standing right there together listening to it. Even when I could hear it as if it were in the next room. I asked him, "Can't you hear that?" He just shook his head, his fawnish brown eyes narrowing in concern; his fawnish spirit afraid, beginning to withdraw from me.

It's hard enough for people to handle it when their partner has a head cold. Sometimes it can feel like they're doing it on purpose to annoy you. So I can only imagine how Darshak must have felt as a seventeen-year-old, watching as his girlfriend began to hear voices, careening between ecstasy and despair, rhapsodizing nervously about the crows that were trying to communicate with her. I was scared. I was combative. We both knew our summer of love was over.

Darshak left. He moved back into his mother's Craftsman full of hand-painted china and leather-bound books. The voices I was hearing were telling me there was a woman at risk, and now I know that woman was me. But at the time, in my visions and messages, as in real life, I couldn't figure out how to rescue her. Instead of helping, I moved. I hoped that if I went somewhere else, the screams would stop. I moved from our little garden apartment into a wooden shed in a stranger's backyard on Sola Street, feeling like Leonard Cohen's "Suzanne," a half-crazy girl hidden between the garbage and the flowers.

Crows signal periods of rupture. At five years old, when the crow had come screeching through the sky and fell at my feet, my world was breaking apart then too. But though my first crow event could be seen as an omen, a signal of the many violations my goddess nature would experience before she would be able to reintegrate, it wasn't my official call to witchcraft. Because as a child, I wasn't old enough to answer it. Our true call only comes when we can respond of our own free will. If we can recognize that call for what it is, we might just find that our trials also present us with the keys that can liberate us from the underworld, and help others do the same.

Hecate stands at the place where three roads converge. As the

Goddess in her crone aspect, avatar of age and experience, the most existential of goddesses, she tells you, "When everything breaks, you still have choices." You can take the road that walks you deeper into your trauma, deeper into the knife, until it kills you; you can walk away from the knife, away from risk and potentially any feeling at all, choosing a life of convention, hoping that the authorities won't notice you and will leave you alone; or take the third road, the shadowy animal path, carved into the edges of a cliff, half covered in vines, a trail you have to forge on your own.

At the time, I didn't recognize Hecate's rattling caw as a call to initiation. "Destroy the patriarchal hordes that have invaded your mind," her crows were telling me. "Show no mercy. Pick the bones clean." These calls were the fanfare that launched my journey. But many more initiations would have to follow before I would be fluent in the *language of the birds*, the mother tongue of occult initiates.

Chapter 5

c c c

ENTERING THE UNDERWORLD

On this day I will descend to the underworld. When I
have arrived in the underworld, make a lament for me on
the ruin mounds. Beat the drum for me in the sanctuary.
Make the rounds of the houses of the gods for me.

From *Inanna's Descent to the Underworld*,
circa 1700 BCE

Inanna, Queen of Heaven, raven-haired Sumerian goddess of
magic and power, travels to the underworld in order to rescue
her lover, Dumuzi. It's one of the oldest myths of initiation in
recorded history. Inanna the Wise shows up at the gates of hell,
ready for an adventure. She goes willingly. Into the earth she de-
scends, into history, where records are kept and stories scar the
earth as water carves stone. Trailing her fingers along the wall,
she can smell the decomposing leaves, hear the bats rustling behind the flow stones. She can hear her demon sister, Ereshkigal,
raging deep below in the volcanic heat. Once the goddess of all
things, under patriarchy Ereshkigal had become a shadow version
of Inanna, demoted. Ugly, rotting, now hers was a palace of grave

stench, her lonely throne sitting between the stalactites, dripping mineral milk into pools of bloodred clay.

To confront her demon sister and rescue her lover, Inanna passed through the seven gates of hell. Each gate demanded a sacrifice. First, her lapis-encrusted sword was taken. Then her bronze shield. Gatekeepers took her gold bangles and hennaed robes. They demanded her silver girdle, her copper crown, even the black kohl was smeared from around her eyes. "Do not question the ways of the underworld," the gatekeepers commanded her. Each item they took represented an aspect of her authority, her station in life, her power. All of it gone, Inanna arrived in the pit of hell, naked and defenseless. Her demon sister turned her into a corpse, a piece of meat, gamey and rancid, hanging from a hook in the wall.

Over thousands of years, the story of Inanna was told and re-told. The name of the goddess changed as the story migrated. In Assyria, Inanna became Ishtar the Bold, warrior and light bringer, demanding entry at the gate of death, "threatening to smash it open and set the dead loose on the earth's surface if her request were denied."[1] In biblical times, Inanna becomes Salome, performing the dance of the seven veils to get the head of John the Baptist on a plate. In Greece, after the triumph of patriarchy, Persephone is the goddess of the underworld, an innocent maiden abducted, dragged to the underworld by force, made into the dark lord's unwilling queen. Always, the story of the Goddess's descent into the underworld reflects the values of the time and culture in which it

---

1   Patricia Monaghan, *The Book of Goddesses and Heroines.*

was produced. Always, the story wrestles with power, sex, death, and the sacred mysteries of regeneration.

Again and again, our goddesses and heroines travel to the underworld. Again and again, we descend in our own lives. Why do we tell this story over and over again? The underworld is where we confront the wounded, exiled pieces of ourselves. The pieces we'd forgotten, hidden, or didn't want to see in the first place. We confront the monsters of our culture, the parts howling for attention and care. We go into the underworld to reclaim the integrity of our lineage, to snatch it back from the hands of those who had taken it from us. Sometimes those takers are our own kin, our own blood, ourselves, our Ereshkigals.

In myths, the Goddess suffers, but as an immortal, she is guaranteed many future adventures. When these underworld initiations take place in our own lives, there are no guarantees of success and the correct course of action is rarely clear. The Goddess in us knows the way out, but our human selves can get lost. Like a bird in a cave, we chase what glitters, thinking it's the light of day, when really it's just a reflection off the water, underground rivers rushing us deeper into the labyrinth, toward the gaping mouths of the monsters that howl there.

After the night of blood, I became sensitive to the passage of time. I felt a sense of enclosure, a need to escape. Everything was urgent. The café job that I once enjoyed became unbearable. Once, I'd loved the burnt garlic smell of the everything bagels and the process of making a cappuccino, drawing the frothed milk slowly up from its cold baseline, not letting the steam head sputter, so that the bubbles would be tiny and slow to melt. I wrote riddles on the chalkboard with elaborate flower vignettes, beaming smiles and free coffees at my regulars when they were able to guess the correct answers. But after the Blood Rite and my breakup, haunted by screams, chased by crows, broke, living in a shed, exiled from my family, eating mainly day-old croissants, one day I had a full-fledged breakdown while making sandwiches.

It was a week after my eighteenth birthday. Painting spoonful after globby spoonful of tuna salad onto ciabatta bread, I felt the hours of my life draining away. I saw a sickness of poverty and monotony stretching unto death: here in this glorious life I would be trapped at the sandwich station, in an endless future of ciabatta and bathroom keys and brokenness, teased by the boys I worked with who felt like they should've been promoted to supervisor instead of me, sexually harassed by the cook who kept trying to corner and kiss me. I got frustrated over some small thing, a rude customer or a coffee spilled into the sandwich bar, and I kicked a mop bucket across the room, pounded the wall, and then crumpled sobbing onto the floor next to the industrial dishwasher in the kitchen. A few of my coworkers stood around me, wide-eyed and silent, not sure what to do, until one of them said, "Go home, Amanda. You should just go home. Get some rest." So I went, back to my little shack on Sola Street, accompanied by a murder of crows who sat outside my house chattering. I never went back to my café job again.

Rent in Santa Barbara was just as outrageous then as it is now. My sixty-square-foot shed on Sola Street with vines growing through the wall, a cot for a bed, a dirt floor, a padlock instead of a door-knob, and bathroom privileges in the main house only, cost $450 a month.

Even after I lost my job, I was lucky in that I was able-bodied, cisgendered, and attractive according to society's conventions. Had I not had those unearned privileges, I don't know what would have happened to me, since working a conventional job while experiencing what was essentially a form of mental illness became increasingly impossible. If I couldn't work, I couldn't pay my rent and couldn't eat. What happens to the people without the advantages that I had? I couldn't keep it together for eight hours at a time, much less forty hours per week plus a full-time school course load. I hadn't yet developed the skills I needed to take care of myself. Simultaneously, though, I had a passion to live, to adventure, to travel, to write poetry. I wanted to be safe but I also had a call to explore the hidden depths, to test myself, to visit the wild country where the witches still live.

Our lives are often determined by chance encounters. Bethany, a girl I'd worked with at the Earthling, only worked at the café one day a week to hide the fact that she was a stripper from her dad. At that time there were no strip clubs in Santa Barbara. Instead, you'd join a service, where guys would call in and then you'd go to their hotel rooms for a "private dance."

Taboo and beguiling, a bit dangerous, impossible to resist, strippers appeared in movies and TV shows: they were tacky and trashy, men tossing money at them. The idea of becoming one seemed an impossibility to me; I'd never even considered it. Yet,

I'd been enlightened to the fact that I would be sexually harassed by men before I even entered first grade. It seemed reasonable to me that if I was going to endure that kind of abuse, I might as well get paid for it.

Had I not met Bethany, I doubt I would've sought out sex work on my own. Even then, I worried that if I became a stripper, it would make me hard and nasty and turn me into a drug addict. Bethany was none of those things. Blond and upbeat, she seemed like someone who'd major in hospitality and play volleyball. She gave me the number of the guy who ran the stripper service, but before I called him, I asked her, "Does it change you?"

Bethany responded with a shrug, "Everything changes you."

The audition process was basically that Jeremy, the owner of the business, came over to my crow-encircled shack. In his over-sized jersey and jeans, Jeremy talked with me about becoming a stripper but it felt more like chatting with a daytime bartender about baseball. Jeremy was matter-of-fact: "Either I or one of my guys will escort you to the door. The client will give me the money. You'll be safe because he'll know we're with you, just outside the door, and we'll keep the money for you until you get out. You just go in, do a little dance. Give the guy a massage. And that's it. It's $415 for the hour, you get $315 and any other money you make in there is up to you."

I thought he meant that if anyone tipped me, I got to keep the tips. Later, I found out that wasn't what he meant.

But in any case, $315 for one hour's worth of work was more than I made in a forty-hour workweek at the café. I told Jeremy I'd give it a shot, and he said, "Fine, I just have to see your tits."

I was sitting on the edge of my bed, barefoot, in rust-colored corduroy bell bottoms, a thermal tank top with little yellow flowers on it, and a Riot Grrrl plastic flowered barrette in my bangs. I paused for a moment, gauging the situation, trying to feel out if I was in danger. It was the middle of the day; I could hear someone hammering something next door and the clink of dishes being washed in the kitchen a few yards away. I lifted up my shirt and bared my chest. Jeremy nodded, neutral. My breasts were small but serviceable. He left a pager on the top of my bookshelf and told me he'd call it when he had a client.

Two days later, Jeremy paged me and told me he'd had an easy one for my first time.

We pulled into the Motel 6 parking lot in Goleta at twilight. In a way it felt safe, familiar. I'd driven by this motel countless times in high school; it was right across the street from the Taco Bell, where I'd slathered my bean burritos in spice packets before going to my afterschool job stuffing envelopes.

Drowsing on the horizon, the sun whispered through the palm trees, electric pink in the hot salt breeze. I sat, thighs sticking to the car seat, my boom box on my lap and the window rolled down, watching a virginal white egret performing its ballet in the reeds of the adjacent lot. Jeremy fiddled with his pager. He hadn't talked to me the whole ride over. He didn't seem to want to get personal. But finally, he smiled at me and nudged me on the shoulder. "You ready?" he asked.

I pulled my boom box to my chest; it felt heavy and good, like a shield. Jeremy was already out of the car, standing up, waiting for me to close the door so he could lock it. "But, what do I do again, when I go in there?" I asked him.

"Paul's a regular. A nice guy. He'll make it easy for you," Jeremy said, coming around to my side and closing the door.

My stomach dropped. I wanted to ask him more. I still didn't understand what was supposed to happen. I'd been trying to visualize it: *Flashdance*. Jennifer Beals coming out onto the stage in '80s power suit and stilettoes, spinning off her clothes like Wonder Woman, baptizing herself with buckets of water, shaking her sopping hair and pounding the floor with all the pent-up rage and Eros the divine feminine had been holding in for eons. I envisioned something like that.

"You don't need to make this a big deal," Jeremy said, shaking his head, telling me I reminded him of his girlfriend. "It can be as chill as you want it to be."

I looked down at my shoes. I couldn't yet afford to buy new ones just for the occasion. I didn't own any high heels—I'd never worn them—so I did the best I could with some wedged linen espadrilles. In my hippy purple paisley sundress, face pale as the moon with messy cropped black hair and lipstick in '90s rust, I looked like I'd just got back from an unsuccessful day at the beach.

"And you'll be right outside?" I imagined him standing outside the door with his arms folded, a soldier protecting something of great value.

"You're a stresser, aren't you?" Jeremy asked, chuckling.

"No, I'm not," I lied. I was, of course, a total stresser. I was vibrating on the edge of everything then, always about to fall off.

"I'll be in the car," he said.

* * *

Paul's room was on the bottom floor in room 5. Five, the number of treachery and struggle. In systems of numerology, five represents humanity. Jeremy knocked; my stomach churned, slick and inflated like bread dough. Heart thumping, I gripped the handle of my boom box, my fingers popping white like gristle. Paul opened the door a crack and I felt a blast of air-conditioning. He stood there, a shade, naked except for his grubby tighty-whitey underwear. Shorter than me by a few inches, but stocky, sunburnt, baffled-looking, and wounded. His brown eyes were itchy and red beneath a thin, brown comb-over haircut. Paul slipped Jeremy a wad of cash with his right hand. His left hand was jammed in his underpants, masturbating.

He was masturbating. Already. When I saw that, the spirit of "Amanda" just switched off. I became neutral, blank, automatic lizard brain operating on instinct. I wish I would've called Wheezer to my side; I wish I would've known I had that tool. I wish I would've grounded and centered, a witch's most essential daily practice, where she calls her full spirit back into her body, where she visualizes herself growing roots to the core of the earth. I wish I would've created for myself a mountain shield, or practiced a Queen of Swords level of discernment, icy and calm. But I didn't. I didn't know how. Like they used to tell me in grade school, I'm a slow learner. And it turns out I often have to learn the hard way.

Clearly, harm lived inside room 5 of Motel 6. Why did I walk into harm? I could've turned around and left. I could've said, "No,

80

this isn't for me." But I didn't. In some way I knew that it was exactly for me. And I knew that because I'd been given harm as my lot at a vulnerable age. The weapon had lodged in my heart while I was still growing. My bark grew over it, but it was still buried there, magnetic, an attractor. Yet this weapon wasn't just mine alone; it was an heirloom passed down to me through generations. My grandfather had plunged it into my mother's heart, until it touched her spine, touched her ancestors and mine. You could walk that wounded heart road all the way back to Europe, to the Inquisitions, to the blood that fell on the smashed altars of the Goddesses of Babylon.

Paul widened the door but I stood outside the threshold, looking in. It felt like I'd seen everything in the room before. Every Motel 6 looks the same, a flimsy film set, pretending to be cozy, where any minute the walls could fall back and reveal...what? The void. Nothing. No one. "Come in," Paul implored. He grabbed me by the wrist and pulled me inside, the door shutting behind him with a binding suck.

Everything in the room was clammy and damp, the air-conditioning vibrating waspish in the corner. I set my boom box down near the television as Paul turned on a lamp, then bustled around moving beer cans and papers from place to place. "I've got some speed if you want some." He flicked his hand toward the bathroom door. "It's on the toilet." I craned my head around to look inside. On the back of the toilet was a little bag of sticky yellow powder, a hypodermic needle, and a tourniquet—lurid, thick, and made of a sickly snot green rubber—dangling off the side.

I was in the motel room of a masturbating stranger. Paul was suggesting that I share needles and shoot up speed with him. Silent, throat dry, I shook my head and focused on my boom box, staying close to it as if it were an anchor or a teleporter, something familiar that was mine. I clicked in my mixtape, expecting it to sound rough. The magnetic tape had grown thin from listening to it so many times: Edie Brickell, the Violent Femmes, Tori Amos, Depeche Mode, The Cure. I wanted to be surrounded by my people. I wanted to hear Tori Amos sing, *she's been everybody else's girl, maybe one day she'll be her own*, like she was with me and she got it.

I scanned the room. Boxy television atop cheap veneer dresser. Strappy foldout luggage table holding duffel bag. Beer cans. Big Gulps. Paul had rolled off his underwear so they dangled on his ankle like an animal he'd kicked and killed. In the middle of the bed he sprawled, limp dick in hand, above him a bucolic print of a country lane. Dappled sunlight, a bridge. It reminded me of the most popular book at one of the bookstores where I'd worked: *The Bridges of Madison County*. One hundred sixty-four weeks on the bestseller list. It got so that when middle-aged women came into the shop, I'd just point to the bestsellers wall in the back and say, "It's over there." They always wanted the same thing. To be truly loved. To be truly seen. If they couldn't have it, they wanted to read about it. Fair enough.

"Should I just…Do you want me to start?" I asked.

Teeth grinding, neck straining like a horse, Paul said, "Yeah, yeah, just go ahead whenever. I'm just going to lie here on the bed and jack off; that's what I usually do. Don't worry, you're going to do great." He lay back and made a swirling motion with his hand for me to *do my thing*. At first he didn't look at me. He jackhammered his dick but couldn't get it up. "It's the speed," he told me, apologizing. I bent down to press the button on my boom box. *Yeah I like you in that, like I like you to scream*...Robert Smith's plaintive voice warbled and died. My boom box clicked off. I shook it and pulled the tape out, flipped it over, and tried it again. Pressed a few more buttons. "It's not working," I told Paul. Maybe that meant I should just leave. I couldn't dance. I should just go.

"Don't worry about it." He smiled at me. Never ceasing his attempts at masturbation, with his free hand he harassed the remote control until he got MTV. The R & B singer Des'ree appeared in a boxy black suit with military buttons. Marching out onto a plain white cove, she pointed at the youths of America, she pointed at me as if she were Uncle Sam claiming me for the nation: *You've gotta be bad, you've gotta be bold, you've gotta be wiser, you've gotta be hard, you've gotta be tough, you've gotta be stronger*. To this day I can't hear that song without thinking of the first time I stripped in that Motel 6 on Hollister Avenue.

Over the next few years I grew to feel that this was what the world wanted of me, this was how it saw me and recognized my value. I should capitalize on what sex appeal I had. I should stop crying. I was in hostile territory. I needed to do whatever I could to survive. Called to war, it was my sex against theirs. I knew my side was at a disadvantage, but I would fight with everything I had. I told myself that many people had it worse than I did. I was right. Even in that situation, by comparison to many people in this world, I was lucky.

Hoping that the dance moves would just come to me somehow,

I tried to do a few from my beginning jazz classes at city college, pumping my shoulders up and down. Paul didn't care what I did. Panting, brow sopping, he made noises like something was scratching him on the inside. I wiggled around and lifted the hem of my dress, spinning in a circle. Untying my shoulder straps, I let the paisley sundress fall to the floor and stood there topless in my white cotton lace-trim underwear from Miller's Outpost. I glanced up at Paul; he seemed to approve, nodding, grinding his teeth. "Yeah, yeah, yeah," he said, as if trying to convince himself. I dropped my underwear, but they got caught on my shoes. So I squatted and wobbled and took those off too. As the song ended, I stood up naked, bare feet sticking to the mysterious stains on the carpet at the foot of the bed. Not even lasting one full song, my strip tease had taken all of three minutes.

I still had fifty-six minutes to go.

The thing about stripping for the first time was that I had expected the world to end. Some part of me had thought I would walk into that room and take off my clothes, and the ground would shake, thunder would blast. I'd be struck by lightning. But there was no cataclysm. My clothes were on and then they were off. "Everything changes you," my stripper mentor Bethany had told me. We expect change to be instantaneous. "From that moment forward, everything was different..." We have this idea that when the taboos of our culture are broken, we'll be broken too. But somehow, unbelievably, even when everything feels wrecked and hopeless, life just keeps going.

What happened next was a blur. "Why don't you give me a

massage," Paul suggested. "That's what they usually do. Come here." I came toward him. He grabbed at my tits, and I said no. "Oh, hmm, usually they let me." He seized my hand and tried to pull me down on the bed. "Let me fuck you," he pleaded. I said no. He snapped, "You guys always say that. Next time I won't ask, I'll just do it." I didn't have time to let his rape threat sink in, or the fact that there might be a "next time," because he rolled over for his massage, ducking his head with embarrassment, saying, "I've got something going on with my…" as he pointed to his shoulders flaming with acne and flaky skin. "It's from work. Diving. I'm a diver. You know? The wells. The oil rigs, out there." He gestured his fingers dismissively toward the ocean.

I preferred it when he was facing down and couldn't reach me. I massaged his back and he told me I was good at it. That was something I heard often throughout my experience in the sex industry. I was a better healer than sex worker. Probably because I liked healing people, but resented interacting sexually with people I didn't know or like, who saw me as some kind of faulty yet still magical fetish object they hoped to use to soothe their fears about their masculinity.

Paul couldn't lie still for the massage; he rolled this way and that and couldn't get comfortable. I was trying to move slowly, so that everything I did would take up more time, but Paul was in a sped up world. It seemed like he wanted to enter my world, the slower one, but he couldn't find a way. He was trapped in his own underworld too.

"Here." He scuttled off the bed and pulled out a cold Budweiser can from the mini-fridge. "Stand up." I got up on the opposite side of the bed. Desperate, he frowned at me from across the room, plead-ing, "Maybe you could hold this cold can of beer under my balls."

I considered his request. If we were standing up and doing something, it might help me avoid being raped on the bed. I walked toward him. His balls were purple and swollen, a lined eggplant accordion. We paced around the room, me holding the beer under his balls, him with his non-masturbating hand thrown over my shoulder as if we were at some sort of perverted prom. We did this for about five minutes. Then he grew agitated. Whatever he was hoping for, this wasn't delivering.

"Let me draw you," he gasped, struck with inspiration. I re-clined on the bed like the Degas I'd seen in my art history classes while he squirmed in a swivel chair and drew some sketches with a ballpoint pen on hotel stationery. They were childish and uncertain. He was talking the whole time.

"Do you have a boyfriend?"

"Do you have a girlfriend?" I responded.

His shoulders fell. "No. Well, kind of. I'm seeing a girl... Actually, I don't. You know. I'm away so much because of work."

"Is that why you're sad?" I asked. I didn't care if or why he was sad. My questions functioned as a shield, deflecting attention away from me. My sadness, my fear, my feelings were irrelevant.

He shrugged, pulling at the skin on the back of his neck as it reddened. "I had a girlfriend once but we had a difficult relation-ship. She wanted things from me and I...didn't know how to give them to her. Nothing I did ever satisfied her. Not like you. I think we have a lot in common." He smiled at me, vulnerable, with his shoulders hunched. "I feel like you approve of me. Do you?"

86

"Yes?"

Seeming satisfied with my answer, Paul stopped and stared at me for a moment, eyes wide like a deer. "You're really beautiful. Would you like to go out to dinner with me sometime?"

"I...umm..." but before I could answer, he interrupted.

"I could never handle it if my girlfriend did this shit like you guys do."

Paul spat on the carpet and stood up. "All this is my mother's fault." He started pacing around the room. "Seriously, I know people always say that, but in my case it's true. She's codependent. Abusive, you know? Manipulative."

While Paul was getting another beer, I got up and peeked out the window. Jeremy's car was gone. I was alone. Pins of adrenaline jammed into my belly in a sudden jolt. I didn't tell Paul. I wasn't sure what would happen if I did, but I didn't want him to know.

"Your mom was mean to you as a kid?" I asked Paul, trying to distract him.

He flicked his hand in front of his face, brushing at the dry skin at the corners of his mouth. "I was an only child; she had high expectations that I couldn't meet."

Paul fell back onto the bed and started squirming, pulling at his hair as if trying to get something out of his head. "Did you know I'm also a poet?"

I shook my head.

"Come here," he begged.

Reluctantly, I inched my way toward the bed, standing just out of reach like a cat. But he lurched and grabbed me and pulled me down, pinning me and trying to pry my legs open. "You're like a fairy with skin so white," Paul chimed. "I try for your honey but it's locked so tight." As I struggled with him and he clenched me, I could feel his anxiety, his shame, his dread pouring into me. I came to understand that this was in fact what he wanted from me—he wanted me to hold his suffering for him. Holding suffering and looking appealing while you're doing it is the main function of the sex worker, it turns out. But I was not equipped to hold his suffering, nor to know what to do with it, and furthermore, I didn't want to hold it. I resisted. I struggled and fought and eventually he tired and let me go. I leapt from the bed and stood gulping for air behind the swivel chair, electricity twisting around my wrists like snakes. I used the chair to barricade myself while I peeked once again into the parking lot.

"I just made that poem up on the spot, you know," Paul told me. I shook my head. Clearly we were having two wildly different experiences.

Jeremy's car crept back into the lot and I pressed my palm against the window, creating a steam outline on the glass. I wanted to touch that car, I was so glad to see it there.

Paul held his fists to his eye sockets in a dramatic Grecian gesture. "I think I'm in love with you," he cried. "Please, please! Will you just hold me? Just hold me for a second, for a few minutes?" He scooted over and patted the space next to him on the bed, pleading and insistent.

"I . . . I can't," I stammered, collecting my things, pulling on my underwear, tying the straps of my dress. There was a knock at the door. "We're done."

I stood with my hand on the door handle, carrying my broken boom box in the other. "Thank you?" I offered.

"Yeah right." Paul scowled, making his way back into the bathroom. "You bitches are all the same. Nothing means anything to you. There's a tip on the table."

The streetlights buzzed as Jeremy and I walked to the car. A seagull pecked ketchup from a greasy wax wrapper and the sky was oily and dark. The streetlamps made everything look grainy, digital, a bad movie on late-night cable.

"I looked outside at one point and your car wasn't here," I said to Jeremy as he unlocked my door.

"I was here the whole time." Jeremy shrugged. When we got in the car, we both ignored the Del Taco bag on the floor that hadn't been there an hour ago. Jeremy reached into his pocket and pulled out the wad of cash, slowly laying twenties down on my thigh. For each bill I thought of the hours I wouldn't have to spend working at a café job, the many hours of my life I'd get back in exchange for this one. "Here," he said at the end, slapping down an extra twenty. "First day bonus, cuz."

He laid the money out on my thigh and it all made sense, a thousand clicks whirring into place. I could have money to the degree that I suffered. I could suffer fast, like I did in the motel room while risking my life, or I could suffer slow like I did at the coffee shop, physically safe but grueling away my hours, not being able to eat well or pay rent or be creative or afford a therapist or medical care, maybe for the rest of my days. I chose to suffer fast.

For many years, I remembered my whole "first time stripping" experience as funny. I forgot about the rape threat. The speed on the toilet. The squalor. I forgot that I went back to my little shack that night and cried, curled into a ball on my squeaky cot, feeling like my life was spinning out of my control with no one I could turn to for help. I forgot how the next night the storms came and I wandered the streets drenched, shook by thunder, walking through rain that came in heavy veils. Around 2:00 a.m., I found myself alone at the end of the pier. I sat with one arm circling a wood post sticky with tar, my feet dangling off the dock into a black oblivion. Water ran down the back of my neck and into my eyes. More than I could see, I could feel the water two stories below me. The great Pacific, heaving and lowing, pulling on my bloody, bloody heart with all the inexorable power of the moon. I thought of the 10 of Swords in the Motherpeace version of the tarot deck, the one my mother had used when she taught me how to read, a gift for my first initiation, the Rite of Roses. In the tarot card, priestesses of the Goddess know the patriarchal hordes are coming for them; they know theirs is a lost cause, so rather than submit to rape and pillage, they toss themselves off a cliff into the amniotic waters of the Mediterranean.

I sat on the end of that pier for hours, feeling it rising and shifting and creaking with the tide, lightning flashing ever nearer on the horizon. I wanted to go home to my underworld Goddess, restored and happy in the oblivion She offered. Then I heard a voice, flashing with the lightning, a crack in my mind. She gave her command: "You're not done yet. Stand up."

For many witches, their first initiation drags them into the underworld. But there are many underworlds. All interconnected. The witch's first experience there depends on where she enters. My underworld was a labyrinth of sex and power and patriarchy. I stepped inside and the demons began feasting on my sense of self-worth. "The only thing that's valuable about you is your sex," they cawed, poking and squeezing, "and even that is defiled and cheap." For seven years I wandered the halls of that underworld and couldn't see a way out. Every attempt at escape just led me further in.

When the Inquisitions of Europe came, they told us that witches were the queens of hell. They didn't know the half of it. We witches *are* the Queens of the Underworld; we've been there so often that by now, collectively, we know its every chamber. Alone and unadorned, the witch has to figure out how to make it out of the maze. The harder her passage, the more powerful her initiation. Powerful initiations amplify her magic when she gets back home. But not every witch makes it out of the underworld alive. Sometimes even the bravest and strongest fall, their bones and tufts of hair littering its labyrinthine pathways. Witches witnessing these bone warding cairns would do well to remember: the underworld does have doors. Keep your guardians close, remember who you are. When the Goddess appears to you, follow Her. Whether you realize it or not, finding Her is the reason you were sent there in the first place.

Chapter 6

c c c

THE EGREGORE

In the movie [*The Exorcist*] the men were repulsed by the devil and the stench of the devil; they told the devil to leave the girl and to cease to exist. Of course the devil couldn't do that. The devil had come into this girl for a reason and it wasn't going to leave.

John Haskell, "The Faces of Joan of Arc"

Within the occult there is an entity known as an *egregore*, a kind of angel. The word *egregore* comes from the Greek, meaning "watcher." Spiritualists and theosophists of the late nineteenth and early twentieth centuries called these spirits *thought forms*: energetic beings created by people's highly charged thoughts and emotions. Simply put, an egregore is the spirit of a group. Egregores can arise spontaneously from a roaring crowd at a football game, a political rally, a church meeting or a concert, and then disperse just as fast. But if enough energy is poured into them, eventually they become immortal. Jesus is an egregore, as is Mohammed, or Aphrodite, who still speaks to us through our dreams and in songs. When we pray to egregores, paint pictures of them, write hymns to them, they take on a life of their own.

Cities have egregores, and houses; even groups of friends can create egregores. Neither positive nor negative, the egregore is simply what it is, like a volcano or a weasel. You might not want to share your bedroom with a weasel, but weasels do prevent the forest from being overrun with rats. Egregores have their purpose, too, as containers of influence. Once created, egregores have their own agenda and don't care whether or not you approve. What do egregores want? The same thing as the devil, the same thing as God. The same thing as all of us. To live, to live, to live. And to be seen. The Watchers want us to watch them back. They want intimacy.

One of the most important initiations for any witch is to recognize that intimacy is synonymous with influence. A witch needs to be able to choose which influences she will accept.

The Fulton Street egregore had been waiting for me to arrive. Fulton ran a few blocks north of San Francisco's panhandle: a narrow stretch of meadows slicing down from Golden Gate Park. Eucalyptus, sycamore, and alder loomed like druids there over the homeless wanderers and gutter punks prowling through the dim glow of the antique streetlamps. My friend William had a room on the second floor of a four-story Edwardian house overlooking the street. He'd been sending me letters sprinkled with the spores of the house egregore, who was looking for new hosts to amplify its power. I opened the letters in my little shack in Santa Barbara and breathed the spores in; they gave me a sudden urge to visit San Francisco.

Towering white and covered in dust, the house on Fulton Street was bound in ornate cornices trimmed in gold. Inside, a sooty stained glass window illuminated the winding central staircase; it gleamed with orange orbs and mounds of Dionysian grapes. William's room was bare. White walls, a mattress on the floor, a desk with a wooden chair, and sheer drapes that billowed and shifted in the briny air. I was platonically in love with William. At the advanced age of twenty-four, he was six years my senior and seemed impossibly sophisticated to me. He'd lived in Paris and traveled through Europe, visiting all the places to which I'd longed to go. He'd moved to San Francisco out of a gut-wrenching (and to me inexplicable) longing for his ex-girlfriend, a busty crop-haired blonde who did something having to do with computers. But William was special. He had curly brown hair and a Roman nose and we sat on the floor of his room playing Leonard Cohen's "Take This Waltz" on repeat as he thumbed through a dog-eared copy of Hesse's *Siddhartha* and chatted with me about Jung and shamanism from within a dense exosphere of Camel smoke.

During a tour of the house, William showed me the narrow staircase into the attic where Colette lived. The house on Fulton Street's longest tenant, Colette was the egregore's priestess. A stylish Bohemian from New Orleans, she ruled the place from her attic boudoir, fingers of incense reaching down the stairs, beckoning us with some secret scent, sulfurous and chemical. As we walked the halls, William pointed out the rooms of the other tenants: Brett, a Chaos Magician who managed a Big 5 Sporting Goods store, and Donna, a gaunt college student who darted furtively past us without comment, clutching her books to her chest as if we intended to rip them from her hands.

Alex, a Jewish mathematician from New York, lived on the first floor. He was studying at UC Berkeley. He saw math as some kind of ecstatic psalm inscribed into the universe by God, and as soon as we were introduced, he started ranting about math's beauty and elegance, eyes wide, hair standing on end as if he'd got his wires crossed while trying to electrify an elephant. I soon discovered that he'd stay up for days in a mania, scrawling advanced mathematical symbols on stacks of loose-leaf paper. Then he'd fall into a peculiar kind of math coma and sleep until deep into the afternoon.

Beyond Alex's room was a long, narrow kitchen where a famished-looking couch lurked beneath the window. On the opposite wall hung a Bernard Buffet painting of a sad clown. It loomed over a church pew, which I later learned had been used in Satanic rituals that previous tenants had held in the basement in the 1970s. On this pew sat the two house gargoyles: Stella, a needy shar-pei with a chronic skin condition, and Fang, an elegant but violent Siamese. As we entered the room, Fang hissed and clawed the empty air before her, fur bristling, eyes wild. On the way out, William showed me the last remaining room in the house. A bedroom. Airy, with fifteen-foot-high ceilings, dripping candle sleeves on the lights, a loft bed, and bay windows framing the mist-shrouded cypress trees in Buena Vista park. "This room's vacant," William told me, smiling.

Darshak had always called San Francisco *the City*, as if there were no other. When I saw it for the first time, all white and shining with pyramids, towers, and tarnished copper domes, I could feel its power before I even got out of the car. Troubled spirits lived in San Francisco. Anton LaVey. The Red Man of the Mission District. To enter the city was to enter the heart of the Romantic, the land of the weirdo and the outsider. The flower children. A boom and bust town, port city and melting pot, full of painted ladies and the barbarous ghosts of sailors and gold miners. A place where many of the rebelling souls of America had come to exorcise themselves, the exiled spirits drifting through the air as fog.

William and I took a street car to Union Square, then snaked our way through Chinatown. Fingering the spiky foreign fruit, silk robes, and woven finger traps: the harder you pulled, the more impossible to break free. Everything buzzed. The tattooist's needle, the jackhammers. Metro power lines sparked like dragons across the city skies. San Francisco was full of egregores, manifestations of the spirit of the times, giving form to the mystical volatility percolating beneath the surface of the city. In North Beach we passed a street garden with a temple to Pan, Greek god of wildness and ecstasy. By that time, the city had seduced me completely.

William took me to Caffe Trieste, a sepia cave with a trompe l'oeil mural of an Italian piazza on the wall and a jukebox that only played opera. The café was named after a port town in northern Italy famous for attracting writers, artists, and other misfits. Behind the counter stood a tall boy with sloping shoulders and angel eyes who kept glancing at me while William and I drank cappuccinos from heavy brown mugs. I was only to be in SF for three days and was eager for a holiday romance. I slipped a dollar bill with my phone number in the beatific barista's tip jar, whispering, "A secret message for you," just before William and I left.

"If that café boy calls me before I leave on Monday, I will move to San Francisco," I told William as we began our walk back toward Market Street.

"I thought you were saving up for Europe," William said.

"I'm open to fateful interventions," I told him.

Cut to three days later. The cute boy had called. I dropped all my classes at Santa Barbara community college, quit my motel stripping gig, crammed all the belongings into the back of my Mustang, and moved to *the City*. I took the vacant room on the first floor of William's house. San Francisco was still cheap then. The monthly rent of my new room cost $50 less than the rotting garden shed I'd called home in Santa Barbara. I draped the windows in thrifted floral silks and decorated the walls with my own ecstatic collages. On *free days* the city's wealthy would leave their unwanted items on the curb. I scavenged a pink desk that made me feel like a writer in a genie bottle and a moss-green velvet love seat upon which I'd scribble drawings in my notebook. I hoped that in this new home I could turn my attention toward bringing my creative visions into the world. I would leave Anxiety and Mental Instability—raven messengers of the initiations I had refused to recognize—in that old flooded shack in Santa Barbara. I would let them be carried away by the rain, never to be heard from again.

* * *

For work, I grabbed the lowest-hanging fruit and got a job at the Lusty Lady, a woman-owned and operated peep show on Geary that paid an hourly wage and required no physical contact with the customers. The "punters" were all safely behind glass, dribbling their hard-earned quarters into slots, raising and lowering the partitions according to their desires. We dancers whirled around naked on a red velvet stage lined with mirrors, shiny ballerinas in a pornographic panoptic jewelry box.

In many tarot decks, Major Arcana XI is called Strength, but in the Thoth deck it's called Lust. The Thoth deck was a favorite of the occultists in San Francisco at the time. They hung out at the Sword and Rose bookstore in Cole Valley and sent messages to each other via arcane symbols spray-painted on sidewalks and doorways, clues to the locations of secret meetings to which only the initiated were invited. Painted by Lady Frieda Harris, under the artistic direction of the infamous Aleister Crowley, the Lust card depicts "the Whore of Babalon," an embodiment of ecstatic life force energy; she is wildness, the essence of nature and creativity. An essence I was attracted to and wanted to embody. Before I hopped onstage in my feather boa and heels, I loved to stomp through the lobby of the Lusty Lady in Doc Martens, sweats, and a black hoodie pulled down low over my eyes as if I were some kind of assassin. That was the stripper way. We all did it. Backstage the girls would roam without their wigs, scratching their heads, slouching spread legged as they gorged on burritos, talking about how America isn't ready for them, their love of other strippers, their college courses, and their activist work with Food Not Bombs. I admired their loud laughs and big personalities, the fact that they knew every band and performance artist, and I admired their beauty.

I specifically remember one dancer named Lolita, a Riot Grrrl, first-generation Chinese, almost six feet tall with straight black hair down to her thighs. Her costume consisted of thigh-high spike-heel patent leather boots and a navel ring. She loved to dance to Bikini Kill and Rage Against the Machine. "Fuck you, I won't do what you tell me," she'd sing along in grouchy serenade to the men behind the glass windows. I remember one time a man pointed at her, commanding "the China girl" to come over. "You mean you would like the attention of the *Asian woman*," she corrected him, kicking her boots at his goggle-eyed face.

Often without realizing it, we accept the influence of our generation. Like most of the city's young countercultural inhabitants of the Gen X period, and unlike today's San Francisco youth who literally live in their Google dorms, we worked hard not to work hard. Most of us did everything we could to avoid "real jobs" so that we could spend our days reading, drawing, falling in love, hanging out in cafés, and in my case, taking every dance class I could find. Contemporary dance at Alonzo King Lines Studio. African dance at the community college. Feldenkrais movement exploration with Augusta Moore. Contact improvisation. And ballet classes led by one of the most defiantly bitchy Queens in the Castro.

Caffe Trieste was just a block or two away from the Lusty Lady, and thus I continued my courtship with the cute guy who worked there: Adrian. Adrian was a real live artist. An ex-heroin addict with an MFA from the Art Institute, he lived in a converted loft space south of Market.

"Hold on a second," he commanded the first time he took me into his studio. Suddenly inspired, he splashed automotive paint from a can on the floor onto one of the large panels strewn about the room, all of them paintings of flying saucers lurking over empty, alienated suburban landscapes. While he worked, I snooped and found notes for a short story written by a woman to whom he assured me he was no longer involved, a writer his same age (twenty-seven) and already famous—in San Francisco at least. Her notes were stashed all over his loft. Snippets of ideas for stories, or scenes of plays scrawled on the backs of envelopes and inside book flaps. He talked about her as if she was an equal, though an arrogant one who may have gotten above her station. To him, they had a real relationship that they were trying to work out, riddled with adult complexities I was too young to understand. I had lugged my typewriter with me to San Francisco and was writing a novel then, too, about a girl who heard voices and was trapped in the underworld. But my writing lived in the world of dreams, while his *friend's* work lived in the world of reality. Writing was how she made her living. I, on the other hand, was a stripper.

"You're going to get so much out of knowing me," Adrian told me humbly. Though it pains me now to say it, he was right. His influence was powerful and through him the city opened to me. During our courtship, he took me to the wave organ: a gulping, slapping stone instrument hidden on a jetty out in the Marina. I could hear the bowels of the city gurgling through its pipes.

We went to underground theater, and he introduced me to a set of his artist friends: Akari, a musician who understood the talismanic power of red lipstick. I never saw her without it; it seemed to function both as a weapon and a shield. Her superpower was that she didn't give the slightest shit what men thought of her. Nevertheless, she had a boyfriend, Sky, a painter.

The first and only time I went over to their little one-room apartment, the three of us sat together on their bed and they introduced me to *Horses*, Patti Smith's urgent battle cry. *Jesus died for somebody's sins, but not mine*, Patti chanted, channeling the defiant egregore of her generation. Akari cut me a small, sharp streak of yellow speed. "You don't have to take this if you don't want," she told me. I'd never taken it before. But Akari seemed powerful and mysterious to me, so I took a dainty sniff. Aside from my heart pounding like I'd just run up a flight of stairs, all I felt was a strong desire to talk. We all gabbed breathlessly for the next few hours, until I felt like I needed to go home and clean my room. Before I left, Sky solemnly presented me with one of his artworks, a translucent blue angel, fist raised, powering across the endless void. "It's Azrael, angel of death and rebirth. It belongs to you. I made it for you before I even met you."

I've found that when a spirit wants to come into your life, someone will present you with its image. Over a decade later, when I was living in Los Angeles, in a century-old haunted house in Echo Park with clapping sounds and rotten smells in the wall, people kept giving me images of a little girl. About eight years old, she always had black bobbed hair and a headband, and was dressed in her 1940s Sunday best. I had a whole altar to her in the hall: paintings people gave me, photographs found folded into used books; a friend even randomly gave me a patent leather shoe, something she wore in every image. By that time, I had been reborn to my witchly nature, and I knew what to do. I wasn't surprised when, one night while lying in bed with my boyfriend, he, who was normally a silent sleeper, woke me up sleep-chattering about murder and strife. As soon as my head again hit the pillow, my body was immobilized and the girl from the pictures appeared at the foot of my bed. By then I knew to stay in my power, to check my boundaries, but also to offer to help her if I could. It turned out she was lost, stuck in the middle world. So I took her by the hand and led her to the threshold of the upper world where she belonged. Soon after that, I moved. My presence in that house was no longer necessary. But back when I lived on Fulton Street, I had no idea what it meant to stay in my power. I didn't realize I was allowed to assert my boundaries, and because of that, I couldn't yet be of much help to anyone.

As the months went by at the house on Fulton Street, I became obsessed with angels. Writing down their names: Anael, angel of air; Barbelo, perfect in glory; Metatron, great one and adversary. Typing out a treatise on the spirits I'd been encountering, I spent days making stacks of collages and charcoal drawings in an attempt to locate myself within their cosmology.

The egregore of Fulton Street was growing more powerful, feeding off our passions and fears. William's heartbreak had opened him up to a viral, psychotic depression ripping open his heart to be feasted upon by the demon spirit of the house. At that point, he'd sit for hours with his head in his hands, slowly stroking his forehead as if he were a grieving statue. "Does my face look gray to you?" he'd ask in a horrified whisper. "Do I smell like rotting flesh?"

Alex's math comas grew ever deeper until it seemed that nothing could wake him. He'd have a dozen alarms going off at a time, until I would barge into his room and try to shake him out of his stupor. In that cacophony of alarms, it felt like the world was ending.

And Donna, the skinny college student with the downcast eyes, started telling me strange stories. She told me she'd seen a taxicab with a sign on it accusing her of killing Kurt Cobain. At the supermarket, over the loudspeaker, voices would yell at her, "Donna, why did you raise the price of lettuce? Donna, we know it was you!" One time, after a few months of living in *the City*, with my own visitations from the spirit realms growing progressively more pronounced, I started seeing a therapist provided by the city four times per week and been put on medication. My mother sent me a photocopied dossier on schizophrenia, where she'd highlighted symptoms she saw as being similar to my own. I forgot the photocopy on the kitchen table for a few days, and when I came to collect it, I saw Donna had left a note in a venomous scrawl, "Maybe I just don't like everybody!" A few days later, Donna vanished.

Soon after Donna's disappearance, Adrian the artist and I drove deep into Marin to see the red tide, a toxic algae that glows when agitated. We trekked through the reeds and swamp marsh out to the beach where the sea roared across a wet desert of sand. A pale blue fire bloomed there, then disappeared, ghosting in and out of the dark like something from another dimension.

We ran through the sand kicking up big clumps that sparked back down to the earth as if the sky were falling. We rolled in those sparks and breathed into each other's mouths, passing our breath back and forth until we felt high and I lay back suspended in a web of stars. He pulled me close, his thick fingers gripping my flanks, and in a husky voice he said, "There's been times when I wanted you so bad I could kill you." I wasn't afraid of him. It was the kind of passionate declaration that, as a woman, I'd been trained to want since birth: a man so overcome with desire for you that he could fuck you into oblivion. Fuck you until you resumed your place as the void from which all things emerge. The birthplace of the world.

"I've never met anybody so ready to be exceptional," he continued. It sounds like a line, writing it, but the way he said it felt real. For many years afterward, I cradled that line, I clung to it when I felt like I was no one, that I'd never get anywhere, worrying that I might be lost in the underworld forever. He drew his fingers to my collarbones and looked me in the eyes. Despite his arrogance, there was something angelic about him. His big eyes, so vulnerable and innocent. I looked past him and the stars were still there. Hanging. Everywhere. As if they were in a jelly. The sky hadn't stopped falling. I felt dizzy. The universe was splitting apart.

"Do you hear that?" I asked him.

"What?"

"That hum. Like everything is vibrating." He shook his head and I could feel his spirit retract back into his shell. "Whoosh," I said. I could hear the universal hum, the rhythmic pulse of the universe, and around the edges I could hear wings beating. The waves and the wind and my pulse and his all mixing, all thrumming in the same rhythm. "Whoosh, whoosh, whoosh," I said. I don't know what happened, I just wanted to sing along to the music. It seemed beautiful, ecstatic. Like maybe finding oblivion really *should* be our goal as humans after all.

With a twitch, Adrian leapt up, afraid. "I think we should go," he said. "It's getting cold." His fear triggered my own. I stumbled along behind him, cold sand kicking up into my eyes as he powered back to the car.

We got in and slammed the doors, shivering in the dark, trying to catch our breath. We began the drive home in silence. After a while, I put on a mixtape my friend had made me that included a bunch of songs from the German industrial band Einstürzende Neubauten. I'd been impressed by that tape; the music felt urgent, destructive, clashing and clanging, fatal and foreign. Adrian asked me who it was, and I was proud to tell him. Proud that I knew about something he didn't. He frowned and nodded, silent for a moment, then sighed. "I've never heard them sound so *pop* before," he said. Soon after that night, he stopped returning my phone calls.

What happened that night? Was I really hearing the universal hum? Was I just some eighteen-year-old weirdo who wanted to impress her date by acting like a lunatic? Did I start to disassociate when threatened with real intimacy? Can I say yes to all of it? Whatever the truth of that night was, the hum didn't stop on the beach, and the sky didn't stop falling. I was still haunted, so porous I could crack open, a fibrous plant full of holes. As my time wore on in San Francisco, any spirit that wanted to visit me could visit me. I couldn't say no. I brought home strangers whose names I don't remember. I had no boundaries. I would sit for hours hypnotized by the spirits coming out of the ceiling and the sky.

In the house on Fulton Street, I would have the sense that I was being watched by a malevolent spirit. Usually I would go upstairs and hang out with William in his room until the feeling passed. But sometimes it wouldn't pass. And I would creep down the hall and enter my room and the presence would be so thick, I'd just have to leave the house.

One rainy day I was alone. The sky danced in low wisps outside my window and I heard a pulse in my room, those same wings beating. I left the house in an effort to escape to Cafe Abir a few blocks away, but as I darted down the street, I could feel the presence above me, hear its silk clashing wings, see its shadow following me on the sidewalk. "The angel of death, the angel of death, the angel of death," the words flashed loudly in my mind like a traffic signal. I tried to walk like an ordinary person but couldn't. I sprinted to the café and threw myself inside, heart racing, collapsing at a table, only leaving when the café closed at 10:00 p.m.

Eventually, hearing the vulnerability in my voice on one of our phone calls, my mother asked me if I wanted to "go somewhere to rest" but we both knew that wasn't possible. We didn't have any

106

money to send me to some kind of garden sanatorium with fountains à la Vincent van Gogh. We were broke. If I got put away somewhere, it would most likely be somewhere with bars on the windows and a TV in the rec room bolted to the wall.

Into Donna's old room moved Neil, a stocky white Taurus with a shaved head who studied Chinese medicine. He kept Indonesian masks on his wall—the kind with wide, wrathful eyes and grimacing mouths—and noise music droning in his room at all hours, day or night. Both of these were supposed to keep the demons in the house out of his business. Neil practiced tai chi, a martial art that aims to help you master your flow of energy and find your center, two essential practices if you want to be a person of power, not knocked off balance by outside forces.

Neil was able to withstand the influence of the house egregore because he was practicing tools of self-mastery. All cultures have them, but in order for these tools to work, you can't just know about them; you have to practice. A big part of being a witch is learning how to hold your ground and take on influence only with awareness. Since my time on Fulton Street, I've learned a thing or two about guarding against toxic intimacy with egregores, or anyone else. Now, before I enter into any kind of relationship, whether it be with a person, place, or thing, I ask myself, "Do I want to take on this influence?" I consider who the influence will encourage me to become. The egregore is always pulling you toward itself, encouraging you to become more like it. Our magical practice encourages us to move toward liberation. It helps us create space and empower ourselves. The daily practices of witchcraft—grounding, centering, shielding, incantations, ritual offerings to enlist the help of our spirit allies—all remind us that we have agency. These practices can help us establish healthy boundaries and remind us that we are not at the mercy of outside forces.

If I lived on Fulton Street now, I would fumigate my room daily with banishing smoke like white copal, frankincense, or dragon's blood. I'd call upon my spirit guardians to protect my space, and I'd leave them offerings of incense and fresh water as thanks. I'd bless black salt and spring water, then use the mixture to inscribe warding symbols on my doors, windows, and mirrors: a pentacle for blessings, the Algiz rune for protection. I'd clean the place up and remove any clutter, which is where stagnant, corrupt spirits like to hide. I'd recite the Consecration of the Sanctuary, one of my favorite protective prayers, borrowed and adapted from the syncretic cult of Santo Daime. *There is only one presence here, it is Love. Everyone who enters here will feel the pure and holy presence of Love...*I'd mind my own energy and if I found myself slipping out of balance, I'd do everything necessary to restore myself to a state of mental, physical, and emotional equilibrium. I'd see healers, meditate, dance, cleanse my diet, call upon my community for love and support. Finally, on my altar, I'd create a council of elders: images of sages and deities whom I wanted to call into my sphere and be intimate with, egregores whose influence upon me I'd joyfully encourage.

All of these practices help create harmony in your environment and make it more difficult for troublesome egregores to gain hold. Kind of like how if you don't want mold in your bathroom, the best thing to do is keep it clean, dry, and well maintained. But some bathrooms are too dumpy to keep clean, and sometimes a place is just too corrupted to be restored. In that case, the best thing a witch can do for herself is leave.

After about six months of living there, I came to understand that Colette, priestess to the egregore of the house on Fulton Street, was struggling with heroin addiction. The first time I saw Colette high, she was in the upstairs bathroom hand-washing one of her mauve mohair sweaters in the bathtub, her pale blue eyes suddenly pupil-less, with an atmosphere of gauze or fog around her. "You look different," I told her, studying all her details. "Did you get a haircut?" I'd never seen anyone on heroin before. Now I know you can recognize the heroin spirit by the veil it lays across a person's eyes. When a person is on opioids, you can never really speak to them directly; you always speak first to the corrupt Spirit of the Poppy.

Colette was *under the influence* of the heroin poppy. Plants have spirits, just like humans do. Like all sentient beings, plants have an agenda, things they want. They want intimacy, connection, and they have territory to claim. They want to spread their seed. Plants have desires. Sentient beings influence each other. People can influence the plant spirits, modify and manipulate them until they become corrupted. Many narcotics are corrupt plant spirits. When you come under the influence of a corrupt spirit, you become their servant. And a servant to the egregore that caused their corruption in the first place. People under the influence of corrupt spirits can rarely maintain healthy relationships.

There isn't enough room in their lives. The corrupt spirits want everything from their humans, until there's nothing left for them to give.

I caught a glimpse of the Fulton Street egregore once when Colette threw a fit and threatened to heave herself off the Golden Gate Bridge. It began with the smell of smoke and maniacal screams wuthering down from the attic. William ran up the stairs and we heard him through the floorboards, gentling her, speaking as if to a wounded animal. But soon Colette came tearing down the staircase, skinning the banisters with her sharp nails. Alex and I barred the front door to prevent her from leaving. She hissed and spat and clawed at us, eyes black with rage, the house egregore trying to get out of her body before she could make it out the front door, screaming that she hated us and wished we were dead.

Raised by a Unitarian witch, I had no strong feelings about Catholicism; I saw it as the most pagan form of Christianity, but beyond that, I knew little. Up the hill from my house, Saint Ignatius Church stood guard on the corner of Fulton and Parker. Not long after seeing Colette possessed by the egregore, I felt called by the Virgin Mary, who lived in one of its side chapels. Candlelit, mainly empty except for a few solitary worshippers, I sat there in the silence, waiting, neutral. Within moments, I was bawling. Huge, heaving sobs. Tears gushing from my eyes. Suddenly, I was overwhelmed with all the heartbreak and beauty of the world; I could feel all its suffering. I wept over everything and nothing in particular, until my eyes were purpled with veins and bruises and almost swollen shut, until an old woman came up to me and laid her hand on my shoulder and told me that whatever was wrong, if I prayed to the Virgin, she would help me. As a witch, I don't distinguish between goddesses. All are avatars of *The* Goddess, source of all love and all life. The Virgin Mary is the same as the Virgin Diana, is the same as Aphrodite, Ishtar, and Isis; when you look at her from different angles, you see her different facets shine. When the old woman looked in my eyes and smiled, I saw Hecate, Guardian of the Crossroads. I began to trust that somehow, someday, she would show me the path out of the underworld, to a place where I was safe and happy and free.

A couple weeks later, Alex the mathematician took me to see *Stomp* at a music hall in Berkeley. Athletic young New Yorkers swung like spiders across the stage, pounding on walls and lids and buckets and whatever else was around. Their rhythm shook our bones and put us in some kind of a healing trance. Shamans throughout history have used drumming to induce trances. Recent studies with EEG machines have found that drumming can cause changes in your brain waves and central nervous system, bringing about feelings of euphoria and lucidity. In other words, drumming inspires shamanic states of consciousness. After the show, Alex and I emerged back onto the Berkeley streets, grinning. I could feel my full spirit flickering in every cell. The egregore's spell was broken. The drumming broke it. Simultaneously, Alex and I turned to face each other. "We can move!" we both exclaimed. Somehow, it hadn't occurred to either of us that we could leave the house on Fulton Street.

We put an ad in the paper for my room, and the next morning

at 5:00 a.m., inquiring phone calls began nonstop. Dot-com had hit. My room with the bay windows and the poltergeists went from $400 per month to $1,200 per month overnight.

After I left, the person who moved into my room had a psychic friend over to stay. William told me that the psychic had to leave in the middle of the night because she couldn't sleep. All night long spirits kept pulling at her clothes, gnashing their teeth, and chattering.

On a recent trip to San Francisco, I decided to walk by the old house on Fulton Street. As I drew nearer, a cold fire erupted in my belly; my feet became heavy and hard to drag. The house was gone, burned to the ground. Nothing was left of it but a ruin of black cinders, fallen beams and broken glass, smoke stains corrupting the ornaments of the neighboring homes. Researching the fire online, I saw that no one knew how the fire began, but it was the largest the neighborhood had seen in decades. One person had died, scratching at the front door, trying to get free.

Chapter 7

c c c

MEETING THE FAIRY QUEEN

"Through love you learned my secret name,
Because of love I shall not hide;
I am the darkness from whence came
The pure Bright Spirit, hot with pride."
  Victor H. Anderson, "Fugat spiritus meus tecum."

Fairies started off as nature goddesses, Old World guardians of the forests, mountains, and virgin springs. In pagan times, fairies were local manifestations of the Mother Goddess, she who was both creator and destroyer. Just as nature herself gave birth to us, nurtured and provided for us all, she could take everything away just as easily. The Goddess was immanent in the fruit of the tree and the soil of the grave, where both human bodies and the seeds of new trees are buried. As Christianity invaded Europe, its policy was to demonize the fairy spirits. Under its influence, ancient goddesses of the wood and spring were diminished and made small and, sometimes, evil. But they could never be completely destroyed. The fairies lived on hidden glades and in the imaginations of the rural peasants. The epic medieval poem *The Faerie Queene* told the story of a beautiful woman who provided the hero with healing potions and gave him magical swords conferring monarchal authority. But she was dangerous too. In some versions, she'd seduce the king and give birth to monsters disguised as valiant knights or gifted poets. Her children *seemed* human, but really they were halflings; they'd have a goat leg, or one tooth curling out like a boar's tusk, or a patch of mink fur bristling on their cheeks.

In Italy, *fata* means "fate"; fairies were descendants of the Fates themselves, as in the case of Fata Morgana. In France, a fairy was a *fey*. The demoted goddesses of Europe appeared in countless forms: Titania, Melior, Palatyne, Mata Mari. The latter being a Basque goddess, the Lady of the Sea, bubbling up from sharp corals and kelp forests, haloed by the moon. Titania, a wood nymph, could transform herself into a hare. To protect her forest creatures, she'd unnerve the huntsman, watching him with her nose twitching from the leaves, then dart off into the dark woods that psychologist Carl Jung says represents the collective unconscious.

In the tales of the medieval period, the two most famous fairies were Melusine and Morgan le Fay. Like her descendent the Little Mermaid, Melusine was a lover and a mermaid herself, who wanted "to be where the people are." She married a prince. But he broke their pact (fairies are fond of pacts) when he spied on her in the bath. He saw her gleaming legs grow scaly and become the squirming tail of a snake. His betrayal brought both himself and his entire land to ruin.

Melusine's cousin Morgan le Fay made her most significant appearances in the Arthurian legends. Associated both with the crow-headed Morrígan, warrior goddesses of Celtic Ireland, and

114

with the Lady of the Lake, she was a sword carrier and swamp dweller with hair down to her waist. She pushed through the marsh reeds on a boat draped in handwoven rugs, strung with lanterns and dripping candles, sailing to the Isle of Apple Trees, also known as Avalon.

Both Morgan le Fay and Melusine came from Avalon. To get there, you enter through the mouth of a cave. This fairy queendom was an underworld land of ten thousand women, a place of perpetual summer, where the flowers were always in bloom. Also called the Land of the Shining Ones, its geography a lattice of secret lakes, glowing orbs, crystal castles, and jeweled mountains. In the Land of the Shining Ones, jewels are always mined by dwarves who love their work. In the fairy world, unpleasant labor doesn't exist. Fairies tantalize their lovers with a promise to put an end to their drudgery. They can spin straw into gold. They can assemble a complicated line of leather shoes with a tip of the hat. *Let yourself be seduced,* they croon. Fall asleep in their fairy circle and you'll wake up at one of their endless parties, ecstatic. Until one day you realize you don't know how to get back home. But then, why would you want to? Maybe because the Summerland is synonymous with the grave. Avalon, land of infinite beauty and freedom, is less free and beautiful once you realize you can never leave.

Whether nature spirit or seductive demon, fairies have had a lasting influence on the Western imagination. The West Coast witchcraft tradition of Reclaiming, from which my mother draws her greatest influence, has its roots in the Faery, sometimes called Feri, practices of the blind poet and shaman Victor Anderson. Based in San Francisco, the Faery Witch tradition is a nature religion. Its rites require the initiate to call upon the elemental spirits, the gnomes of the earth, the water undines, the sylphs riding the wind like dandelion fluff, the salamanders twisting in the bonfire.

Fairies don't just inspire us; they still exist. Long ago they mated with mortals; their genes still travel through our bloodlines. Some of us just inherit a little bit: a gap in the teeth, a pointed ear, a crooked finger. But sometimes the recessive fairy gene appears in pure form and a full-blown fairy creature pushes forth from between the legs of a mortal woman.

The Jewelry Store was in the Mission District, not too far from my new apartment. I'd found out about it when three women, three Fates in loose pants and slouchy dance shirts, caught me on the traffic median as I was walking across the street. One cupped my face as the other ran her fingers down my arms and along the back of my neck. "Come to the Jewelry Store this Friday," the gray-eyed brunette told me, stuffing a flyer into my palm. "We're performing *The Enchanted Garden of the Empress Zoë.*"

Around the turn of the century, the Jewelry Store was an indoor mall glittering with gemstones in golden glass cases lined with velveteen. By the time I moved to San Francisco, the space had become derelict, squatted by a bunch of young artists in performance collectives, fire-breathers and unicycle riders. In order to have a little money to live on, twice a month they held illegal raves in the basement. Upstairs was a meditation studio and rehearsal space; the jewelry theme lived on in the bedrooms, all of which were painted in the colors of precious stones, turquoise, garnet, and peridot. The communal kitchen was carnelian, always crowded with people playing the guitar and singing, chopping onions or sitting on the countertops smoking a joint. The entire building smelled of Nag Champa, marijuana, coriander, sweat, and smarmy theater makeup. Most of the residents of the Jewelry Store had the permanent residue of grease paint around their eyes and hairline. Simultaneously vaudevillian and mystical, everything was play for the kids at the Jewelry Store, who'd spend their days drifting between meditation, dance, sex, and psychedelics, each activity generating a state of mystical intoxication. Soon after meeting them, I was often over there performing with a collective called Dream Circus. Created by a young impresario named Paradox, a twenty-three-year-old lanky double Gemini who always wore a red and white striped nylon unitard and had the movement style and the spiritual essence of a squirrel monkey. Dream Circus was spooky; it was spectacle; it was subterranean entertainment and a total way of life. It was hedonistic rites in celebration of Bacchus, magician's card tricks and sleights of hand. Every action was in allegiance to a decaying form of Romanticism.

The Romantic sensibility, I've come to understand, is one major reason for the contemporary intellectual's disdain for the occult. Occultists are considered dinosaurs, monstrous prehistoric lizards clinging to the Romantic as if it were a rock. Historically, the Romantic movement represented a turning away from reality. Art history in the West forked in the 1800s, splitting into Romanticism and Realism. Realists depict "reality as it is," with its economic dialectics, materialism, and class struggle. It deals in facts, in science, in things we can prove; it is not ecstatic but

117

pragmatic, political. Realism tells the stories of real people, the factory worker, the industrialist architect, the provincial house-wife having an affair. Not fairies, not women who talk to spirits, certainly not witches. The Romantics, on the other hand, turned away from the modern world as a reaction to the ugliness and bru-tality of the Industrial Revolution. Retreating into the world of folk and fairy tales, into the exotic, "the Oriental"; the Romantics lived in an opium den of avoidance.

In one of Romantic painting's most famous works, Caspar David Friedrich's *Wanderer above the Sea of Fog*, the hero, a roman-tic genius, a windswept blond dandy in a velvet suit, turns his back to the viewer and to the world, gazing out over an endless land-scape of fog and forest, as if into a primordial wilderness to which he longs to return. The Romantic seeks the mysterious, the divine, and traditionally does so from the position of a white upper-class man who has the privilege of choosing to reject the world of work and manners, preferring to retreat into a wild yet terrifying sub-lime, a space of somehow still uncolonized "colored people" where he can reign like Colonel Kurtz, or father children with a thirteen-year-old in a grass skirt like Gauguin.

That's the criticism: people turn to the occult because they either (a) don't want to deal with the real horrors of the world and have the privilege of turning away from it, unlike the oppressed who have no choice but to face reality, or (b) are losers who can't hack it in industrialized civilization and so choose to play Dungeons & Dragons instead. Western post-Enlightenment civilization defines itself as being rationalist and therefore against magic, but all cul-tures have magical practices, including our own. Christianity is full of magical practices, and the language of economics is permeated by spirits and invisible hands. Magic is everywhere; it's just that the central power figures of a culture get to determine whose magic is considered "real" and whose is just considered embarrassing. Further, magic is not just a practice of the privileged; otherwise only the privileged would practice it, and that just isn't the case, as you can see by visiting the fetish markets of Togo, the witch markets of Brazil, or any botanica in Los Angeles.

For me and many of the people I knew at the Jewelry Store, performance *was* a kind of magic; it was the practice of entering ecstatic and altered states of consciousness at will. The spaces we performed in were often illegal, under bridges, in vacant lots. Or else we invaded the orthodox spaces of the art world, showing up uninvited to opening events with fountains and canapes. We'd slip smoke-like through the crowds, hiding in corners and shadows, naked, painted white, with pointy ears and sharp teeth. Pixies at their soiree with no explanations.

Rehearsals at the Jewelry Store would rarely start on time. You'd go over and hang out, talk, maybe an impromptu jam session would be going on, so everyone would sing for an hour before rehearsals began. Or some other group might be practicing their fire-breathing techniques in the space you wanted to use, so you'd have to wait. It was all about process and enthusiasm, not about end results. Everything was possibility; there were no boundaries, hardly any form, just ideas and activity tangling in the air like kites.

One afternoon, I waited in the basement rave hall for our rehearsal to start, a dank underworld, doused with glitter and sweat. Two girls were already down there in the neon half-light, sitting on a blanket as if they were having a picnic. I started practicing in the shadows, casually doing some dance moves while the girls stared at me, giggling.

Both petite and very pale, one of them had a face full of piercings, big brown cow eyes, and dreadlocks down to her waist dyed various shades of orange with bits of brass and leather smuggled within. She spoke with a British accent. After everything she said, she'd glance at her friend, waiting for a signal that she was allowed to proceed. More androgynous street urchin than ordinary girl, her friend stood just over five feet tall, with fine strawberry-blond hair grazing her jaw in a pageboy haircut. She wore baggy knickers in a soft violet canvas, leather suspenders, and a cotton T-shirt worn thin with holes, repaired by hand multitudes of times with violet thread. Thin white stockings slouched on her shins under leather boots that looked like they'd been pilfered from an eighteenth-century Parisian flea market. She spoke loudly, drawing out her words, throwing her voice to me as if it were a crystal ball she wanted me to catch, bragging about her frequent luxurious intercontinental travel.

I was used to hanging out with broke people. These girls didn't look like people you'd expect to fly first class. "What do you do for a living?" I asked the orphan girl. She shrugged and looked at her cow-eyed friend conspiratorially. The orphan girl cocked her head at me. "I have a paper route," she said. In fact, she did look like a 1920s paperboy who'd shout, "Extra, extra, read all about it!"

She stood up to introduce herself, loping a bit from side to side like a ferret. Her name was Isla Otterfeld, and the girl was

120

strange. Her legs bowed wide, her toes pointed outward. Batting big blue eyes rimmed with thick, dark lashes, she'd smile, and I don't know how else to say it, she'd coo. "Mmm, awwww, cooooo," and then she'd break into peals of laughter one would expect to hear from beneath a toadstool in a Bavarian wood, rather than a dank basement in the Mission, its floors sticky with spilled beer.

It was uncanny the way people were instantly hypnotized by this diminutive little creature, snapped under her spell. They'd fawn over her and bring her cups of tea and offerings of skunk weed. They'd laugh at all her jokes and defer to her judgment. Though smaller than everyone by about a foot, she was clearly a leader in the Jewelry Store's band of misfits. She told me her band was playing soon at a space downtown. That I should come. "You should give me your phone number so that I can remind you," Isla said.

"I'll remember if you tell me when it is," I told her.

"Give me your phone number, just in case." She grinned at me, and I complied. Soon, we were speaking on the phone every day.

During these phone calls, I would tell her stories and she would listen and laugh as if I were the most fascinating person on earth. She'd tell me how creative I was and how what she loved best about me was my imagination. When the time came for her show downtown, I was so grateful for her friendship, since I always felt like an outsider with the Dream Circus clan, that I found myself wanting to bring her a gift. From the esoteric shop on Polk, I selected an assortment of polished purple amethysts and put them in a gold silk bag I embroidered with an acorn. Fairies live in Oak Trees.

* * *

121

Her band was playing at a dive bar. Just barely nineteen, I could only get in because some girl I'd been dating a while back had got me a fake ID. While Isla was setting up, she kept flashing her eyes at me, blushing and shrugging while she tapped the pedals to test her guitar. I talked to a girl nearby who told me she wrote short stories about the sex lives of insects and earthworms. Isla kept shooting me dirty looks as I was talking to the writer girl, frowning and huffing and shaking her fist. I couldn't tell if she was kidding. I didn't know that Isla already thought of me as belonging to her.

After the show, I presented Isla with the bag of amethysts, and she took it as if it were a tithe she was owed. She poured the stones into her hand and held them up into the light and cooed and giggled. "Good! You *should* bring me gifts."

"I should?" I asked, puzzled. Although I was fascinated by her, and grateful for her friendship, I also found her strange, mystifying, and if I was being honest, a total weirdo. I didn't expect that she would feel I owed her a gift.

"Yes, of course you should," she responded. "And you should come back to my place right now. It's just around the corner."

Isla lived in a converted mechanics shop on Minna with a roll-up door made of corrugated metal. She lived there with two other guys: Dave, whom she'd known since she was a teenager in her Georgia homeland, who had a pug nose and mullet and wore shirts with the sleeves cut out to show off his muscles, and this other guy who was somehow affiliated with that band Brian Jonestown Massacre. The guys mainly lived in two little cubby rooms upstairs while Isla had the entire ground floor to herself.

She took me on the grand tour. First, there was the recording studio, all set up with mics and mic stands and drum sets and amps and equipment with knobs and dials and cords and cables and carpet on the walls to absorb the sound. "You have to be careful in here," I told her.

"Why?" she asked, eyes opening wide.

"Because of the gremlins. Gremlins love technology," I told her. "They love to chew at the cables and hide behind all the gadgets."

Isla giggled and squirmed, grinning up at me. "Aww, but that's okay. I'm friends with the gremlins. We're brothers! C'mon." She curled her fingers around my arm and pulled me up a winding metal staircase. Gesturing to a door on the left, she said, "That's the dark room, but you can't go in there right now."

"Why not?"

"Narcisse is in there. He might be in the middle of something."

"Something, not photography?" I asked her.

"Let me show you my *Gallery of Lost Souls.*" Isla redirected me to the hallway. Hanging in a line along the wall was a series of prints she'd made herself. A dark-haired girl in a sheer white dress walked through an empty meadow. They'd been in love, Isla informed me, but now the girl was in a mental institution. In another photo, a punk boy with wounded eyes had an orange Mohawk collapsed across his skull as if he were a defeated rooster. "He broke my heart. Stole from me, tricked me," Isla said with tears in her eyes. "He died of a heroin overdose last year." Narcisse from the photo room was one of the people in the prints. A young Frenchman, he was so pale and blond he looked like he might be an albino. Gaunt and ghostly, he only wore white and ate only white food; if he ate potatoes, he'd take off the skin. Mostly his diet consisted of white cheese and skinned apples. Isla told me that when Narcisse shat, it would just be fuzzy white pellets. Nuggets of calcium the size of walnuts clogged his back and neck because his diet was making him sick. But Isla thought it all was adorable, so hilarious, and, in fact, perfectly reasonable.

Other people were there too; some pale guy with bushy eyebrows kept coming up to her, pulling her away, frowning, whispering urgently in her ear. Isla'd roll her eyes and tell me to hold on. Eventually she led me to her bedroom where, after a flurry of apologies, she told me I could wait.

My intuition was correct; amethyst was her color. Everything about Isla's room was lavender. The walls. The rugs so purple they were almost black, thick as bearskins. Beeswax candles dripped off wrought-iron candelabra, their heat shimmering up toward the skylight and loft bed where she slept. Beneath the loft hung a hammock of undyed wool swiveling in slow loops, as if it trapped a lethargic, invisible demon. The room even smelled lavender. Lavender infused into the air with handmade incense, or rubbed into flesh with essential oils, or lathered from the luxurious soaps in her bathroom. I peeked into her closet—a small room the size of the shed I'd lived in in Santa Barbara. It had a mirror surrounded in carnival lights and was packed with leather jackets and silk nightshirts and calfskin booties small enough for a child. Below the dressing table, like the treasures of a modern-day leprechaun, were three canvas mailbags. Each one was overflowing with stacks of money. There was easily over half a million dollars in those bags, which she'd casually nudged under the table with her essential oils and eye creams.

Heart racing, I ran over to the other side of the room, afraid. I knew I'd seen something I shouldn't have. Something that made the enchanted life on Isla's fairy isle possible but that I sensed we were never supposed to discuss.

"Sorry about that," she said, shuffling her way back into her room, oversized shirt slouching off her shoulder, a child wearing her mother's clothes.

"Nothing," I stammered, turning to face her CDs. "I was just looking at your music."

She closed the door with a kick. "Find anything you like? Anything you want you can have." She came up to me, so close I could smell her lavender musk. "I need a do not disturb sign." Stroking the tips of her fingers down the small of my back, she told me, "Go upstairs. I'm going to find some music to capture your spirit."

We lay by candlelight on her indigo blankets, opium swirls of incense crowning our heads as we drifted along to Pink Floyd's song "Echoes," a twenty-minute epic to rival Coleridge's "Kubla Khan." It begins:

Overhead the albatross hangs motionless upon the air
and deep beneath the rolling waves in labyrinths of coral caves...

Isla was stretched out, leaning on her elbow above me, eyes violet and hypnotic. "You know, we met before that time at the Jewelry Store," she told me, her gaze gripping mine, charming my cobra soul.

"When?" I whispered back.

"At that Butoh performance. I saw you in the parking lot. I was

125

driving in with my friends, and we all saw you from the car. And we all said, 'Who is that?' But I…I knew you. I recognized you and I knew you were mine. A creature from another place. From the fairy world. Don't you remember? In the lobby. We spoke."

Known as the *Dance of Death*, Butoh was created by the Japanese as a reaction to Americans dropping nuclear bombs on Hiroshima and Nagasaki. And I did start to remember, vaguely, leaving a theater of grimacing white figures, as if leaving a dream in a graveyard, entering the wet light of the lobby that shone all over everything, and through that light appeared a strange loping figure. A petite girl, dressed like Oliver Twist. "Oh yeah, now I'm starting to remember," I told her. "You were so friendly. I thought you were trying to pick my pocket."

Her eyes narrowed, petulant and fierce, as she leaned in. "I knew from that moment we were supposed to be together. My intuition is always right. I figured you knew the Jewelry Store people; that's why I went that one time. I knew you'd be there."

My stomach lurched. A jungle adventurer who realizes the panther has been tracking her for days, hiding in the undergrowth, leaping from tree to tree. Caught in a sudden delirium, I was sucked into the music, echoing pings, the calls of birds. Isla lay back in a dreamy fugue. "I love that line about the lullabies," she said, but she seized her throat and turned her face away.

"I used to love it when my mother sang to me," I whispered. "I still remember the words."

But no one sang to Isla as a child. Raised by a single, drug-addicted mother with a series of pharmacist boyfriends in Savannah, Georgia, under hanging trees and kudzu vines and Spanish

126

moss, in dingy houses where she felt alone, there was no one to discipline Isla. No one to make her close her eyes. She entered the fairy world and never returned. She was the fairies' favorite child. And she called out to the other fairy creatures in this miserable world like a beacon. And when she saw me walking by in that parking lot, she recognized me: a creature from another place, from the fairy caves of Avalon, from the Summerland, from the land of Tir Na Nog, the first territory on the other side of death.

"Summertime. And the living is easy. Fish are jumping and the cotton is high," I sang.

Before my eyes, Isla became a watery creature, white bellied and slippery. She curled her fingers in my hair and pulled me close, placing her lips on mine. Eyes fluttering backward, she sighed. "I want to treat you better than I've ever treated anyone," she declared. My dual citizenship with the spirit world, the porous nature of my reality, which had so terrified Darshak and Adrian as it tugged me in and out of the realms of the imagination, did not scare Isla. It fascinated her. For her I glowed in the dark, a prehistoric fish at the bottom of the ocean.

She lay propped on one elbow, gazing down at my face, hand stroking my forehead. "Would you rather choose or be chosen?" she asked me gently. I wasn't sure. Be chosen? "Good." She smiled, satisfied. "I'd rather choose." She placed one of her fingers on my third eye and tapped. "I choose you."

Soon, Isla and I were spending all our time together. Dashing through the pines on our way to Big Sur in her 1974 electric blue Alfa Romeo with custom-painted star hubcaps. She taught me how to drive a stick. The car was temperamental, with a sticky clutch and gas pedal so responsive just a nudge would send it throttling forward in a thick perfume of gasoline. She took me to the mineral hot springs at Esalen. We bathed in the starlight and held hands while young women massaged us on the midnight cliffs, the ocean sucking and slapping at the boulders below.

Isla bought me a sapphire-blue acoustic guitar with electric hookups and I'd practice until my fingers were calloused and bloody. We'd write romantic songs about secret gardens and lovers trysts gone awry. Sometimes we'd spend days holed up in her room listening to music and drawing. Since completing her undergraduate degree at the Savannah College of Art, Isla had been obsessed with drawing sunflowers on thick, velvety paper stretching sometimes over twelve feet tall. She'd inscribe the flowers in tight, photorealistic precision, their petals trembling and gasping like sea anemones. At the center of their buds would always be these sad, veiny eyes. They were beautiful, and I wanted to like them, but they always creeped me out. She'd pin them to the wall and the flowers would watch us from a garden of horror and disappointment.

When we weren't writing our own songs or making art, we'd spend the afternoons listening to music and making love. Isla was a rebel in most ways, but she was conservative in bed. Innocent, almost childish and yielding. Very shy. When she looked at me, her eyes would be wide and hungry, like I was some bright and floating thing she couldn't believe was actually there, as if *I* were the fairy and she the huntsman.

* * *

One night, Isla took me to a party up near the Russian River in Sebastopol, a coastal town about an hour north of San Francisco. We drove down a single-lane road, our headlights glancing off the whirls of fog and silhouettes of black pine. We parked alongside the road and could hear the throb of trance music coming from a wooden house with a winding front porch strung with brightly colored Japanese lanterns. Isla clomped up the steps in her heavy boots and thrust open the door without knocking. A crowd of revelers sent up a cheer when they saw Isla's face: now the party had truly begun.

Inside, it was all wood walls and wood beams and stained glass lamps with lots of art collected from everywhere: brightly painted Balinese dragons hung above antique Berber rugs, geometric designs in cranberry, turmeric, and indigo. Everyone there, all genders, was long-haired and sleepy-eyed, draped in undyed linen blouses and fringed shawls, with brass rings tangled in their hair, skirts slung low to show off their yoga-toned, ringed belly buttons. No one around Isla ever seemed to have a job. Everyone was a traveler, having just come back from Spain, or Tokyo, or a trip through the Peruvian Amazon. The last time I'd left California was when I was twelve and I went on a camping trip to the Grand Canyon with my dad.

"Here, try this," Isla said, pulling me aside and spooning a generous dollop of honey into my mouth. Crammed with little bits of something mysterious, it tasted like it'd been scraped from the roots of an old, smelly tree.

"What is it?" I asked, dubious. We hadn't really even entered the room yet.

"Just wait," she cooed, stroking my face. "We're going to have so much fun." A flock of women swooped in, surrounding Isla, smiling in their big floppy hats and heavy beaded necklaces. With names like Luna and Lorelei, all of them dazzled her. I watched from the corner as they pulled her off into another room.

The music continued in its psychedelic whirl. I began to feel a gnawing in my belly. Soon, everything was alive. The woods around the house, the plants, the crystals on the shelves of the library, all vibrating and active. I searched the house but Isla was nowhere to be found. When I asked the beautiful people where she was, they'd give me blissed out smiles, sometimes gesturing toward this or that door, then shrugging and turning away, my anxiety harshing their vibe. Eventually I found myself called outside by a towering ancient redwood. The tree stood just beyond the back deck, where there was a hot tub on one side and the fairy dark woods below. I heard a giggle and suddenly two childlike hands covered my eyes. "Where have you been?" I asked Isla. When I opened my mouth to speak, she slipped a round tablet that tasted like baby aspirin into my mouth.

"Swallow," she commanded, then, "Get in!" Joyous, she stripped off her street urchin attire and splashed naked into the aquamarine glow. We kissed in a froth bubbling up from the center of the earth. Water streaming off our shoulders, our legs entwined in a candy cane of white and pink and red. This was the world I'd been searching for. Everything was beautiful here, with this fairy creature next to me, stroking my face and telling me that we could live in the Summerland and never leave.

"I know this place in Spain," Isla said, "where you can live on the beach in caves. People have them all decked out with blankets and rugs and lanterns, and they eat fish straight from the ocean. We can go live there for a while, and then afterward I have a friend who is a count. He lives in a castle in Aix-en-Provence. That's where all the most beautiful people in France live; we can go live there too."

I told her that I'd heard about medieval cemeteries in Italy where you could go on the night of the full moon and see blue will-o'-the-wisps escaping the marble vaults.

"We'll go there! We'll stay in a villa and eat wine and melons!" she exclaimed.

"At night we'll prowl through the cemeteries in cloaks, our necks wreathed in garlic, calling for the aid of Aradia, Italian goddess of wildness and witches," I agreed.

Pulling herself dripping up onto the ledge, she grabbed a nearby towel. "I'm going to get us a glass of water," she told me.

I rested my arms on the edge of the tub, paddling my legs out behind me and asked her, "Will it come from a spring guarded by nymphs, surrounded in iris blossoms?"

"Yes," she whispered, cupping my face, reaching into her pocket for a white tab of paper and slipping it with her baby fingers beneath my tongue. "It's going to be the most magical water there is; I'm going to get it for you."

I waited in the hot tub until eventually I felt that I would faint. Years later, that's the way one of my uncles would die, drugged and passed out in a hot tub. I hauled myself onto the deck, disoriented and weak, barely able to tug my clothes across the friction of my still-wet body. Inside the house, a techno banshee was shrieking. I didn't want to go in, but I needed to find Isla.

The house seemed endless, fake somehow. It was trying to trick me. To hide her. I couldn't find her. And I began to panic that she had left me there, that I'd never be able to get back home. The people around me were starting to come down. You could see it. Smiling no longer, their eyes were wide and black, their lips a straight line across their gaunt faces.

I left the house and felt with my bare feet along the ladder leading down into the woods below. I followed the humming insects and the sighing of the pines. Soon I lost all sense of direction. The trees whipped and whirred like in those Vietnam movies when the helicopter lands in the jungle meadow. It was the Angel of Death. Finally. I knew it. My own personal fairy master, my Fata Morgana. I felt its darkness envelop me. And I felt, rather than saw, a thousand animals come, opossums and raccoons and centipedes. They ate away my flesh, my eyes, my brains, until all that was left was dry bones. I was nothing. I was dust.

But somehow, even as dust, I woke in the morning.

I rose from the earth covered in leaves and dirt, eyes circled in mascara, and heard a terrified screaming coming from the river. Cutting through the thicket of trees to the east, I passed along the icy banks as the river gurgled around my ankles. There, I found a man and a woman in a canoe wearing puffy orange life vests, clearly abducting a child.

"What are you doing with that baby?" I shouted at them.

"He's fine," the woman said to me, annoyed as she struggled to keep grip of the howling toddler trying to squirm free of her arms and plunge headlong into the water.

"Why's he crying so much then?" I demanded.

The woman scowled, impatient. "He's afraid of the water."

The man, the child's father I now presume, took one look at me and started paddling hard, trying to escape upriver as swiftly as possible.

The abductors, I now understand, were the child's parents. Looking back, I realize I must have seemed threatening to them; a wild night creature creeping out of the lonesome woods. What if I had plunged into the water and tried to grab the child? Fairies are known for taking children. That night I had crossed the River Styx, waded away from the ordinary realms of existence. I had become a fairy too. Like Isla. A monster. An amoral creature of Tir Na Nog, and as such, I was a threat to those who still lived in human reality. It's not an unfamiliar story for the youths of America. For many of us, self-administered, drug-induced initiation ceremonies are the best we can manage as we fumble toward spiritual awakening, even when mentorship in these processes is what we need most of all. We look around and can't find anyone we trust to help us; without elders to look to for guidance, it's easy to get lost.

Eventually I made my way back to the Banshee House. I stalked into the kitchen, barefoot, trembling, covered in dirt, only to find Isla giggling with Lorelei at the kitchen table as they nibbled their biscuits. "How'd you get all that mess in your hair?" Isla wondered at me, smiling sweetly. She hadn't even noticed I'd been gone.

* * *

I'm just going to come right out and say that Isla was a drug dealer. Haunted by the ghost of her mother, an addict with a constant hunger for drugs, Isla grew up to become the supplier. She could feed her mother's need, and everyone else's. But Isla had a code about dealing. She refused to touch the drugs that had so incapacitated her mother: the barbiturates, the speed, the opiates. She would only deal in "nice, sweet, friendly drugs." She told me, "I always want to do it on the up and up, and be a really good helpful drug dealer that just supplies people with things that are beneficial." Ecstasy and acid, sometimes mushrooms. Though the latter didn't make her any money, she believed in the benefit of distributing the "little teachers" to the people. With the acid, she mixed the potion herself in her darkroom. She called it "laying acid" as if she were laying eggs. The acid was laid in books, like the one the High Priestess of the tarot holds containing the knowledge of good and evil, heaven and hell.

Isla would tell me she was blessed because she made a lot of money and didn't have to work, but in my opinion, she worked constantly. There were always people hanging around, pretending to be there for friendly reasons, when really they were coming to score. No one could state what they wanted, get it, and leave. There had to be this whole big song and dance about it. We'd try to record a song and the phone would ring off the hook. We'd try to go away and we'd constantly have to cancel our plans because of some shipment or another. Our lives were constantly interrupted.

We'd have dinner parties. Isla would enjoy them and insist on inviting everyone she knew. But I'd end up slaving away in the kitchen sprinkling our dinner with gray finishing salt gathered from the marshes of some medieval town in the Loire Valley, only to bring it down and find her making out with one of the random assortment of her model-type friends.

We fought because I wanted to leave for Europe, land of beauty and romance, of vampire theaters and ballet slippers and cobblestones, where tract homes and junk mail could never reach me. I'd been saving up to go for years, money scraped off the sticky floors of sex clubs; I felt like I earned the money in sweat and humility. But being with Isla, the money flowed from my bank account. She always told me not to worry about it. She would pay me back. It upset her that I might leave for Europe without her and if I mentioned it she'd give me the silent treatment for days. There wasn't enough funding for the arts in the U.S., I lamented. But why did I need government funding when I had her to support me? she'd complain. Thing was, I didn't trust her to support me. She was capricious. She'd offer to pay for something one day, then forget she'd ever mentioned it the next. To ask again made me feel greedy. Besides, if she did get me something fancy, she'd be likely to hold it over me if I was ever angry at her and say, "But I bought you this or that or the other thing," how dare I be mad at her? Even if she was making out with someone else. Even if she grabbed my dinner from my hands or left me on the side of the road because she saw me talking with some other woman.

Most of our fights circled around three themes: (a) the imbalanced power dynamics in our relationship, (b) our vastly disparate levels of willingness to let ourselves get completely out of our minds on drugs (she loved the idea; I was terrified), and (c) faith in the benevolent attitude of the Universe. Regarding the latter, she had absolute faith that the Universe had her back, which is probably what made her magic so strong. I, on the other hand, was skeptical that the Universe even liked me, or wasn't on some perpetual trip to teach me a lesson, which is probably why my magic was volatile and often terrifying.

Isla loved to jet through the city on her Harley roadster, her pride and joy. She'd dart in and out of San Francisco's ectoplasmic fog, zooming around corners into the blank white void with me clinging to her back, face scrunched between her shoulder blades, praying to every god I knew of but feeling the wings of the Angel of Death vibrating in the engine roar. She was pure will, and she didn't question it. Isla wasn't afraid of dying.

Still, she did have her fears. Isla had a morbid fear of ugliness or ordinariness. She couldn't handle poverty or suffering. One time we were walking through the Tenderloin district and she clutched my arm as a toothless homeless man came up to us and growled. Isla yelped. "Run, Amanda," she called at me over her shoulder. "Calm down," I told her as I walked behind; the man was clearly strung out, would probably die on those streets, even though he ran after her, laughing. "You're just making it worse," I told her. Isla's impulse was to run away. To return to her fairy lair with the incense smoke and silk hammocks.

Fat, too, was a moral failure. Isla had issues not only about controlling her own food but also the food of her friends. As everyone knows, fairies and food have a special relationship. She had a sweet tooth and loved to eat candy and ice cream and pastries galore, but if she found *you* eating ice cream she'd be just as likely to rip it from your hand and throw it out the window as she would to have a bite of it. If you weren't up to her standards of beauty and civility (she loathed coarse behavior), you'd soon be out the window with the ice cream, a sticky mess melting on the sidewalk.

Because of her allegiance to beauty, I had more freedom in the world than she did. I could go to places where she couldn't, ugly places. Places with metal and machines and rats in the gutter. Places like New York City. She always said she would never go there. That she hated to even set foot inside it, she found it so unaesthetic and grueling. And so in our most violent fights when I felt the most afraid of her, I told myself that if I ever needed to hide, I could move to Manhattan.

When Isla and I got together, I was working at a strip club just off Market Street called the Chez Parée. After our escapade at the Russian River, Isla became more and more agitated every time I went to work. "You don't have to do this job," she'd tell me. "I'm going to take care of you." But her promises meant little. I couldn't even trust her not to leave me by the side of the road if we had a fight. She'd done it more than once. Finally, after a series of particularly grueling arguments, she demanded I quit, and I gave in.

Together, we went to the Chez Parée. I went backstage to collect my costumes from my locker. "Are you quitting?" the women backstage asked me. I told them that I'd met this amazing pixie girl who happened to be rich and that we'd fallen in love and that we were going to go live in castles in France and caves in Spain and that in a few weeks we were going to Burning Man. The girls continued putting on their mascara. Mandi, who would always admonish me to "stop making that face!" while putting on my liquid eyeliner, smoldered jealously, deliciously, in the corner.

Isla burst into the room. "What are you doing, Amanda?" She was manic. Being in this tawdry place upset her. She didn't like all the men out front sulking in their plastic chairs, or the girls in the back room smearing body makeup on their razor burn. "Come on!" she shouted, ambling toward me with her strange bowlegged walk. "Let's get out of here."

"I'm almost done," I said, pulling the last remaining G-strings and heels out of my locker.

"You don't need that stuff!" she exclaimed, her face growing red. She started grabbing things from my hands. "What is this?" She held up a black sheer negligee with fringe around the hem. "You don't need this! This isn't even long enough to cover your butt. You don't need this anymore. Here!" She shoved the negligee into the hands of Marmalade, a quiet girl who'd just started stripping.

"I love it," Marmalade said, proudly holding the garment up to her chest.

I didn't know what to do. "You can't just give away my stuff," I said in a low voice.

"Why not!" Isla yelled. "I'm going to be paying for everything for you, taking you to Europe, wining and dining you, and you can't even share these pieces of trash!"

She pulled my clothes from my arms and began handing them out in a festival of generosity. "Here!" She handed Mandi, the girl who hated my makeup face, my most expensive dress.

Isla had outsmarted me. I couldn't very well insist on keeping my clothes after I'd just bragged to everyone about how my girlfriend was going to take care of me in the most extravagant way. The trouble was, without clothes, I couldn't work, even if I wanted to. Those clothes were expensive; it took me a long time to build up that wardrobe. Now I was completely dependent on Isla's caprice, which, it seemed, was exactly what she wanted.

Not long after Isla threw away my clothes, we went to Burning Man, where clothes weren't necessary. When I was young, my mother would take me to the Burning of Old Man Gloom, a city bonfire San Luis Obispo held each fall. People would stand around in the autumnal smoke, sipping hot cider out of Styrofoam cups, scribbling their worries down on bits of paper, then tossing them crumpled into the flames. At the center of the pyre was "Old Man Gloom," stuffed with repossession papers, biopsy results, divorce forms, and delinquent notifications. Flames would lick up the Old Man's legs, eating his center, devouring his jeans, his flannel shirt. People would stand around joyfully watching all their worries disappear in a catharsis of flames.

It's a tradition that goes back millennia. Julius Caesar reported, erroneously, that the druids stuffed their wicker men with human sacrifices before they lit them. In India, they burn an effigy of the demon Ravenna. In Latin America, a puppet of Judas is paraded through towns, then torched. The desire to destroy "The Man," the betrayer, monster, and troublemaker, to light him on fire and make him disappear, is one that cannot be repressed in our species. Creating effigies and burning them is a magical act: taking a symbol, charging it with emotion and meaning, then manipulating it by burning it, dancing 'round it, decorating it, bathing it in milk or water or wine, piercing it with pins, or venerating it on an altar. We can't help but do it. It's not enough just to *know* that everything changes and that everything ends; we want to *see* the old man burn; we want to *make* it happen. Even when we know he'll just reappear again next year and that our worries will never really go away.

Black Rock City was already in full swing by the time we pitched our tents. The place was set up in a series of concentric circles around the central "plaza" where the effigy was being built, a fifty-foot-tall man made out of wood that they were going to set on fire on the final day of the festival. Dream Circus had been tasked with building a three-story castle around which we would cavort in a five-hundred-person-strong performance of *The Seven Deadly Sins.*

By the time we arrived, the scaffolding for the castle had already been erected out of plywood and swaddled in chicken wire. At a nearby hot springs, we spent the day scooping mud with buckets into the back of a pickup truck. We took the mud back to the castle and slapped it onto the wire mesh like drywall until the whole thing was caked, covered completely. As the mud dried over the next few days, it became pale and cracked so that eventually it looked like the structure had emerged as a natural form from the dry lake bed.

Once we'd erected the castle, we began rehearsing. It was too hot to rehearse in the middle of the day, so we spent the hottest hours sleeping and lounging under makeshift yurts and awnings, drinking chai and sharing sourdough pancakes with lentils and giving each other tarot readings and massages. All afternoon we were serenaded by the folks in the next tent practicing their accordion. Sand storms kicked up around us, swirling little djinns, mixing with the scent of roast cumin, cinnamon tea, and gasoline from trailer exhaust pipes. Motors were everywhere. People zipping around on motorcycles and motor skateboards and Jeeps. I even saw someone who'd motorized a sofa. Three people reclined on it, kicking up dust on the barren desert plain, using their remote control to avoid the stoned pedestrians. A lawless temporary autonomous zone, the entire scene was Mad Max meets hippie dream village.

One afternoon, rehearsal got postponed until the next day and so I was hanging out under the Dream Circus awning, naked for whatever reason, when I heard the trumpeting blast of Isla's Harley. I rose from my beanbag chair and walked out, shading my eyes from the desert glare.

A Tasmanian devil trailing a white streak of dust cut across the central medina, Isla saw me from about twenty yards away and stopped. Her mouth gaping, she brushed the back of her wrist across her eyes. "Get on!" She jerked her chin toward the back of her motorbike.

"I can't," I laughed.

Isla was stricken, baffled. "Why not?"

"Because there's a girl on your bike already."

The girl on the back of the bike slapped Isla on the head. Hopping off, she growled, "I'll walk, thanks."

I climbed on and off we shot, to tour the gallery of ice sculptures: angels slowly dripping their disappearance into the coming twilight.

The next night at the Bindlestiff Family Cirkus, the players contorted themselves through meshless tennis rackets while Isla plied me with drugs. Acid and ecstasy and mushrooms and mescaline. Later, I was a crumpled mess in our tent, terrorized by the endless motors outside, pleading with her. "I'm afraid I'm going to die. Am I going to die?" I kept asking her, gripping her skinny little arms.

"Don't worry," she told me, hushing and soothing. She shared with me her trick: "Don't think of anything bad. If you don't think of anything bad, nothing bad can happen. Try to only think of nice things. Do you want me to sing to you?" She started to sing, but I couldn't do like she did. We both knew bad things happened, but only she had the will to always pretend that they didn't.

The next night, I was still coming down during my performance with Dream Circus. Our chariots rode in endless circles, drawing a procession of hundreds of people performing Bacchanalian orgies, people decked in wings and animal masks and feathers and beads, painted in glitter; eyes lined in kohl; arms circled in gold bracelets; performers swinging on trapeze from the burning castle or riding around it on unicycles. Thousands of people cheered as the castle went down in flames, followed by the wooden man himself, until it seemed that everything was an apocalyptic blaze of destruction.

At Burning Man, the whole point seemed to be, simply, "spectacle," a spectacle of destruction for the teenage spirits of America. One could imagine some outraged parent stampeding into our civilization, demanding, "What is the meaning of all this?!" And the rebel children responding, "There is no meaning, Dad. You just don't get it." Except, in Isla's case, no parents would ever barge in, because her mother was dead and her dad was, in her own words, "just some toothless hick farmer," whom she barely knew. And who were the parents of our civilization? Clinton was president then. My gay uncles had named their convertible after Monica Lewinsky.

On the playa that night, watching the last flaming two-by-fours collapse onto the sand, I felt like the burning man was a symbol for the entire Western world. Capitalist patriarchy likes to build things just to watch them fall. We extract resources and use them to build spectacular toys and then destroy them in a nihilistic bonfire. The burning of the man was cathartic, and an ancient custom, but there seemed to be a hopelessness or a despair about it. Like our civilization is wild and out of control and we might as well just let go and enjoy it because there was nothing real, no parent, no leader to save us. The planet is going to go down in flames; we might as well dance around the fire.

Europe, finally. Isla brought the Dream Circus clan to Scotland to perform street theater at the Edinburgh Festival Fringe. Our decision to go on the trip was last minute, and so, for the first few days, despite Isla's wealth, we couldn't find anywhere to stay. The city was packed with tourists. Our first night, we slept in a graveyard, not so different from the ancient Italian ones we'd envisioned in the hot tub at the Russian River. Stone obelisks and mourning angels, aged marble crypts streaked with time and rain. I bedded down in a circle of Celtic crosses half covered in moss. All night long I was tortured out of sleep by strange spirits: orange biting gnats and angry bulls. But Isla was tortured worse; the fairies of the Old World were outraged by this New World fairy intruder.

By the time a few of her friends from London arrived the next afternoon, Isla was exhausted and outraged. Jessica of the orange dreads appeared—Isla's partner in crime—and Angelique, who dressed in bloomers and bonnets like Raggedy Ann and had just spent the summer busking around Europe, dancing like a marionette on top of a makeshift music box. Angelique's father had rented us a big dorm room at the university, and so no more cemetery nights sleeping in the rain for us.

That night, Isla, Jessica, and I went prowling the streets. We found an old church, its stones black with soot and time, stained glass shimmering in its Gothic arched windows. Inside was silent and empty. Isla and Jessica were walking on the pews, rummaging through the sacristy looking for treasure. I felt anxious watching them. "We shouldn't be doing this," I protested. "What if we get caught? What if we get thrown in a Scottish jail?"

"C'mon, Amanda. Churches are bad," Isla said, trying to soothe me. "You know how much suffering they've caused the world?"

Jessica, who was lighting matches from the altar table and wafting the smoke through the air, added, "I bet they burnt witches like you right outside their front door not even that long ago. They probably got the money to build this thing by robbing brown people in some South Sea colony."

They had a point. But I couldn't watch. I went outside and sat on the front steps. A few minutes later they came out, Isla with a pewter candle holder and Jessica with a red glass bauble, both of which they soon grew tired of and left on a stone wall abutting a tea shop.

* * *

My Faery Queen was an outlaw. "We shouldn't have to obey laws we didn't write," Isla would say. We shouldn't have to obey rules written by old white men who only created them in order to preserve their wealth and power. At one point it was legal to enslave people; legal to rip a Native American child from her mother's arms; legal to beat your wife. At the time Isla raided the church, it would have been illegal for us to get married. From Isla's perspective, fairies didn't have to follow human laws. The laws weren't written for our benefit; they were created to protect the rights of the oligarchic few. Because which laws, throughout human history, were ever written by the vulnerable? By the outsiders, by the enslaved, by the witches, the women, the people with disabilities, the mentally ill, by the poor? None. Not ever.

To exist outside the Law was, for Isla, a rejection of the evil hypocrisy of white supremacist capitalist patriarchy. I wanted to exist outside of the Law, too, but I also knew that while we rejected the Law, it hadn't rejected us. We still lived on its land; we were still its property. This trope of the outlaw ran through American culture, a deep red vein throbbing through its white puritanical marble. The outlaw is the one who stands outside the corral of civility. The one who is wild and free. Maverick cops and mafia bosses and fighter pilots and wily cowboys like Jesse James. Even intellectual culture has its outlaws, Hunter S. Thompson, William S. Burroughs, Jean Genet, all of whose vulvas are conspicuously absent. I recognized the trope of the outlaw in Isla, but when women are outlaws in our culture, they're always punished for it. Thelma and Louise, Joan of Arc. The narrative balance isn't set to rights again unless the woman ends up punished for her hubris (*The Scarlet Letter*) or submitting to a man (*The Taming of the Shrew*).

For a long time, I saw the witch as a kind of outlaw. She stands outside the church; she stands outside patriarchal authority. But though the witch is an outlaw and outsider, I don't see her as a criminal. Crowley's law was, "Do as thou wilt shall be the whole of the law. Love is the law. Love under will." Witches of the twentieth century added, "Do as you will, but cause no harm." Fuck who you want, take the drugs you want, wear what you want, live how you like, but do your best not to hurt anyone. I thought of a priest coming to his church, finding things missing, and feeling violated and sad. Even if I didn't agree with the church in principle, I didn't want to cause harm. Isla's law was rebellion, rebellion against the Law of the Father. She stood on the cliff, her back turned against his world in disgust.

Chariot races and torches burning. The physical theater company Chaos Troupe performed Albert Camus's *Caligula*, wearing simple black jeans and shirts, their faces and hands luminous in the dark theater. Without a set, or any spectacle at all, they conjured Rome to the stage with its columns and villas and amphitheaters. The themes of the play were clear: decadence and selfishness, an oligarch's willingness to let the whole world burn for his fleeting pleasure. The show was tight. Rigorous. I doubted very much that any of the players had dropped acid before the performance.

Afterward, my misfit clan and I roamed the streets in our buffoon costumes, clowning and miming for the crowds as they walked between theaters. But I couldn't give it my usual gusto. Paradox kept teasing me that I was performing the role of the mopey clown. He'd come up to me and grimace, and crouch down and sob silently, then leap up and beam at me, expecting me to laugh. I couldn't tell him what I was thinking. That our little band was running around, sleeping in cemeteries, stealing from churches, clowning on the streets, living a kind of chaos, but unlike with the theater company we'd seen that day, our chaos had no meaning.

Isla's energy WAS chaos. She embodied the spirit of the Fool. In tarot, the Fool is wild, unbridled, amoral, an uncontained electricity jolting through the air looking for a conduit. Isla needed no structure, no form. She didn't have to communicate anything or work in service to anyone. She was the cosmic elf, a creature of the void. When we were high, Isla was happy. It wasn't tripping for her. It wasn't a "trip" to Avalon. Her journey to the Land of the Shining Ones was a homecoming. She liked to let her entire self dissolve and be pulled apart in the waves. In contrast, the energy of Chaos Troupe was contained, harnessed to pull chariots of meaning, to move people on a deep level, to advance and *go somewhere.*

Suddenly, the carousing I'd been doing with Dream Circus seemed childish to me. I wanted my work to be intelligible. It wasn't enough any longer to rebel and reject; I wanted the work I did to mean something to people. I was so withdrawn that evening, Isla kept asking me what was wrong. She went into a shop and bought me two beautiful cashmere sweaters, one the color of Scottish heather, the other a pumpkin orange cardigan with buttons made of mother of pearl. But my smile upon receiving it wasn't big enough. "Nothing I do is ever good enough for you," she lamented, once again darting off into the crowd. Once again leaving me to

147

wonder if she would just leave me in Scotland somewhere, without any money, without a wallet or even my passport.

The next day Isla rented us a car and drove us up the coast, stopping at a pile of yellow boulders arcing in a cove around the gray North Sea. We ran down a path, stripping off our clothes, rushing headlong into the water, blasted by the northern coldness of it. The tide lifted and lowered us, our bodies burning pink, our teeth chattering. We held hands in a circle. Each taking turns, we held each other, baptizing each other as undines. Giving each other new names. Someone would float on their backs, sun blazing above. We began a spontaneous chant of hums and clicks, a fairy language that came from Mata Mari, fairy goddess of the sea. These were the moments I lived for with this clan. I lay in the cold, light shimmering on all sides, my fellow fairy children dancing in a circle around me, lifting me and singing. Faces silhouetted by the sun, I could see the shine of their eyes, burning love through the shadow.

Rebelling, choosing the life of the artist, outsider, or witch, causes many hardships. So much self-doubt. But then there are moments like this. Moments of such raw and spontaneous beauty, when you feel like you're living the way humans were intended, in joy, in freedom. And it seems worth it then. No other life seems possible.

That night we arrived at an eighteenth-century estate in the Scottish Highlands Isla'd booked to prove good on the promise she made at the Russian River. We *would* sleep in a castle. To the east, a small river hugged a hillside covered in purple thistles, heather, and a small, mossy wood. Snowy horses pranced in a pasture of emerald grass, and all to the north stretched fields of grain, waist high and rolling, a golden sea stretching off into the horizon.

The castle estate was made of pale gray stones, smooth as doves. Banners snapped above a round drive, with men in chauffeur's caps waiting to escort the wealthy from their Lincolns and Porsches and Aston Martins as they arrived. If they were surprised to see our ragtag band tumble out of our rented Mini Cooper, tripping in our platform clown shoes, Paradox in his unitard, all of us still damp from our North Sea baptism, they gave no indication. They simply tipped their hats and pointed us toward the concierge.

Our room was at the top of the keep, a series of suites with a heavy wooden door. As soon as we arrived in our rooms, Kiara— one of the Fates who'd introduced me to Dream Circus, and Paradox's paramour—took a shower, then came out wearing nothing but a towel around her head as we all sat drinking the champagne waiting for us in an icy metal bucket. Later, as we were lying in our bed before dinner, Isla giggled to me, "That Kiara's always running around naked. I feel like she's always trying to get us to have some big free love party or something." Isla was scandalized. I hadn't really even noticed that Kiara was naked but Isla was baffled. "I mean, she knows we're going out. She knows you're my girl, so why would she do that?" No one was supposed to come between us. No one should even hint at it.

On our last afternoon in Scotland, we sat on boulders, chanting over the mushrooms in our hands, the kind known as the "pixie

149

caps." We were scheduled to leave early the next morning to catch our flight from Edinburgh later in the afternoon. The river gurgled and sang as we ate the fungus, waiting for the shift to come, the shift into the fairy world, where you can see that the trees and stones and wind are alive. Where the clouds speak and the earth reveals its secrets.

As soon as we entered that realm, Isla appeared in her true form, with pointy ears and switching tail. Stomping all around us, stampeding to and fro. We walked the path alongside the river until we came to a small thistle plant, standing proudly in the center of the path. A little over ankle height, with a fuzzy purple head, its neck wreathed in a collar of upward spikes, its leaves furled and unfurled like living lace, full of life and twinkling brightly. I knelt next to it. "Look at this adorable little warrior," I said, marveling. It was a challenger, a knight, daring us to pass.

Everyone gathered around, admiring the thistle's ferociousness. Isla reached out to caress it, then yelped, "It bit me!" She leapt back, her face bruised with rage, lips pulling back from her teeth as she roared. Isla and the thistle seemed well matched until she set upon the little plant in a fury. A force of nature, stomping, leaping, bloodthirsty, hailing a storm of stomps in her steel-toed leather work boots. Her fury didn't relent until I pulled her back and we all stood around, gaping while she panted, catching her breath. The thistle was destroyed. Its purple blossoms ground into the mud, its stalk bent unnaturally, its roots torn from the earth.

"What the fuck, Isla!" Paradox shouted at her.

"It hurt me," she protested, glowering.

"You didn't have to kill it," Paradox said.

Kiara added, "It was such a beautiful little thing." She knelt next to the thistle, frowning, gingerly lifting its limbs to see if it could be salvaged.

"You all care more about that stupid plant than you do about me!" Isla cried, kicking a spray of dirt at us, then shooting off down the path in a rage of smoke.

After an hour or so, I felt like I should go find her. Leaving the wooded river, I found her standing at the edge of a meadow, watching two white horses stomping at the center, majestic and magical, as if in a fairy tale. I observed her for a while, admiring her ability to be so immersed in the moment. She could lose herself completely to beauty. Focused. No fear. None of the anxiety and doubt that were my constant companions.

I came up and took her by the hand and we walked toward the horses. With each step the landscape changed, the ground beneath our feet growing sticky with mud. The emerald grass becoming weedy and sparse. Finally, we got to the center. I'd expected the horses to be valiant and tall, manes shimmering, nostrils velvety. But the animals were short, more like mules or ponies. Muddy, grumpy, and sway-backed, they mashed their cud with yellow stained teeth, swishing flies away with their tangled tails. "They tricked us," Isla declared, aghast, and took me by the hand as we skulked away.

A dusting of stars appeared above us. Warm wind from the hills urging us toward the endless waves of grain to the northwest. We ran into the never-ending purple sunset. We ran in circles through the field, in wide arcs, ducking and diving through its amber dampness. Finally, when we were deep inside and could see nothing and no one in any direction, we collapsed to the earth, coming upon each other in an embrace. In a fevered rite, we pressed our bodies to the earth. I felt certain that a thousand pagans had lain before us in this field. In the summer rites of Beltane, the fertility rites of fire, where pagans would leap over the flames and then grab a fellow reveler or several and baptize the earth with the libations of their lovemaking. When we were finished, we lay on the ground and slept entwined, waking several hours later to gaze at the stars in the clear night air, wondering who was staring back at us from faraway galaxies.

When we returned to our hotel room, it was early morning, around 3:00 a.m. We found Kiara and Paradox sprawled on the carpet outside our hotel room door. The concierge had refused to give them the key, since their names hadn't been added to the room register. Paradox was fuming, Kiara shivering and exhausted.

"You didn't put our names down. Why?" Paradox demanded.

"I didn't think about it." Isla shrugged.

"We've been waiting here for hours."

"Can we talk about this inside?" Kiara pleaded. "I need to pee."

Isla gritted her teeth but chose not to argue. She felt in her pockets for the key, then turned to me, eyes wide. "Do you have the keys?" she asked.

I shook my head. Paradox stiffened.

"Fuck," Isla said.

"Can't you just get extra ones at the front desk?" I asked.

It was late at night. There was no one at the front desk when we entered. The hotel staff was small. There were few guests. "The trouble is," Isla said reluctantly, "the car keys. I attached them to the hotel keys." She looked at me. "We must have lost them in the field."

Paradox was aghast. "You lost the car keys too?"

"Just give me a second to figure this out." Isla glowered at him.

"We're leaving the country in the morning. How are we going to do that without a car? We're in the middle of nowhere."

"Jesus Christ! You're so ungrateful! I'll figure it out," Isla said, pounding on her little skull as if it were a broken TV.

I watched all of this with dismay. We'd been traveling together for several weeks by then. Everyone looked like they were about to cry, then punch each other.

"I'll get the keys," I said.

"From that field?" Paradox scoffed.

"No, babe." Isla shook her head, smiling at me, her endearing pet. "There's no way. It'd be like finding them at the bottom of the ocean."

I went out into the night. I don't know what possessed me to say I could find those keys. Dawn was approaching, the field shivering and shimmering. I stood at its edge and looked out. I could feel a presence there. Male. A different kind of father than the ones I'd been used to. Ancient, generous, and benevolent. Holy. I felt something click over in me. A sense of purpose.

To the guardian of the field, I said:

"O! You, harvest guardian, father of the grain. Wise one and benefactor, I honor and acknowledge you. Come, join me. Guide my hands and lead me. The keys are here somewhere. Guide me to them."

I waited until I sensed an acknowledgment from the Spirit of the Wheat and waded in, the golden strands rustling around my waist. I let my eyelids fall heavy. The presence felt like love, pulling me like a magnet as I trailed my fingertips along its stalks, shifting in the bronze morning twilight. They dipped in a wake behind me as I walked, as though there were someone following behind me, also trailing their fingers through the grain. I was alone, but the guardian was everywhere. The hairs stood on the back of my neck, my hands flickering with electricity, as they always do when Spirit appears. Behind me I could see the castle in the distance, small and sparkling against the hills nearly half a mile away. Something snagged me on my right, a sharp pull. I looked down and saw a piece of white on the ground that I first mistook for trash. It was the keys. THE KEYS. Hiding, there in a tangle of roots. Once I had them in my hand, I had the sense I should leave immediately. I strode back toward the castle feeling a new sense of power and purpose, stopping only at the edge of the field to kneel and give thanks to the spirit that had helped me.

The magic I felt so keenly in the wheat field began to dissipate the moment we arrived back in San Francisco. I grew increasingly dissatisfied. Isla felt me pulling away from her. She kept saying we could go back to Europe whenever I wanted, but her business always got in the way. Our fights increased. Isla grew ever more outraged and self-destructive, pounding her head against the wall and scratching at her arms until they bled. In those moments, I couldn't help thinking of what happened to that thistle.

One night I had a dream. I was standing on the street during

154

a parade; all my friends stood around me asking, "Where should I go, Amanda? What should I do with my life?" A prophetic dream, since now, twenty years later, these are questions my clients commonly ask me. But back then, I didn't have answers. In my dream, a fire truck came blazing down the street with a man standing on top of it wearing a suit and a top hat: a magician tossing tarot cards to the crowd below him like folks toss beads from Mardi Gras floats. In the tarot, the Magician is the first of the major arcana, the archetypal cards that make a tarot deck a tarot deck. The Magician encourages you to make choices, to take the first leap that launches you on your journey. In my dream, I said to myself, "How can I tell anybody what they should do with their life or where they should be? I don't even know where I should go." As soon as I said these words, the Magician held up a big sign that read: "Amsterdam! Amsterdam! Amsterdam!"

A few days after that dream, I found myself at a party talking to this guy who'd just gotten back from working with a dance company in Belgium. I told him that I wanted to study dance in Europe but that I didn't know where I should go. "You should go to the School for New Dance Development," he told me.

"Where is it?" I asked him.

"Amsterdam," he replied.

Chapter 8

c c c

SIGNS, SPELLS, AND OMENS

> She was the daughter of the Virgin of Montserrat,
> and she felt instinctively and of course heretically that
> the Virgin herself was only a symbol of a yet greater
> sister-mother who was carefree and sorrowful all at
> once, a goddess who didn't guide you or shield you but
> only went with you from place to place and added her
> tangible presence to your own when required.
>
> Helen Oyeyemi, *What Is Not Yours Is Not Yours*

I have a client whom I love. She has a pink bedroom, a menagerie of pets, and does raw, fierce performance art, dancing naked and hate-fucking Marlon Brando. She often texts me to ask what things mean. What does it mean, for example, when she keeps seeing the same numbers over and over again? 11-11-11. When the boy she has a crush on shows up wearing a unicorn shirt and she was *just talking* about unicorns? If the thunder that cracked at the moment of her breakup means that she made the right choice or the wrong one? Are these signs? What do these signs mean? "Now is a powerful time in your life," I usually tell her. "You've got the magical heat. Be careful. And go slowly."

A sign's meaning is contingent on context and quality. Of course, we *want* our signs to mean that we're going to get everything we want, that we're doing everything right. But while it's true that our Spirit Allies *do* send us messages, usually they're saying something like, "Look up, pay attention, consider the nuances." If the boy you have a crush on shows up to the party wearing a unicorn shirt, you would do well to remember that unicorns are elusive, often temperamental, and difficult. Some say only a virgin can tame a unicorn, while others say unicorns are imaginary. His unicorn shirt *is* a signal that there's something of significance about this person in your life. But I wouldn't start naming your future fur-babies just yet.

Everything around us is constantly communicating, singing of its history, its composition, its desires and experiences. The Universe is made of information. Signs appear when, out of the universal hum, we pay attention to that one voice: Spirit's serenade just to us. And those signs mean something. But if we ignore our signs, their meaning collapses, trees falling in the forest with no one to hear them. Had I disregarded my Amsterdam dream and chosen to stay in San Francisco or move to New York, my dream wouldn't have meant anything. I may have forgotten it altogether. If we fail to recognize them, there are no signs.

Most often, we only look for signs when we are uncertain, when we lack confidence that we are making the right decision, or when we really want something but aren't sure that we can get it. When we have everything we want, we stop paying attention to the messages. In tarot readings, people often want to keep drawing cards until they get the message that they want to hear. But interpreting the messages as they come to us, rather than as we wish they were, is the whole point of divination. It's in the interpretation of signs that we become oracular, and it's in acting with confidence on those messages that we become witches.

When I arrived in Amsterdam and checked myself into Bob's Youth Hostel, I had $200 left to my name. I'd been traveling around Europe for months by then; Amsterdam was my final destination. Beds in the girls' dorm were 12 guilders a night. If I spent no money on food or anything else, my money would last just over two weeks. My intention was to search out and conquer the School for New Dance Development, the school the dancer I'd met at that party in San Francisco had told me about nearly half a year before. As soon as I arrived, I started getting signs that I was in the right place.

My first morning in Amsterdam, I ate breakfast in my youth hostel dinette. The basement room was packed with travelers all bundled up in scarves, their wool hats pulled low, the air damp with their breath and melted snow evaporating from their nylon backpacks. I sat writing in my journal. I leaned quietly against the back wall, willing myself to be unseen and anonymous so that I could focus amidst the din. I was about to write, "I wish that I could get a job at this youth hostel and work here for free board." I began the sentence, but didn't have time to finish it, because of all the people in the crowded room, the owner of the hostel sat down next to me and asked me if I wanted a job.

158

Mission accomplished! Amsterdam was beginning to welcome me already; clearly I was meant to be there.

Next problem: even with free board, if I bought a couple of hot dinners, a proper winter coat, and a new book, I'd be destitute. Not being Dutch, there were few jobs available to me. I had no interest in working Amsterdam's sex industry. The women in Red Light paced their little glass dens, eyes wild, hearts desperate; they grimaced and flashed their teeth at the men hovering outside their windows like predatory moths. Walking by, I could see that it was just a thin pane of glass (and my American passport—most of them were from the former Soviet Union or the global south) that separated me from the women inside. Geography is destiny.

The only other jobs open to foreigners were in what the Dutch referred to euphemistically as "coffee shops." The coffee they sold was watered down Nescafé. What they really sold was hashish and marijuana. Since pot had been legal in Holland since the 1970s, the Dutch were mainly bored by it. Few Dutch people had any interest in working in a coffee shop, and so you would find many foreigners working there.

Most of the coffee shops in Amsterdam were in the Red Light District, next to the prostitutes, sex shops, and torture museums hawking medieval iron maidens and thumbscrews. The commerce of the area stood in stark contrast to the picturesque canals, arched bridges, and houseboats so cheerfully lining the streets. Entering the Red Light from the Damrak, Amsterdam's main thoroughfare jutting out from Central Station, I began my search for employment with confidence. My plan was to begin at the first coffee shop and work my way up and down the streets until

I found a job. I entered coffee shop after coffee shop, each one playing trance or techno or jungle, selling space cake glowing beneath green neon lights, murals of bug-eyed aliens smoking spliffs painted on their walls. I went into shop after shop with no luck, eventually fearing my luck at the youth hostel was just a fluke.

As I pushed my way east and neared the far edge of the Red Light, the shops were thinning along with my morale. My toes had grown cold and difficult to bend in my Victorian lace-up boots and thin cotton socks. Ahead was the last coffee shop in the district. It would be my seventy-first attempt to get a job that day. The place was called De Oude Kerk, named after the street it was on, Old Church Street, but all the regular clients called it Rasta Baby, like its sister shop down by the docks. Unlike the other coffee shops I'd been to that day booming techno or the Grateful Dead, this place was Rastafarian. Reggae bass nudged ceramic teacups toward the edge of the tables. On the back wall was a mural of a defiant-looking Prince Emmanuel, the solemn child prophet of the Rastafarians, arms folded, head cocked. He glowered with dismay at the stoned tourists slouched low in their seats, giggling to each other as if they were getting away with something as they tried to roll their joints.

Orlando, who owned De Oude Kerk, was Surinamese. He spoke slowly with an air that was both amused and patient, like everything was an inside joke he shared with whomever he was speaking to. He ran gambling upstairs and liked to have girls working the bar of the coffee shop by themselves. Though dangerous for the girls, it was good for business. As soon as I walked in, he offered me the job. After pounding the pavement all day and finally getting a job, I thought to myself, *We make our own luck.*

Aside from the girls working alone, it was mainly a male clientele. Initially I'd stand behind the counter, taciturn and unfriendly, constantly on guard against someone taking advantage of my vulnerability guarding money and weed in a room full of inebriated men. Half the clients were European, American, or Australian tourists; they would order the strongest weed they could get, and then swiftly slump, foreheads crashing to the table. The other half were immigrants from the former Dutch colony of Suriname. They'd moved to Holland to find a better life but had ended up selling hard drugs on the cold, bitter streets of the Red Light District. The Surinamese always bought the weakest weed available, *a tinq Colombian,* and then would hang out and chat with each other for hours. Their relationship to the plant was social, in contrast to the tourists looking for escape. Mariella, an Italian girl who looked like a stunned opossum, worked the day shift. Mistrustful and sly, my first day at work she warned me that the drug dealers would try to steal from me and belittle me. "You have to watch them every second and be very hard with them or they will take advantage of you," she told me sourly. They'd try and do heroin in the bathroom. They'd turn the place into a drug den. And in fact, in my first week, I did catch one man doing heroin in the bathroom, which was strictly forbidden by the owner. But when I tried to make him leave, he roared and towered over me by a foot, threatening and protesting, while the other men in the room sat silently rolling their joints.

Initially, following Mariella's instructions, I was grouchy with the Surinamese. They would command me, "Woman! Bring me my tea." I would respond, "My name is not woman!" When I tried to play my The Cure tapes instead of the reggae that was constantly on rotation, they'd shout, "Woman! This is not music!" Then they would joke with each other and place bets on whether or not I would play Bob Marley, because that was the only reggae white people knew or could understand. Usually, they were right; I *was* about to play Bob Marley. Now I want to go back and shake myself. It was their hangout; why should I get to commandeer the stereo? It was a *Rastafarian* coffee shop.

Lion, a twenty-three-year-old Jamaican with dreads down to his waist, who always wore a knit beret in the colors of the Jamaican flag, would sit at the bar sketching. For work, he drew caricatures of tourists on the Damrak, but he'd come into the Oude Kerk on his breaks and sometimes he would draw my portrait and tell me not to worry what the other guys said. "Bob Marley was popular for a reason," he'd grin at me with a sleepy smile.

After a while it was too exhausting to be en garde all the time. I was too cold. I started to be gentle with all the customers, especially the Surinamese drug dealers. We started choosing the music collectively, and I trusted them to tend to their own business with the drugs in the bathroom. When they called me woman, I'd just tell them my name was Amanda. Almost immediately, the vibe at De Oude Kerk changed. The clients were kind back to me. I would pass them on the street on my way home late at night and they'd shout, "Hey! Rasta baby!!"

I teach a class now on psychic self-defense, and one of its most important principles I learned in De Oude Kerk: Be on good terms with the other beings in your environment. When you speak sharply to a person, you make them your enemy. Kindness is a powerful ward and can help you learn many secrets.

Once on good terms with the Surinamese, they taught me about reggae. They spoke to me of the complex post-Colonial politics of Holland and the best place to get gado-gado, a vegetable and rice dish slathered in lemony peanut sauce. Empathy is a spell that creates intimacy and connection, a free exchange of information. Protection spells are sometimes necessary, but their objective is to keep things out. Create peace, and protection becomes less necessary.

One afternoon while at work, I leaned against the wall describing to Lion the kind of bike I wanted. Because of their popularity, bikes weren't even that expensive in Amsterdam, but they were still more than I could afford, and I never had time to go look for one because I was always working. I wanted one with a basket and a bell like the old women I saw pedaling through the city with their black socks pulled up to their knees and their square-toed shoes. I wanted a cushiony seat and wide handlebars. Thick tires were a necessity, too, since the tram lines for the streetcars engraved shallow trenches in the streets; narrow tires could easily slip inside them and get caught. I'd seen more than one cyclist skid out and eat it that way. Just as I finished describing to Lion my perfect bike, a man pushed open the shop door. With his right hand he wheeled in a bike with a basket and a bell, wide handlebars, and fat tires. "Does anyone need a bike?" the man shouted into the room.

"How much?" I asked him.

163

"Ten guilders." At the time ten guilders was equivalent to about $8. Sold.

Beaming, I wheeled my bike behind the counter. "Lady, you are powerful." Lion smiled at me. "Remind me not to cross you."

The bike was the color of key-lime pie, a Soviet model from the 1980s, sturdy and simple, with thick tires and a padded seat. Probably it had been well loved by some babushka back in the motherland. It was not unusual, I later learned, to have a junkie offer you a cheap stolen bike in Amsterdam. But the fact that it arrived moments after I said I wanted one seemed like a loving sign from a benevolent universe.

Once I had my bike, I took my first opportunity to travel to Zone 2 to scout out the School for New Dance Development, the sacred heart of my European pilgrimage. The dancer at the party in San Francisco had given me the cross streets; I figured I'd be able to find it from there. But the closer to my destination I drew, the more confusingly residential the neighborhood became. Finally, I came upon a house, like every other house on the street, tall and narrow, made of brick, ordinary except for a small handwritten sign in the window that said SNDO and a big padlock on the door to keep out the squatters.

Wiping a circle of grime off the window, I pressed my face up against the glass. An empty room, no furniture, no signs of use. It had an aura of vacancy about it that told me it hadn't seen use for months, if not years. As far as I knew, the SNDO was no more, and from the cramped room and the condition of the building, it looked like it had never been much to begin with.

I kept feeling like someone was going to pop out from behind a bush and yell "Surprise! Just kidding, it's right here!" And then gesture across the street to a grand and beautiful studio that would welcome me and pull me into a class right then and there. Instead, I just walked around until it was time to go to work, where I answered the pot-inspired quandaries of the tourists with a disinterested shrug.

I wasn't ready to give up yet though. I knew the Magician had sent me to Amsterdam for a reason. But I was sick of sleeping in crowded youth hostels full of snoring travelers hacking their winter coughs and stumbling into the dorm room drunk at 4:00 a.m. I wanted to get my own apartment, or at least a room somewhere. But there was no Craigslist then; there was barely an Internet. Still clinging to my witchy roots, I decided to ask the spirits for help.

One afternoon, when all my fellow travelers had left the dorm to go explore the city, I pulled out my notebook and called for the guidance of a spirit. O! Reader. I did this the incorrect way. I should've grounded, centered, and shielded first. I should've called on a spirit I'd worked with before. I should've been more clear about what I wanted. But I did none of these things. I was still a baby witch then, inexperienced and cavalier. My practice was intuitive and unstructured. And…it worked.

I closed my eyes and let the spirit move my hand across the paper in a practice the Surrealists, occult aficionados that they were, called "Automatic Writing." To do it, you close your eyes and ask a question, then let your hand wander across the page, pen in hand scribbling as it wills. Almost immediately, I started getting results, my pen scratching and circling. Finally, the movement stopped. I opened my eyes expecting a great revelation. All I saw was a bunch of chicken scratches, spirals, hatch marks, and just one word—*Clifton*—written over and over again in a halting, childish hand. It meant nothing to me.

The next day at work, I again described my dilemma to Lion. Lion didn't know of any rooms for rent. I think he lived with his family. As we were discussing, enter yet another man standing in the doorway of De Oude Kerk, his neck looped with a dozen gold chains, wearing a red and white nylon tracksuit. "I have a room for rent," he announced to no one in particular. Lion looked at me with his eyebrows raised. "I think I'm a little afraid of you now," he told me.

The gold-chained one introduced himself as Mustafa. He had a strange warble to his voice as if it was difficult for him to get his mouth around the words. Mustafa did not inspire a great deal of confidence. But even though he fronted like a movie gangster with the gold chains and the loping walk, he didn't seem dangerous, just a little defeated and sad. When I asked for more information, he told me the place was a two-room apartment in the southeast and that I would have it all to myself for 350 guilders a month. Because it came just after I announced my need, I thought I should at least have a look at it. My bike was a true gift from heaven; I hoped I'd feel the same way about my new apartment.

The next morning, I called the number Mustafa had given me to schedule the appointment. An elderly woman with a thick Caribbean accent answered the phone. "This is Mrs. Clifton," she said. Clifton was Mustafa's surname. I took the apartment.

166

* * *

One thing I've long since learned about magic is that just because you're receiving signs and messages, just because you're experiencing synchronicity, doesn't mean you're supposed to take every opportunity that comes your way because of it.

Both magic and synchronicity thrive in situations of uncertainty. Like a frozen river, in times of stability nothing can move. When facing a period of strife, the good news is that you're likely to have a lot of what I call magical heat: a surplus of magical coincidences and connections. When things are stable and your life is settled, there's less room for the magic to maneuver. When your situation is volatile, anything can happen, and too, it's at those times that we're most inclined to look to signs for help. The more we pay attention, the more meaningful coincidences appear. Problem is, the more stressed we are, the more likely it is that that troubled energy will be reflected back at us. Our magical field is influenced by the state of our psyche. If you're upset, your magic is liable to manifest opportunities and relationships that just bring you more chaos. As a witch matures, she comes to understand that meditation is her most important practice because it stabilizes her mind and makes her more peaceful. Ironically, the more stable and happy you are, the less you need magic to attain your desires, but also, the more likely it will be that your magic achieves the intended results.

The room I rented from Mr. Clifton was on the fourth floor of what was essentially a derelict housing project in the southeastern part of the city. Whenever I came home, Mustafa would try to sell me one of the radios or television sets he had lying out on the tarmac in front of the building. He was a hustler, but his hustling wasn't getting him very far. Whenever he offered me a television or a radio, he did it with an air of futility. He knew I wouldn't buy it, probably no one would, but at least he was trying.

In fact, the whole building the Clifton spirit had led me to was full of desperate people. Across the hall from me was a couple I heard but never saw. Since they spoke Dutch, I couldn't under-stand what they were saying, but I knew whatever it was, it wasn't good. They were constantly fighting. The woman would cry and the man would yell. One day I came home to find a hole punched through their door.

The doors were flimsy. Mine had a chain lock, which locked only from the inside. I couldn't lock it when I left. There was no handle on the door; you could see into my room through the little circle where the handle was supposed to be. Eventually a French girl stole my sleeping bag. Though the windows were double paned, the place was drafty, cracked floor boards rife with splinters. And there was no toilet. Instead, there was a dirty industrial sink in the hall. I could pee in a pot and empty it there.

But the worst, and most deadly, thing about my new apartment was that it had no heat. It was the coldest winter they'd had in the Netherlands in twenty years. I'd ride home at 2:00 a.m. after De Oude Kerk closed, in temperatures 20 degrees below zero, navi-gating frozen canals where in the day Dutch folks would smile and swirl on ice skates, looping around the city. At night, the canals would exude a soft mist, and I'd go out to the middle and lie there, staring up into the low dark sky, feeling the enormity of life resting on top of me.

I was never not cold. I didn't have proper clothes. I would layer on every article of clothing I had, skirts and dresses over jeans, sweaters on top of that. I'd wear knit caps and wrap scarves around them like a turban, and then throw a second scarf over that as a shawl to cover my neck and shoulders. When I went to work, I'd cling like a barnacle to the heater running behind the counter at De Oude Kerk.

"Woman! Where are you from?" the Surinamese drug dealers would question me.

"California," I'd say with a shrug.

"Oh, we thought maybe West Africa," they'd respond, baffling me. Eventually, I found out they asked because of the way I was dressed: layers and layers of clothes, like the Herrero women of Namibia in their Victorian petticoats and shawls and aprons and turbans galore. That, and because of my name, Amanda, which sounds like the freedom chant, "Amandla!" shouted at protest rallies across the south and west of the African continent. "Who named you that?" the Surinamese would ask me. "My mother," I'd respond. And they'd look at each other, confused.

When my shift ended, I'd go home and strap my Walkman beneath my bra and dance in my freezing apartment until I was sweaty and panting. I'd dry off and then race into bed, hoping my internal heat would last. I'd pile everything I owned on top of the thin mattress I used as a bed: all my clothes, blankets, my sleeping bag, cardboard. Then I'd sleep *under* the mattress to try and keep warm. Lips blue, I would shiver, teeth chattering the whole night. Sometimes I'd chant the witch chants I remembered from my childhood, the words cording out across oceans, across continents, to my mother, to my familiars:

> *Hoof and Horn*
> *Hoof and Horn*
> *All that die shall be reborn*

> *Corn and grain*
> *Corn and grain*
> *All that fall shall rise again*

> *We all come from the Goddess*
> *And to her we shall return*
> *Like a drop of rain*
> *Rolling down to the ocean*[1]

It got so bad that I couldn't empty my chamber pot. By the time I woke up, my pee would be frozen solid. I'd have to heat it on my hot plate in order to dump it out. I had the belief that I should be able to endure anything. That to get what I wanted, I must withstand the worst. My culture had trained me to believe that the greater your sacrifice, the greater your virtue. The chants I used to soothe myself were a thumb, frostbitten and red, skewered into

---

1   The original version of this chant was written by Ian Corrigan, but then it was amended and added to by many people throughout its years in use in pagan communities.

170

a dam about to burst. If I pulled my thumb out, if I stopped chanting, the dam would collapse. I'd be swept away in the freezing waters of poverty and despair.

Magic improves your odds, but it doesn't erase the odds. We still live in the material universe and we must obey its laws. Just because magical practitioners don't always get exactly what they want, exactly when they want it, doesn't prove that magic is pointless. Getting what you want is not the only reason to practice magic.

If magic worked, cynics might argue, then the voodoo priests of Haiti would be leading their rites in an unsullied tropical paradise, rather than the poorest country in the Western Hemisphere. If magic worked, then the Winti ceremonies of the Surinamese, with their perfumed gifts to the ancestors and their possession rites, would've landed them in jungle palaces, lounging poolside as they smoked fresh *tinqs Colombian*, rather than hawking ecstasy to tourists whose fancy backpacks cost more than a month's rent of their apartments. If magic worked, the Eastern Orthodox women trafficked to Amsterdam from Belarus could smash the glass of their Red Light prisons with a simple prayer whispered to the Virgin. If magic worked, then the American Instagram witch making Delphinium potions to heal her sexual trauma could focus her efforts on her art instead of just scratching her way back to baseline mental health.

Though magic does often bring us the things we desire, satisfying our cravings is not magic's primary purpose. Magic connects people to their roots, to their spiritual ancestors and allies, to the hundreds of thousands of beings who have gone before them

experiencing similar struggles. A creative act, magic brings rich-
ness to your life. When you're cold and alone, your chants might
be all you have to keep you alive. Even when it feels like all of civilization has conspired in its effort to take it from you, magic gives
you hope, magic gives you pleasure, and most importantly, magic
helps you remember you have power, even if you can't see a way
to use it yet. The fact that magic connects people to their power is
the main reason most systems of oppression attempt to ban it.

New Year's Eve, 1996. Alone, I wandered to the Leidseplein,
one of Amsterdam's biggest public squares, where I planned to
perform a spell. I knew that at the stroke of midnight, all the cel-
ebrants would release an explosion of energy and goodwill. In
an ideal world, witches practice their spells in nature, beneath
canopies of leaves and moonlight, where the power comes not
from the people, but from the rocks and the stones and the wind
and the trees. But we don't live in an ideal world, and the
enthusiasm of the people of Amsterdam was all I had.

Teeth chattering, swathed in head scarves and my thin wool
jacket, I headed to the center of the square where spidery leafless
trees decked in fairy lights held circle around the perimeter.
Snowflake Christmas decorations arced over the narrow streets,
channeling revelers into the plaza. Sounds of whistling, a distant
drumbeat. The crowd became denser and denser. As midnight approached, I stood at the center of the throng and faced each of
the four directions. I turned to the north, closed my eyes, and visualized the ice giants and the steppenwolves, fierce eyes blazing.
"Great Ones. Guardians. Spirits of the North. Come. Be here with

172

me." I whispered the invocation and turned clockwise to my right, calling in the spirits of the East, South, and West, naming their qualities, singing their praises, asking their favor.

10-9-8-7-6... As the countdown to 1997 approached, I stood, palms pressed together before me as the crowd seethed and sobbed. A girl in a puffy down parka and knit cap pressed mittened hands against the cheeks of her boyfriend, preparing for their kiss. Drunken Brits stumbled together arm in arm like sailors, bellowing their football chants. A queer party crew in their feathers and rainbow streaks of eyeshadow bounced and pranced near an illegal fire guarded by grim police officers in gaudy yellow jackets. My intention for the spell was simple: I wanted comfort. I wanted a protector. I wanted someone to look me in the eyes and tell me everything was going to be okay.

Note that it didn't even occur to me to ask for a solution to my problems or the confidence to solve them. I believed a solution could only come through someone else, so that's what I asked for. And as any scientist will tell you, the question you ask largely determines the outcome of your experiment.

Arms raised toward the fireworks exploding their sulfur and sparks across a sea of exuberant faces, tears streaming down my cheeks, I watched the crowds kissing and swinging each other around. Wetting the surface of my palms with my tears, I offered their salt water as libation, saying, "Please, by the powers of the Goddess and the God and the Holy Androgyne, send me a protector. Send me someone to help, someone who will love me and keep me warm, even if it's just for one night."

I clapped my hands together and then flung them up to the sky, releasing the Guardians of the directions to find my protector and bring them to me. Even before I left the plaza, I knew my spell would work.

A mentor of mine, Robert Allen, a ceremonial magician in the tradition of the Hermetic Order of the Golden Dawn, says spells have three components: emotion, intention (symbolic thought), and action. At any of these points, the magical practitioner can go wrong, but the trouble often starts with the emotion. If your emotion is anxiety or desperation, look forward to a wild ride ahead. In any case, generating emotion in the first place is often difficult to achieve. Now, when I do spells with my clients, sometimes they feel shy, or find it difficult to access the emotion that brought them to me in the first place. Being able to access emotion on demand is why witchcraft takes practice, just like theater takes practice. To be able to call upon a powerful, authentic emotion at will, and to have it be the right emotion for the job, is not easy to do. All the most effective spells have real emotion behind them. Like most engines, spells need combustion to make them go. Emotion ignites the spell; action sends it out into the universe to do your work.

Soon after New Year's Eve, I checked myself back into Bob's Youth Hostel. Homeless people were freezing to death on the streets, and my apartment was only a few degrees warmer. Given that it was the holiday season, I was lucky to get a bed. I took a bunk in the crowded girls' dorm room, grateful to sleep amidst the blazing bodies of two dozen strangers. I noticed on the bunk below mine someone had left her guitar case. Someone had been so committed to her music that she was willing to lug her guitar around with her while she was traveling. I wanted to be that committed to my own art practice.

Later that day, I sat at a cheap café in the Red Light District, blowing steam off salty spoonfuls of French onion soup, watching the snow dance beneath the streetlamps outside. *I wonder how long I will have to wait,* I thought, *before my helper appears.* At that moment, a diminutive figure bustled into view, emerging through the whirls of snow on the dark city street, strawberry-blond hair peeking from beneath her cap, pointy upturned nose reddened by frost. It was Isla. My Fairy Queen and Fairy Monster. Appearing through the snow like the White Witch of Narnia.

No. This can't be right, I thought to myself. My Fairy Queen disappeared into the veils of shivering white. I hesitated. I was terrified of this woman. When I'd arrived in Europe, I worried that she'd hire a hit man to come find me. We hadn't communicated since I'd left for Europe nearly half a year before. In that time, she'd come to represent to me absolute chaos and the potential for annihilation. How could this be the angel the Goddess had sent for me? And yet, I reasoned, to reject this messenger would clearly be to reject the Goddess's will. After a long moment's hesitation, I leapt from my chair and chased after her into the red maze leading toward the city center.

When she saw me, her eyes widened and she shook her head, blinking, as if I were an apparition. Without speaking, we wrapped our arms around each other, spinning and tracing circles into the snow. It was clear. We were together again. Now. Maybe forever.

* * *

175

It had been Isla's guitar that I'd seen on the bunk below mine in Bob's Youth Hostel. She had only been planning on staying in Amsterdam for three days. On the night of our reunion, she rented us a room down the street in a five-star hotel. I saw the choice to go after Isla as an inevitable one. As if the Goddess had chosen for me simply by placing her on my path. When we're unstable or traumatized, we might not see the opportunities that magic presents us with; our expectations and patterns can blind us.

Within a few days of running into Isla, I'd also received a reply to an inquiry I'd put out on a message board about nannying. A Dutch woman was looking for a nanny for her two kids, ages six and nine, to live with her in her central A'dam flat and mind the kids for half the day in exchange for room and board and some petty cash. I met with the woman and the offer seemed good; she was an artist and had a sense of humor. Her flat was cozy, full of good books and ceramics and brightly colored wall hangings made out of yarn. She said that she had planned on getting a nanny the following month, but when she saw my message, that I was here in the city now and desperate, she wanted to help.

I turned the artist mother down. Isla had already started looking for an apartment for us, and there was the idea that I would start to dance again. I assumed, without asking, that the artist mother wouldn't allow me time off to dance in the evenings. Without ever seriously considering that the artist mother could've been the helper that I'd prayed for, I declined her cozy house and joyful kids. Instead, I chose Isla. The choice was mine. The magical heat was telling me to slow down and pay attention. The magical heat was a sign from Hecate that I was at the crossroads. On our

176

life paths, signs are abundant. It's when we stop paying attention to the details of these messages that we take the wrong road, the road with the ruts in it, carved from all the times we've moved toward our wounds instead of toward healing. Hecate had placed the signs before me, but only I could choose which way to go. While unintended detours may still lead us to good places, if your road sign says *Slippery When Wet*, the wise witch would do well to slow down.

Isla and I moved into a newly remodeled flat on Spuistraat in Old Town, right near the city center. Long and thin as a railway car, our front window looked out onto a street festive with flower-boxed windows and people bustling by in their brightly colored scarves. Isla immediately began to remodel, painting the white walls lilac and replacing the sensible slate gray shag with a carpet thick and twisted as the wool of a black goat. She strung up her hammock and painted the ceiling, wood beams and all, a dark indigo. The dark ceiling and carpet made me feel like I was prostrate between two anvils. Isla soon got up to her old antics, bringing lowlifes around and presenting me with an all-night fairy buffet of mind-altering chemicals, but at least I slept beneath a down comforter and could blast the central heating to tropical temperatures.

At Waterlooplein, the outdoor flea market, Isla bought me a sheepskin coat out of a fairy tale: hooded and crimson with a lining in long, silky black wool. On our way back from the market, I discovered a shiny, new building, all glass and steel in jutting angles like a ship: the *Hogeschool voor de Kunsten*. The new performing arts school. Outside was a sign for the School for New

Dance Development. Inside, the School for New Dance Development had an entire floor. Not only that, but they were also currently enrolling for their six-week intensive course. It would begin in a month, after which they would hold auditions for their BA program.

All of a sudden, everything I'd longed for, I had.

Spring came and Amsterdam was alive. The canals melted, trees lined the streets green and fragrant. We rode our bikes past the buskers dressed as medieval suns, light shimmering off the cobblestones wet with spring rain. I danced every day and made friends with my fellow dancers. Ines, an Austrian intellectual, who spoke slowly and deliberately from beneath a mane of coarse blond hair. Nerea, a birdlike Basque, eyes always shining, always ready to embrace you as if her life depended on it.

It was in a video viewing room at the SNDO with Ines and Nerea that I saw the choreography of Pina Bausch for the first time. *The Rite of Spring*. The videotape was at the end of its life span. Stravinsky's sound score crackled with static, white lines of digital decay rolled through the image. But it didn't matter. I could still smell the broken bones and raw carnage through the screen. Dancers ankle deep in red earth, split into tribes of male and female, the former sacrificing one of the latter. They offered up the body of a woman to appease the ravenous gods of nature. Trembling, the women shunted between them a red dress, a hot thing that hurts to hold. Whoever ends up with the dress must sacrifice by dancing herself to death. Dancing oneself to death being a common trope for the Western ballerina, someone who smiles as her toes crackle and she bleeds into her shoes. Ballerinas make the pain look easy. But it does not look easy when Pina's dancers do it. Pina's choreography slits the belly of ballet's patriarchal undergirding so we can see inside. "I show you brutality so that we can see the opposite," Bausch says.

Dance, the body, our immediate physical experience, constitutes the essence of this glorious life. Witches don't seek to transcend material reality. We know that the material world is where the work happens; we want to wring its juice and drink it. We don't seek a spiritual existence in a golden cloud surrounded by angels or virgins. Nor do we abandon our bodies for an abstract realm of mathematical forms. Witches know that it is in our relationships with each other and with our planet that the true magic occurs.

If nothing else, I needed to be in Amsterdam so that I could have that one brief moment with Pina Bausch. So that she could show me that even though material reality can wound and terrify you, even though it screams in our face with its brutality, we can redeem its crimes. We can heal our ancestral wounds. We can even rectify our own mistakes. No need to confess our sins, or make the deity suffer our burden for us. When we create beauty, we become our own redeemers. The Goddess speaks through our deeds. If we can bear to see the brutality we humans have rained down upon this world through our acts of destruction, then we can resurrect its opposite by taking creative action.

By the time audition day arrived, I was confident all roads of my life led to Amsterdam; this was my place and my purpose. Though a hundred dancers from all over the world lined the walls of the audition auditorium, and though the school would select only nine new students, what were numbers when I had Fate on my side? Fate laughs at numbers. She *created* all the numbers in the universe. My desire to be at the SNDO would surely trump anyone else's talent. All the signs had told me so.

Of course, I didn't get in.

"We've been watching you, Amanda," my interviewer told me. "This is a school for dancers. We think you're more choreographer than dancer."

I shook my head in disbelief.

She continued. "We create collectively here. We see you more as a solo artist."

"No," I said, then repeated, "No. That's not true. I'll do what you tell me. I had a vision that I was supposed to be here."

"You clearly have a strong vision," she told me, matter-of-factly. "And that's what makes you not right for this school."

After the audition, my reason for being in Amsterdam, and my reason for being in general, collapsed. All my magical heat had added up to nothing. In the bargaining phase of my grief, I questioned the Universe: Why would I be given all those signs? Why have that dream, why meet that dancer who told me to go to Amsterdam? Why suffer through all the cold, the years of being lost? Why be given a longing to dance supernatural in its proportions, if I was never going to get what I wanted? Why would the Goddess, the Universe, the powers that be, make me want something so badly if it was always going to remain outside my grasp?

Magic and synchronicity had led me to Amsterdam, and then

they abandoned me there. Or at least that's what I believed at the time. But the signs had been accurate; it was my interpretation of them that had room for improvement. For instance, in the dream that led me to Amsterdam, I should've noticed that magicians are known to be tricksters, and fire trucks follow fire. The dream was telling me about the *quality* of the time I'd have in Amsterdam, rather than telling me where I should go. Knowing that wouldn't have necessarily led me to make a different choice, but it might have led me to have different expectations.

And, too, my spells *had* worked. While rereading my old journals during this period of my life, in my late teens and early twenties, I kept coming across an explicitly stated intention of living life to the fullest. Of experiencing as much of life as it could offer me. That doesn't mean getting your way all the time, or always having everything be easy. Adventure is rarely comfortable. And I achieved everything I had set out to do. In my stated intentions, I didn't say, "Graduate from the SNDO with a bachelor's degree in dance." I said, "Study dance at the SNDO." Check. Did it. For six weeks. Magic is the ultimate adventure, because even if you get what you want, you rarely get it in the way you expect. Still, now that I'm older, adventure seems less appealing. Today, when I do any kind of spell, I always make sure to include the phrase, "This spell shall cause no harm, nor turn on me. For the greatest good of all concerned and for the greatest good of all beings. This or better. Victory to the Goddess!" I've learned the hard way how important it is to include caveats. Sometimes, I even ask that the changes my magic bring about be *gentle* and *easy*.

Magic is a duet between you and the Universe. A romance.

Signs are the way the Universe speaks to you; they're sweet whispers, not orders. Still, as in ordinary life, if your lover gives you a bouquet of roses, it doesn't necessarily mean you'll be together forever. It can have a dozen different meanings: apology, gratitude, obligation, affection. Most importantly, it means connection. It means relationship. And relationships require listening, not just for what you want, but also what your partner is trying to say. When you receive a sign, your interpretation matters. And then, how you act on that message is just as important as the fact that you received it in the first place.

Our stories don't end when we don't get the result we want. I didn't get in to the School for New Dance Development. At the time, I believed that my magic had failed me. When really, my dream, my signs, my spells, opened up my life, got me to Europe, and so much more. Even these words are part of the message of that initial dream. Turns out, as it always does, my Magician's magic words were the right ones.

Chapter 9

ℭ   ℭ   ℭ

ENEMIES AND ALLIES IN THE ASTRAL REALMS

Now women return from afar, from always:
from "without," from the heath where witches are
kept alive...

> Hélène Cixous, "The Laugh of the Medusa"

The princess died a few days before I arrived. England was in mourning. Prince Harry and Prince William walked solemnly behind their mother's funeral car, wading through streets knee-deep in bouquets of flowers. Flowers piled high along the road. Flowers waist-deep outside the palace gates. At the time, I looked like Princess Diana. Hair short and dyed blond. People would come up to me on the streets crying, offering me their crushed bouquets. I identified with their grief. I identified with Princess Diana. I loved how she'd said, "I like to be a free spirit. Some don't like that, but that's the way I am." As a child, I used to have a paper doll set with the princess in all her outfits: her fur coat, her prim high-collared blouses, her tiara, her wedding gown. Princess Diana's death was a signal, for some of us at least, that the myth of the princess—rescued by the prince and then living happily ever after—was over. No one was going to come save us. Patriarchy had tried to sell us on the princess myth, and we could see where it ended: in flames.

I arrived in England, the isle of my ancestors and the birthplace of modern witchcraft in early September 1997 and took a room in the home of a widow in New Cross Gate, South London. The widow was an elderly woman, jolly, who'd once lived at Westminster Abbey when her husband was alive and a deacon there. Now she let her spare rooms to students. It was a Victorian tangle of a house, made of brick, each house on the street pressed up against the other with no space in between, no front yards, but the back gardens all joined together in wild joy that reminded me of Peter Rabbit. Each lot was separated only by low white picket fences and gardens full of willow ponds, purple cabbage, Queen Anne's lace, and a host of ravens that would snicker and snarl at each other, swooping on hunched black wings to gobble up the snails.

During the Blitz, Nazis had strip bombed South London because it was near the docks. Each block in our neighborhood had strips of modern buildings that had sprouted up in the 1950s, scars from the war slicing diagonally across the streets for miles. My landlady had been in London during the Blitz. Her father had been a priest, rushing from house to house of his parishioners, offering them bread and succor as the buildings around him trembled and fell. My landlady told me she certainly would have joined the clergy herself, only the church wouldn't allow it since she was a woman, so she did the next best thing and married a deacon. She raised his children and baked the bread he ate while ministering to his people. In the sixteenth century, Christopher Marlowe had been murdered in a pub down the street from my house, and William Blake had seen a tree full of angels in an overgrown cemetery just over the hill where I would often walk to remind myself that no torment would last forever. Given time, the hungry vines and crumbling crosses told me, nature solves all riddles.

My room was pokey and narrow, the walls papered in a William Morris mesh of birds, vines, and pomegranates, with a dim northern light tiptoeing through the lace curtains. On my first night, I lay in a bed lumpy and misshapen from the sweating bodies of a dozen other students before me. I couldn't sleep. All night long, bloodcurdling screams hailed from the back garden. The next morning, I told my landlady that someone had been murdered beneath our willow tree and she said, "Oh yes, that's the foxes. They do make a racket, don't they? But you'll see in the spring their pups are darling; roly-poly balls of red fur."

After my failure to get into the SNDO the previous spring, Isla and I broke up, but she'd offered to pay my way back to New York if I finally agreed to pose for her "Gallery of Lost Souls." I was to emerge from a lake in Somerset, England, like a nymph, the images capturing my soul and placing it forever in her fairy circle. Devastated as I was at the time, I no longer worried about putting my immortal soul at risk with Isla's fairy magic. I was basically like, *whatever*. She brought me to England to take the photographs, but before we made it to her fairy queendom, I'd called the Laban Centre for Movement and Dance on the off chance they might be willing to give me a private audition. They were.

I went in and took a first-year Graham class with Marilyn— a former Graham dancer in her fifties. I'd never danced Graham before, but I gave it my best. About ten minutes in, Marilyn asked me to take off my sweatpants so that she could see my turnout and alignment. "But I'm not wearing anything underneath," I protested. I'd been dancing in studios where everyone wore loose-fitting clothes, thread worn and held up with a shoelace. "Well, that wasn't very sensible of you, was it?" Marilyn frowned, unamused.

Terrified I was losing my last chance to dance, on my next turn across the floor I took off my pants and danced in my underwear. If she wanted to see my turnout, there it was. I danced across the floor in my saggy period underwear and did what I could with it. At the end of the class, Marilyn winked at me and said, "You dance with a lot of heart." Dr. North, the school's dean, offered me a place in their Dance Theatre BFA program later that day. Unlike the program in Amsterdam, the Laban Centre offered a BFA degree that was as rigorous in academics as it was in choreography and technique. And if I decided to move back to the States, the credits from England would still count. My failure to get into the SNDO had worked out for the best.

Since dance was my religion, it seemed fitting to me that my new school was in a converted church. My favorite studios had arched ceilings and stained glass windows the color of sand, sea foam, and moss. We leapt, drumming our feet across wooden floors in studios muggy with breath and sweat as the rain fell against the windows and the pianists called our souls heavenward with the pounding of their keys. The BFA program was three years, five days a week, 8:00 a.m. to 6:00 p.m., sometimes later with rehearsals. In all three years, I never missed one class. Fridays were my least favorite day of the week, because it meant that I wouldn't get to take class again until Monday.

At seven in the morning I'd jog to school through the fog and rain carrying a little yellow rucksack I'd sewn for myself and embroidered with the eye on the Fool's bag in the Motherpeace tarot deck. After all my trials, I wanted to be like the Fool, to start again—as Vicki Noble says in her book about the cards—fresh and new, without any ideas of sin or transgression. Carrying the bag of the Fool meant that I was on a new adventure, that I would not be plagued by old stories, that I had broken with my past karma, that I trusted the Universe to take care of me. Inside the Fool's pouch, she carries everything she needs. Of course, I'd already encountered the Fool with Isla, and then been directed to Amsterdam by the Magician. Technically, if I was going to follow the teleological trajectory of the tarot, my next card should have been the High Priestess: the witch of the tarot deck, keeper of knowledge and adept traveler between the worlds. When you calculate my soul cards using tarot numerology, my cards are the High Priestess and the Fool. I was always meant to be the High Priestess, but with all the Fool in my psychic DNA, it's no wonder I always want to take the scenic route, the circuitous path that leads in and out, away and back again.

* * *

At first, I tried to get by in London without stripping. I knew sex work damaged me, stressed me out, took a big hunk of my soul and kept it locked in a cage somewhere (sometimes literally), far away from me. The worst part was that it made it difficult for me to integrate my upper body with my lower half. Somewhere around my hips, my upper and lower body got confused and didn't know how to talk to each other. Often, I would lose my balance. I thought, *If I use enough force, maybe I can pound my two halves together.* We'd be doing pirouettes and I'd knock myself over trying to do as many as possible. "A thousand falls make a dancer," my teachers would say as I lay prostrate on the floor.

One day I asked one of my ballet teachers if I could get her signature to sign up for more Pilates classes provided by the school. We already took one Pilates class a week, but I wanted more. "Nope. You're strong enough, Amanda. You don't need to work harder," she told me, shaking her head. "You need less stress. No extra Pilates for you. Try meditation."

Sadly for me, and for anyone I dated at the time, I did not yet try meditation as she suggested. How could focusing on my breath make any difference at all? What I needed was more muscle, more core power. In our civilization, it's drilled into our skulls that if you don't succeed, it's because you didn't put enough muscle into it. But of course, that ignores all the people who attain their trophies not through hard work but through privilege. Not to mention those who do *nothing but* work and can barely keep their heads above water because our economic and political system is structured to keep them down.

I had many jobs. I worked waiting tables in Piccadilly Circus,

I worked at a bar in Soho and at a tourist's restaurant on the South Bank. For a time, I worked at a House of Magic as a stage magician's assistant, making martinis disappear and pulling an endless stream of scarves from a shadow dog's mouth, strapping yowling women to a chair while the magician lobbed off their heads to roll on the floor like melons. But London is expensive. I couldn't support myself that way forever. I always owed my school money for tuition. I often couldn't afford to eat. I didn't want to see one more potato. I'd walk up the Thames, along the cobbled streets of Bermondsey and London Bridge, and pass an iron cage hanging over the door of some tiny prison museum. In medieval times, debtors and criminals would be locked inside, unfurling their spectral hands, begging for scraps or sips of water from the child laborers scampering below, their faces black with soot.

I toiled as an escort, briefly, showing up at wealthy men's houses in the middle of the night when their wives were away. I'd leave the house of my Christian landlady, taxiing out in the middle of the night to go to the house of whatever hedonist the agency put me in contact with on my pager. A former Monty Python producer who favored Russian girls because they "really knew how to work." A Swedish oil millionaire who had a medieval bed with a compartment beneath it where they'd keep the hounds to warm the bed. I worried, "Will he shove me in there?" A disfigured man, a pilot, who was scarred all over his body from the time he ran into a burning building to save a child and as reward for his heroism had to pay women for sex ever after. Even then, *I have not told you all. I have not told you everything.*

I always felt in danger. The body I worked so hard to train was constantly under threat. As far as I could see, my body was the only thing I had that the world wanted, but often what it wanted was to misuse and then destroy it. But I was willing to do whatever was necessary to stay in dance school. I told myself I would become a dancer, or I would die trying.

Now that I am a witch, I understand the power of words, and the spells we cast in our minds, with our intentions. I recommend no one ever say, "I will do X, or die trying." The Universe will take your maxim as a challenge. It will delight in testing to see just how serious you really are. And if you keep telling yourself, "Whatever doesn't kill me makes me stronger," your trials will never end.

I spent years of my youth in various sorts of underworlds. Sometimes literally. The Astral, one of the strip clubs I worked at in London's Soho district, while named after a transcendent plane of existence, was actually a bougie bar in a basement filled with gilt mirrors and leather chairs and a central stage with a brass pole.

In the Greek myth, Tantalus was a king who was sent to hell for stealing the fruits of the gods and delivering them as a feast to his people. For this transgression he was punished, made to stand starving beneath a tree heavy with fruit, just beyond his reach; surrounded by a pool of fresh water that would recede every time he bent to drink. In the Astral, the women I worked with experienced a similar kind of torture. Above all, they, *we*, wanted to be seen and valued. And what we experienced came so close to that, but ultimately it was always a trick. Sex workers are witches, powerful, yet frequently traumatized. Wild and unhinged, ankles

190

circled with parole devices, they wake up in the beds of strangers, still wearing their stick-on rhinestone jewelry. The magic of the wounded is chaotic and thirsty, flung out in every direction. Magic like that often turns on the sender.

The Astral was an arty club. No fake tits. All the girls with differing daring forms of beauty, all of them hungry to be adored. The club attracted celebrities: restauranteurs, YBA art stars, famous actors, musicians ranging from Eminem and Snoop Dogg to Britpop stars from Blur and Pulp, and old-school punk impresarios like Malcolm McLaren. A bunch of actors from *Band of Brothers*, the HBO miniseries about young men finding opportunities for heroism and valor during the nightmare of war, were regulars while they were shooting at Pinewood Studios. Even famous women would come in: Kate Moss wanted the dancers to teach her how to "work the pole," until my friend Cassandra, a feisty Scot, threw a drink in her face in the women's bathroom.

The wealthy and famous would compete for us, throw money at us, beg us to go home with them. But at the end of the night, they'd hustle us out the back door of their heiress girlfriend's apartment and we'd go home to our shitty flats in Elephant and Castle. Every girl there dreamed of becoming famous: an actress, a pop star, a writer. Not because we all had a passion for our craft necessarily, or that we even had a craft, though many of us did, but because we saw that there were people who counted and people who didn't, and we knew which shitty side of the window we were currently on. We had our noses pressed up against the glass.

* * *

191

The class divide is made especially clear in London. Just around the corner from the Astral were the Groucho Club and Soho House, "Members Only" clubs my friends and I could get into if we were with the right people. The illusion was that behind those discreet unmarked doors was the land of milk and honey, where everyone took you seriously, life was easy, and every creative ambition you had could be fulfilled. But I was young and naïve; now I know that isn't true. The underworld is everywhere. Even in the Groucho Club.

I remember meeting an older man at Soho House, some peripheral film figure, who bought me and my friends drinks. He wanted us to go home with him but we refused. "Get us into Soho House some other time, and who knows," we told him. A week or two later he came into the Astral and bought a dance from me, glowering the whole time.

"What's your problem?" I asked him.

"I came here to get a dance from you, to humiliate you," he told me. "To see you naked whether you wanted me to or not."

I laughed. I didn't give a shit who saw me naked. "Why did you want to do that?" I asked him.

"Because you were using me. You just wanted me to buy you drinks and get you into Soho House."

"Pshhhh," I scoffed. "Did you buy me drinks because you wanted to get to know me as a person? Because you cared about me and just really wanted to make sure I wasn't thirsty?"

A smile broke across his face; I could see his heart bursting rainbows of joy. "That's right," he exclaimed. "I was using you! I don't care about you. I just wanted to have sex with you. I was

192

using you, and you were using me!" He squirmed, elated; he wasn't just being duped by some strip club slut; he was actually using her as well. He was so thrilled, he didn't even finish our dance; he leapt up to hurry back to Soho House while I finished out my night hustling for the limey dollar. It always amazes me how people don't see the power they have and in fact feel that they are victims of the world. Truly, that amazement extends to myself as well. I didn't see the power I had at that age; I thought I was at the mercy of silly men like him, and so I should scramble for whatever scraps I could get. But a witch needs to recognize her own power. If she doesn't, she can never escape the underworld.

For years I was surrounded by sex workers who wanted to be celebrities and marry film directors. Sex workers raising their children alone. I danced next to a woman who had a pointy face and slanty eyes like a friendly fox. The men were crazy for her, even though most dancers couldn't figure out why. We'd ask the clients what they saw in her, and they'd say, "She's just so kind." What they didn't know about her was that she'd seen her entire family shot to death in Kosovo.

All around me, girls dropped like flies. The beautiful Russian twins, nineteen years old and identical, willowy with high full tits, blue eyes, and manes of tawny hair. They only spoke Russian and never left each other's side. They finished each other's sentences, sharing their lingerie and the cherries in their cocktails. They smiled at how easy it was to make money while the other girls watched them jealously from the DJ booth, worrying that we wouldn't make enough that night to cover our house fee. But within months they'd started to look harder. Their eyes darting and nervous. The slob of a middle-aged man who had married one of them to bring them to England was a porn producer. He got the twins to have sex with each other in videos. To get them to do it, he got them strung out on amphetamines. Their once lithe bodies became gaunt, their eyes hollow. Soon they stopped working altogether. I don't know what happened to them.

Many people who enter the underworld never make it out alive.

Once you're abducted into the underworld, you're constantly reminded you have no right to complain. There's always someone who has it worse than you. Don't feel sorry for yourself, Persephone. At least you're not having sex with your sister, married to a porn producer and strung out on crack.

By the time I stripped for the first time in that dingy Motel 6 in Southern California, I'd already been force-fed the fruits of the underworld. Thus, I was bound to it, and eventually succumbed to its temptations. My Scorpio nature lured me into the cracks and crevices. Eventually, I came to believe that if I traveled in deep enough, I might be able to conquer the final monster. Maybe I could rescue my own princess. Maybe I could beat the game. The underworld is supposed to yield men defining moments, moments of courage. I thought the underworld would teach me strategies for overcoming despair, that I would be confronted with the most profound realities of existence and grow larger because of it. What I hoped to find in the underworld was a bigger, more badass version of myself. In its depths, I wanted what the young male hero hopes to find in war.

But the deeper I went in to the underworld, the harder it became to find my way out again. The more I participated in it, the more it took from me, and the more fragmented I became. In fact, my fragmentation was the entire point. People who perpetrate sexual abuse might believe that they're doing it to scratch a personal itch, but the consequences of that abuse sprawl out across our entire civilization; abuse has far-reaching political consequences. Abuse makes it so that the very people who might grow up to be powerful resisters to the status quo instead expend their energy searching the underworld for their lost fragments, trying to sew the pieces back together with disintegrating thread. When the Medusa's head was severed from her body, she no longer posed a threat. Not only that, but her power was co-opted by the "hero." Whoever held the head of the Medusa held her power. The real power the patriarchy wielded over me was the way it made me see myself.

The deeper I tunneled into the underworld, the more I realized that there was nothing there, just a vast, dark wasteland, filled with ghosts, abused children, torments: proximity to wealth and value but no ability to attain it. The walls of my underworld nightmare would only come crashing down when someday, some prince would come and kiss me awake. When someone recognized the value in me, saw beyond the costumes of the underworld that I wore and recognized that I was worthy of protection and love. I didn't know that in order to break the spell, that someone needed to be me.

One of the best things about England is that the museums are free. On my worst days, I'd wander the streets. It would be raining, it always was, and I'd end up in the Hayward Gallery, a brutal-ist goblin castle squatting along the river. London is crowded and urgent, but inside the Hayward was silent as the grave. I'd press my palms and my forehead against the cold stone walls in the stairwell, drawing in their power. Inside the walls of this fortress, weirdness reigned.

Wandering the galleries, I'd walk through rooms stained pink with neon, voices chanting from the walls, spectral figures loom-ing in the corners with horned crowns, holding fur teacups. West-ern civilization had worked hard to disenchant the world. But the realms of enchantment still persisted in art. The art objects flew against the dim window of ordinary reality and cracked it. Art is magic because it makes the things we imagine visible to us; it pulls them into material reality and changes the way we experience the world.

But the difficulty with all this was that I was straddling the worlds, the art world, the dance world, the world of relationships, the world of women and sex workers, the safe houses of ordinary reality and the hinterlands of the exiled witch. Though I loved to dance, the dance world didn't feel like home to me. I didn't fit in with the other students, so many of whom had come from shel-tered backgrounds. The art world was beautiful in theory, but in practice, both from the YBA artists I'd encountered at the As-tral and in the stories that I'd heard, the art world was just as misogynistic as anywhere else. I didn't know where I belonged.

People have been practicing magic in the British Isles ever since they took up permanent residence there fourteen thousand years ago. Ancient Britain was inhabited by the Picts and the Britons and the Celts, and its magical practices were shamanic celebrations of nature, the animals, and the seasons, and were passed down orally, through songs and dances, folk tales, and symbols painted on the walls of caves. When the Romans colonized the island in 43 CE, they named it Britannia after Brigid (Brigantia), the tutelary deity they found there, goddess of fire and of poets, keeper of the sacred flame and guardian of the wells. The Romans brought with them their own gods and magical practices. They built temples to the lion-headed god Mithras, born from a rock, and Minerva, virgin goddess of wisdom and war. They even built a temple to Isis in London, the Egyptian goddess of magic and wit, Queen of the Underworld, whom the Romans had fallen in love with on their sojourns to northern Africa and then adopted as their own.

When the Romans withdrew four hundred years after they arrived, the Roman Empire had already converted to Christianity. They'd imposed their Christ cult on the Celts and the Picts, but the people of Britannia quickly cast the new religion aside. Instead, they favored the magical practices of the Germanic tribes who'd given them the language of Old English and their god Woden, god of the storm and one-eyed master of the runes; now they had Freyja, goddess of love and magic, and the goddess Eostre, bringer of the spring.

Even before the Vikings, before even the time of the druids, there were cunning women, known as *hags*, or *runans*, *leodrunes*, or *wicces* (pronounced "witches"), all words for sorceresses of various types. They practiced divination with runes, knew the secrets of

197

the medicinal plants, and served as priestesses to their people. England didn't become Christian until the seventh century CE, when missionaries from Rome insinuated themselves back into the political structure of the feuding lords, eventually ending the pagan reign.

Around that same time, the word *witch* began to take on a negative connotation, the other words for magical women disappearing from usage entirely. With the Inquisitions of medieval Europe, magic went underground. It would reappear sporadically over the next millennia, via the practices of John Dee for instance, court magician to Queen Elizabeth. A mathematician and wizard, he and his co-conspirators channeled an elaborate system called Enochian magic, which allowed the diligent practitioner to talk to angels.

Whereas the magical practices of the pagans were folk traditions, involving medicines for the people, love charms, and midwifery, the magical practices of John Dee were informed by the values of his time. The Enochian magic for which he's most remembered entails an elaborate system of calls and invocations rivaling calculus in its complexity. The purpose of this magic was to call angels and demons to do your bidding. You had to know their names, Azazel and Focalor and Ashtaroth, and understand exactly what office they held in the legions of demons if you wanted to command them. The magic of John Dee reproduced the hierarchies and systems of domination so common to feudal England. Though Dee was interested in asking the angels about the universal language of creation, which was supposed to bring about world peace, most of the time, Dee toiled for Queen Elizabeth in poverty. Even in Tudor England, spells for money were second in popularity only to spells for love. John Dee wanted to focus on unraveling the mysteries of the universe, but he had many mouths to feed in his large household. Much to the annoyance of the angels he worked with, he spent a lot of contact time asking them for money, even just to borrow a little.

Our magic today is not immune from similar requests, and like John Dee, our practices reflect the time and place we're living in. Today our magic is uneasily multicultural, anxious (rightly) over cultural appropriation, often delivered in bite-sized platitudes for expression on social media. The modern witch can also be, like our culture, oriented toward objects of consumption like crystals and candles, essential oils and magical jewelry, rather than on achieving justice and the restoration of the natural world. As is true of all humans, the contemporary witch is fallible, and I am certainly no exception.

Even though John Dee was exiled for a time and died in poverty, magical practice in England was never completely destroyed. It would return again and again. In another example, most witches today include some practices drawn from the Hermetic Order of the Golden Dawn, a group that emerged from the Freemasons in fin de siècle London and included many prominent people of the period, like the poet William Butler Yeats. Its members traveled through ancient cities and the catacombs of the British Museum to unearth magical papyri inscribed with spells in ancient Greek. Members of the Order of the Golden Dawn drew their magical techniques from a synchrony of sources: spiritualism, the magical papyri, Roman antiquity, Celtic and Germanic lore, Arthurian legend, psychoanalysis, and of course, the magical practices of their forefather John Dee. They had secret rites of initiation and practiced tarot and the Hermetic Qabalah, astrology and astral projection, visiting the planets in our solar system through their visions.

Many modern witches draw from the Golden Dawn's ceremonial magic, not by choice, but rather from necessity. Over time, the folk magic of the ancient Celtic cunning folk was lost. It was forbidden to speak of it, and the rare fragments that were written down were mainly destroyed. Colonizers and enslavers though the Romans were, they were excellent historians. Most ritual and magic that survives from the ancient west comes from them, because they wrote everything down, and their practices were well-preserved by comparison to the Nordic and Celtic oral traditions, and have thus been picked up by occult practitioners today.

By the time John Dee was practicing his "High Ceremonial Magic" in Elizabethan England, witchcraft, considered by the politically powerful to be a form of "low magic," had already been persecuted in Europe and England for hundreds of years. In *Caliban and the Witch*, feminist historian Silvia Federici argues that the persecution of witches was based less upon a religious or moral hysteria over pagan magical practices, and more upon the rise of capitalism. The rising capitalist class needed to control the workforce. The capitalist need for a steady supply of labor power meant that women who controlled their own reproductive capacity through herbs and midwives (many of whom were witches) needed to be brought into submission. Further, capitalism required a division of labor into two camps: workers and repro- ducers of the workforce (i.e., the women who birthed and cared for babies and tended to the sick and the elderly). The former be- ing paid labor, the second being devalued almost entirely. In other words, the work of women lost its value, women's subordination to men had become an economic requirement, and the witch hunts were used strategically to make women accept their new role.

Further, women should have no access to money. Anyone with access to money had access to political power. Because prostitutes had access to money, which wives who had sex for pleasure or obligation did not, prostitutes also became vilified as witches. Fi- nally, and perhaps most importantly, Federici argues that hidden unpaid labor, such as the work of women, indentured servants, and slaves, is a *requirement* of capitalism. Every bit of wealth accumu- lated in the United States, for instance, is only possible because of the land. No land, no industry, no business, no buildings, no resources to exploit, no products to sell. Most of the accumula- tion of surplus wealth that gave rise to the American empire was only possible because it took place on land stolen from indigenous people, cultivated through the unpaid labor of the enslaved. Even though capitalism pretends to base its economy on the free and rational exchange of labor for wages, most of the accumulation of wealth under capitalism requires an underclass forced to work for free, or at least under debt. Once women were completely subju- gated in Europe, the capitalist raptor turned its eye toward the rest of the world, enslaving and pillaging in the name of the "free" market. People who practiced magic were considered primitive, and fair game for enslavement by the colonizing capitalist regime.

Magical practices were always part of colonized peoples' tactics of resistance. In the "New World," for example, the syncretic folk magic practice of Hoo Doo was one resistance tactic of enslaved Afro-Caribbeans who were prevented from gathering their own resources and wealth by rule of law.

During the medieval period, when witches were being interrogated and burned, a lot of the time money was actually the root source of the problem. The witch's prosecutors often wanted a widow's land, or to prevent the old women of the village from reminding everyone that there once was a time when land was commonly owned, and everyone could graze their herds for free. Witches were accused of causing blights to grain, or killing cattle (living symbols of the capitalists' wealth). The practices of the witchcraft can never be separated from the economic conditions in which they exist.

Now that I am a full-time witch, a good third of my clients come to me for financial reasons. Most of them have other things besides money that they'd prefer to focus on: family or creativity, or activism or their life's purpose, but the fear of being poor dangles over our heads like a sword. Yet, when I was in London, I didn't do spells for money or wealth, because I was conflicted about it. Deep down, I resented money, hated it, and also fundamentally just didn't believe it could come to me any other way but through men. Before I was old enough to reason, the belief that my sexuality was the only thing I had of value was enforced both physically and in the culture at large.

Magic happens in a field, a system of energy. We can't go outside that system to do our work. Magical practices always reflect the social values, anxieties, and hidden beliefs of the culture in which they are produced. If we want to be able to focus our magic on more beautiful things, like communing with Spirit or celebrating the earth or liberating all souls from servitude, we need to focus on changing the larger systems that manipulate and exploit us. To do that requires a group effort. The spell of one witch alone, or even a hundred witches, is not enough. We need thousands of witches, in every city, in every nation, to participate. The struggles we experience don't happen just because we as individuals are failing. The fact that we are so often convinced that our misery is our own fault, and not the direct consequence of deliberate political and social oppression, is one of the greatest examples of mind control magic the world has ever seen.

England is the home of traditional Wicca and Ceremonial magic, both of which I knew about but didn't turn to for help. I mistrusted them. I was brought up a witch, but not Wiccan. Wicca is a new religion, invented in the 1950s by Englishman Gerald Gardner, drawing heavily from the Order of the Golden Dawn and other traditions. He claimed it had been taught to him by a crone, a keeper of the old ways in a remote rural village, and maybe some of it was. In his version of the Sabbat, the High Priest and High Priestess led their coven in rituals practiced sky clad (naked), sliding their ceremonial blades into chalices, and other more literal practices of hieros gamos (sacred marriage). My mother always resisted the idea of the High Priestess, High Priest, or High anything. She felt it was against the communal, egalitarian ethos of witchcraft. Furthermore, those dynamics of power, particularly in the company of mixed genders, were too open to abuse. Even though today I am inspired by many of the early Wiccans—like Janet Farrar, Doreen Valiente, or Maxine Sanders—during my stay in London, I found no group that I resonated with or could turn to.

Traditional Wiccans have a procedure for everything. Raising their athames (ceremonial knives) as tools of discernment and clarity to call in the Guardians of the East, or their chalices to call in the Guardians of the West—Guardians of love and of emotion, elemental spirits of the imagination. Traditional Wiccans often have a hierarchical structure and exclusionary nature, very much informed by the ethos in midcentury England. But I was a seventh-generation Californian; I had a native mistrust of systems of authority. Furthermore, and I think this is still the case for many interested in the occult, many of the folks in the magical scenes I found felt like ungrounded wishful thinkers or worse. Male Chaos magicians trolling the aisles at Watkins Books, an occult bookstore that's been there since the 1890s, who felt like low-level scavengers trying to get pussy with their sigil magick.

The notorious Aleister Crowley was an outcast member of the Order of the Golden Dawn, who then went on to found his own occult organization, the Ordo Templi Orientis. He had a lot of influence on the magicians practicing in London when I lived there. Initially I was intrigued, as his work is brilliant and powerful, but whenever I investigated deeper, the feminist in me would rebel. Crowley created the text for the Thoth tarot deck, but Lady Frieda Harris painted and created the cards, and it was her idea that the deck be made in the first place. But she rarely gets the credit she deserves. Many of Crowley's acolytes argue that he was an early feminist, but there's ample evidence to the contrary throughout his works.

Pamela Colman Smith, a London-born artist and occultist, painted the Rider Waite (now known by most witches as the Rider Waite Colman Smith) tarot deck, the most famous and popular tarot deck, upon the request of British occultist and Golden Dawn member Arthur Edward Waite, and she died penniless, not taken seriously by the organization. Though I felt magic all around me in England, I knew I would not be able to get at it along the traditional routes.

Wandering through London's underworlds alone, I gravitated toward anything that could shift me out of the ordinary world, the world of hierarchies and oppression, of subway gropers, empty consumerism, melting ice caps, and mass hypnosis. Starhawk, one of the leaders of the Reclaiming tradition I inherited from my mother, says that magic is a shift in perception. I wanted to live in the world of the sublime, the extraordinary. I could feel it bleeding into my life sometimes; when I practiced magic or entered a gallery, I could feel it pulsing.

I felt the magic, of course, when I danced. When through the rhythm and the drum, the ordinary world would fall away. In voodoo ceremonies, they say the initiates are mounted by the gods, ridden like horses by powerful deities who don't care about the laws and rules of this world. When they appear, the air grows fragrant with plumeria; poverty and squalor cease to exist. The dirt parking lot of your life is turned up by the gods' stampeding hooves.

I could even feel the pulse of the divine when I was dancing at the Astral. Mounted by a wanton, fearless sex goddess, no rules to bind me, no scorn could reach me. But when I descended from the stage, the spirits would leave me. Nudity and eroticism were no big deal; it was talking to the customers that was the problem…and the management…and anyone in my "real life" who ever found out I was a stripper. Like Sartre says, hell is other people. It was other people's judgments and their behavior toward me that made the sex industry hurt, far more than the work itself.

And hurt it did. By the time I reached my final year of my BFA, I was in shreds. I got pregnant by the assistant manager of the Astral and had an abortion. I fainted in ballet class because I'd done too much coke the night before; then I got up and kept dancing. But I'd grown angry at dance. I saw dance like the jealous god in the Bible that commanded me to sacrifice the thing I held most sacred. If I wanted to dance, the Spirit of Dance seemed to be demanding that I sacrifice my body, the very thing that made dance possible, the very reason I existed. I knew that if I were to continue as I had been, I'd kill myself. I kept my suicide note with me, wrapped in plastic in case I ever jumped in the Thames, so my mother and my brothers would know it wasn't their fault.

Before a witch becomes a witch, she is abducted into the underworld labyrinth. At the center of every labyrinth is a minotaur, a monster. We each have our own monster; we each have our own underworld. In order to become a witch, the initiate must confront the monster, and then return to the upper world stronger and wiser. Neither hero nor heroine can escape the underworld without help. In fairy tales, when given an impossible task, the heroine turns to her allies: mice who sew her wedding gown, ants who sort her rice. But just as frequently, fairy-tale helpers are not to be trusted. You may eventually become a princess, but your helpers might want your firstborn child in return.

I never knew who to trust while I was in the underworld. I had friends, some from school, some from work, but the time I'd spent in the underworld had made me mercurial and sharp, full of fury, desire, and need. Too much for most people to handle. The women I worked with at the clubs were a certain kind of witch: mysterious, hypnotic, hungry vultures at the carcass. Damaged and struggling, flinging our power in every direction, waking up in rooms filled with smoke and strange men, throwing ourselves at them relentlessly until they got scared and ran away. Our energy was chaotic and undisciplined. We were fire-starters, but not reliable allies to one another.

There were men in my life who were just friends, whom I knew from around town, not the Astral. They knew my situation and wanted to help me. One of them, for example, wanted to help me pay for school by attempting to pimp me out to his rich brother (unsuccessfully, as I said no). Another said he would help me pay for school if I went with him to Paris for the weekend; neither his wife nor his mistress would ever need to know. Some of the men I knew were gentle, and to them I must have appeared monstrous: calculating, suspicious, defensive, even dangerous. If they were too nice to me, I'd sleep with their friend or disappear into the night. In the myths, it's the heroes and princesses that get the allies, not the monsters. But monsters, too, have their goals. It's just that the heroes have the gods to help them; the monsters have to figure out a way to survive on their own.

Enter Medusa.

Ovid tells the classical myth of Medusa thus: Medusa was a woman, beautiful and wise, a priestess of Athena, goddess of the arts, civilization, and just causes. One day Poseidon, the God of the sea, came ashore and raped Medusa on the floor of Athena's temple. Outraged, Athena, a goddess frequently used as the mouthpiece of patriarchy, punished Medusa for her indiscretion. She should have been more careful, she shouldn't have worn that dress, she shouldn't have been drinking, she shouldn't have smiled like that...Athena turned the priestess Medusa into a gorgon, a hideous monster with blazing red eyes, a gaping mouth, and hair writhing with venomous snakes. The gorgon retreated to an island in the Mediterranean to hide her hideous face in shame.

But Medusa's story didn't simply end with her exile. Men came from far and wide to try to slay this snaky demon and thus earn a heroic reputation for themselves. But any man who looked upon Medusa would be instantly turned to stone—their expressions of horror and repulsion recorded in sculptural form for all eternity. Every time Medusa passed these grimacing statues, it would serve to remind her just how repulsive she truly was. How shameful. How repellant.

In Ovid's version of the myth, Medusa has no feelings, no thoughts, no desires of her own; she is merely there as an obstacle for the hero Perseus to overcome. Ovid didn't tell the story of Medusa to record the injustice of her experience. The only reason he mentions her at all is because, on one of his adventures, Perseus finally managed to hack Medusa's head off as a favor to a king whose daughter he wanted to fuck.

In the end, Medusa was brought down by a mirror. Athena gave Perseus a hot tip. He should use his shiny shield to reflect Medusa's own face back at her. Upon seeing her reflection, Medusa would be stunned by her own ugliness. The trick worked. As predicted, Medusa was frozen in disappointment and alarm; she was hideous. Perseus cut off her head and shoved it in a bag. Occasionally he'd pull it out to show off at parties, or as a weapon against advancing armies in his myriad other adventures. By the end of the story, reality was as it should be. The hero won, the monster lost, the crowd cheered.

But in school, I began to learn about a different version of the story. We were studying French feminism: Luce Irigaray, Julia Kristeva, Hélène Cixous, and Catherine Clément. I read Cixous's essay "The Laugh of the Medusa," and I began to realize that the Medusa that had appeared to me at my first abduction was not my tormentor, but my ally.

In ancient Greek, the name Medousa translates as "guardian," or protector. When Medusa appeared to me, coming out of the closet in my childhood, she appeared because she knew what was coming for me; she'd experienced it herself. Medusa is an avatar of the Dark Goddess of the Crossroads, and she comes as a guardian and guide for those whose selves are fragmented and torn away piece by piece.

In "The Laugh of the Medusa," Cixous talks about how the space of the imaginary, the magical, "the other" (i.e., women, gay people, people of color, people with disabilities, non-neuro-

normative folks) has been defined as something that stands outside of the ordinary realms that she and the other French feminists call "the Symbolic Order." The Symbolic Order is a term
originally coined by psychoanalyst Jacques Lacan and then developed by French feminist philosophers. The Symbolic Order is
another name for what they call "the Law of the Father," where the
child is given "a symbolic identity and place in the human universe
of meaning."[1] The child is born blameless and unformed, then becomes both an independent subject and a subject of the laws of
her culture, by fiat of the language that orders her universe. She
is a girl. She throws like a girl. She wears a girl's clothes. She
isn't funny. She's made of man's rib. She's sugar and spice. She is
named, and through that naming, like the demons of John Dee,
she is compelled to behave according to the Father's laws. As soon
as language ensnares us as children, we are caught in the web of
the Symbolic Order: a prison of language and symbols from which
the subject cannot escape. Witches, women, and all "others" are
exiled to the dark swamps that surround the Symbolic Order. We
who stand outside the Symbolic Order are affected and influenced
by it, still subject to its whims, but never allowed to wield the
magic wand (the phallus), that scepter of power, for ourselves. But
rather than try to protest our Medusa-ness, our witch-ness, our
monstrousness, and fight our way to a place at the hero's round
table, Cixous argues that we should claim the shadow realms for
ourselves. Outside the Symbolic Order, our uncharted territory

---

1   Emily Zakin. *Psychoanalytic Feminism.* https://plato.stanford.edu/entries
     /feminism-psychoanalysis/.

extends into infinity. The islands of Circe and Medusa and Morgan le Fay are in this wild space, the land of the witch.

"Stop looking for a way out of the underworld," the Medusa told me. "Instead, start looking for a way to claim your dominion. If the Lord exiled you into the desert, the Goddess can transform that sandy wasteland back into a garden of delight."

Once I heard the Medusa speaking to me, I started to realize I wasn't alone. I had allies all around me. Maya Deren. Hannah Wilke. Sylvia Plath. Katherine Dunham. Nijinska. Hélène Cixous. Sandra Cisneros. Audre Lorde. Martha Graham. Remedios Varo. Dorothy Cross. Simone Weil. Phoolan Devi. Wendy Houston. Frida Kahlo. Pina Bausch. When I'd first been introduced to the work of Pina Bausch, I hadn't known that she was my ally. I'd seen her as my North Star, a guiding light perpetually out of my reach. But my situation began to turn, my London initiation complete, when I started to realize that I had the power not just to follow her, but *to be with* her, to be a part of her coven. That is the shift in perception that Starhawk was talking about. The moment you stop seeing yourself as a supplicant and start seeing yourself as a *participant*, a co-conspirator, an agent, that shift marks the moment you become a witch.

Pina Bausch tunneled straight into the most vulnerable, feminine parts of experience and exulted in them. I'll never forget the first time I saw *Café Müller*. The scene where a woman, in love with a man, desperate for his acceptance and support, throws herself into his arms, and he refuses to catch her. She falls to the floor like a sack of hammers. But she doesn't stop. She keeps flinging herself at him again and again; again and again and again falling to the floor, brutalized by her own need and his lack of interest. It gave form to a feeling I'd had, of throwing myself upon men, begging for their mercy, their care, their help, and being rejected, scorned, dismissed, "not caught," and then treated as if, by the very fact of not being caught, and of being wounded by not being caught, I had rendered myself worthless. Damaged goods. A bruised apple left out for whatever scavengers would deign pick it up. But recognizing vulnerability as a strength made Pina an oracle and witch of the first order. When a witch comes to power, her vulnerability, her vision, cracks the world open and changes everything. Wands appear for her everywhere, sprouting up from the earth. In the myth of Persephone, Hades abducts the maiden to the underworld just as she is reaching for a flowering narcissus. For the world order to be maintained, he can't let her reach the flowers. Her flowers are her magic wand, the instrument of focused transformation. Its seeds are carried in the wind. When all the witches of the world seize our flowering wands, the patriarchal order will fall.

Just as classical mythology is filled with stories of hideous monsters slain by the heroes of the Symbolic Order, classical dance is filled with stories of magical women who meet their death in the fairy realms, the deep dark woods, places where you can dance yourself to death. *La Sylphide, Swan Lake, The Rite of Spring*: all originally composed by men. As a young woman, I often felt like one of the dancers in Pina Bausch's version of *The Rite of Spring*, flinging the cursed red dress at each other, not wanting to be the one who gets sacrificed at the altar of patriarchy. In the end, one of the dancers in the story dies, she loses, but Pina found a way out of that binary of win or lose, because Pina made the dance. Pina told the story.

In another myth, Ovid tells a story of Apollo, the god of patriarchal civilization. He fell in love with the Cumaean Sibyl, a prophetic priestess of the snake goddess, but she scorned him. In attempt to woo her, Apollo promised her eternal life; the Sibyl refused his advances. Apollo punished her for rejecting him. Thinking himself generous, he still gave her the gift of eternal life, but then he withheld eternal youth. Over time the Sibyl shriveled away, becoming first a bent old woman, then shrinking to the size of a cricket, then a withered leaf; finally, she crumbled into dust and blew away. All that was left was her voice, hushing in the wind. But the Sibyl still lives. We still breathe her in. In defiance of Apollo, the Cumaean Sibyl declared, it is "by my voice that I shall be known."[2] Through us, the Sibyl can find form again. Through us, she can speak and create and be heard. The voice of the Sibyl travels by wind and storm. She shakes the leaves; she flickers your candle flame; she looks for witches through whom she can speak, those of us who are attuned enough to listen. The voice of the Sibyl, the voice of the Goddess, is like the wind, never-ending, always moving, always present. She says, *Create works that give form to me, bring the Goddess back into the world.*

* * *

---

2   Marina Warner. *From the Beast to the Blonde.* 1994. P. 10

People get confused about the idea of a spirit coming to you. We're trained by the media to expect it to come as a vision, like the Ghost of Christmas Future, to stand in the room gesticulating with firm and bony arms. But just as often, Spirit comes to you through coincidence, or as witches like to think of it, synchronicity. During my London initiations, Medusa started appearing to me everywhere.

I'd see her face painted on the side of buildings, on the cover of books, in artworks. And soon, she started appearing in my own work. My final dissertation was on deconstructing the classical narrative through performance; the dance piece that accompanied it was called *Medusa Recalcitrant.* Recalcitrant means "willfully disobedient." As a twenty-three-year-old, the idea of willful disobedience against the Classical Narrative and the Symbolic Order it helped to reinforce exhilarated me. In my piece, each dancer embodied a different aspect of Medusa's spirit. In the classical version of the story, Medusa is decapitated, her mind, her subjectivity, severed from her body. My piece was an intervention, a way of keeping Medusa alive, and ultimately, an effort to reunite all her fragmented parts. To re-member her. If, as poet Audre Lorde said, "The master's tools will never dismantle the master's house," my desire was to toss aside the master's tools and to use a witch's tools instead: wands, cauldrons, the body, the imagination, community, breath, life force, my allyship with Medusa and the other exiled beings wandering the mist-shrouded isles of enchantment.

I began to remember rather than reject my roots. My dancer friend and classmate, Joanne, and I had talked about witchcraft and my growing up as a pagan. We'd have breathless conversations down the local pub, in smoke-filled rooms lamenting the inquisitions of Europe and the women who were killed—a big part of the mythological legacy of my childhood. Joanne came from a solid, happy, upper-working-class family in Somerset, without much religion, but she was fascinated by the idea of witches and made a dance piece about them, which she invited me to perform in. After graduation, I decided I wanted to make a film inspired by the piece.

I wanted to commemorate the women who were killed during the Inquisitions. To celebrate their lives and memorialize those who had been forgotten or who were never recognized in the first place. We went out to Glastonbury Tor at midnight on a moonless night, on a wild hill, overgrown with weeds and shrubs. Glastonbury Tor, where Morgan le Fay lived in the mists of Avalon. Known to be a necromancer, Morgan le Fay was a sorceress able to summon the spirits of the dead. I aimed to commune with and learn from her. I wanted her help resurrecting the spirits of witches from time immemorial. In the opening shot of my film, Nikki, one of the dancers, emerges from the dark, her hair lashing in the wind. By calling out to the witches of history, I summoned my ancestors from the earth, both the genetic Celts from whom I descend and my spiritual ancestors, the wild women and sorceresses who've existed throughout the world across space and time. I could feel their fear and their hunger. I could feel them come to me, asking to be heard, to be reborn.

In Laurie Cabot's book *Power of the Witch*, she discusses the African American botanist George Washington Carver. He knew the secrets of the plants; they would reveal their purpose as medicines when he spoke to them. He said that the way to hear them was to love them. "The secrets are in the plants. To elicit them you have to love them enough ... I learn what I know by watching and loving everything." The same is true of witchcraft, of magic, of the Goddess herself. I love witches. I love the Goddess. If we turn toward what we love and listen, if we walk in her direction, the Goddess reveals her secrets; she whispers and a path of flowering wands bursts forth to lead us home. And as every witch knows, wands are the tools of initiation.

Chapter 10

ᚲ ᚲ ᚲ

THE DEMON LOVER

They had not sailed a league, a league,
A league but barely three,
Until she espied his cloven foot,
And she wept right bitterly.

Author Unknown, "The Demon Lover"

I had a demon lover once. They often appear when a witch is about to step into her full power. A Scottish folk ballad tells the most infamous version of the demon lover story thus: a woman abandons her husband and child to leave with her lover on a ship across the sea. She thinks she and her seafaring man are going to live together forever on a shining island of lilies and gold. Turns out her lover is actually Satan, and he's taking her to the black, dark hill of hell, where she will suffer forevermore. In literature, when the demon lover appears, it always upends the world of the heroine. Everything she thought was real turns out to be false. Finding herself tricked, she is made to know that she can't rely on her own experience or perceptions.

Demon lovers are not new. Some occult traditions call them

incubi, male demons who press like heavy stone upon the chests of sleeping women, luring them into acts of fornication. The incubus appears in ghost stories throughout the world. Hungry, night-walking spirits in the forests of the Amazon; shape-shifting creatures with the wings of a bat in the Spice Islands of Zanzibar; in each case they come to seduce their prey and tear their worlds apart. In the Sumerian *Legend of Gilgamesh,* the eponymous hero was spawned by a mortal woman and her demon lover Lilu, a night spirit who coursed above the wastelands in the shape of a foul black bird. In 1948, Shirley Jackson wrote a short story about a demon lover, as did Elizabeth Bowen, in 1945, moody works strangled with anxiety, set in airless spaces or frantic cities with broken chimneys, bombed out buildings, and cold shafts of light. In the stories, the demon always comes to punish the woman in some way. Women who are single, who want to leave their relationships, or who didn't wait for their partner as long as they should have. Women who are not under the protective aegis of patriarchal authority. In literature, demon lover stories often revolve thematically around anxiety over women's role in the political world: the desire for freedom should not overrule the obligations of one's gender. Anthropologists believe the story of the demon lover was created as a cover for pregnancies conceived during incest. Even Dracula was a demon lover, hypnotizing Mina Harker and stealing her partner away from her. The demon lover is the devil himself.

In general, witches don't believe in the devil. As pure evil, the devil is a Christian invention; pagan gods have more nuance. Deities that are difficult in the pagan world are not necessarily evil; they just have agendas that work in opposition to our own, or sometimes, on rare occasion, in antagonism to the life force itself.

In the classical Rider-Waite-Smith version of the tarot deck, the Devil is the trickster character, the shadow at the gate. He's the guardian you must battle before you achieve your break-through. The Devil is evil if you give in to the fear he generates, but he becomes Lucifer, light bringer and wisdom snake, when, through dealing with him, you realize your own power, that you have choices and that you are at no one's mercy. In most versions of the tarot, the Devil is depicted as the deity Baphomet, a winged hermaphrodite with the breasts of a woman, the muscles of a man, the head of a goat, and the Latin words *solve* and *coagula* written on his forearms. *Solve* meaning to dissolve, to destroy, to tear apart, and *coagula* meaning to bring together, to make whole again.

Supposedly once worshipped by the Knights Templar, in many tarot decks the Devil card depicts Baphomet sitting atop a pyra-mid with a reversed pentagram emblazoned on his forehead. Be-neath him, a couple, who once appeared in sacred union in the Lovers card, now reappear bound in chains; sometimes hordes of people appear, all of them bound in some way, either tricked or forced or otherwise compelled to act against their own interests for the benefit of the devil himself.

I know that this person, my demon lover, had his own reason for existing. He didn't just appear in my life, as women so often do in the narratives of patriarchal literature, as a catalyst for my self-realization. He had his own existence and agenda. Still, for witches, events have meaning; the people who come into your life have messages. To be a witch is to live inside your own personal myth...even if you know you're creating it yourself.

As in myth, my demon lover was a monster, a vampire, a powerful, ugly, otherworldly figure that my friends and I often referred to as Nosferatu. A shape-shifter, he was only ugly sometimes. He had no problem getting women, a fact that contributed, for obvious reasons, to him being my nemesis. One time, he and I were looking through a box of his things and there was a Polaroid of a famous '90s punk rock model sitting in some secluded field in what looked like rural England, squinting and smiling and shielding her eyes from the sun; she looked like she was on a romantic picnic. She looked like she'd just had sex with the photographer. "I took that picture," my demon lover told me, affecting nonchalance, confirming what he could see I already suspected.

He was handsome: tall, with peppered graying hair and brown eyes full of longing, hidden behind circular spectacles that made him look like a turn-of-the-century Austrian intellectual. But also, he could seem almost grotesque at times, like the Hunchback of Notre Dame. He would snort and push snot back up into his nose with the heel of his palm like he was in second grade; he would slouch and seem dehydrated and gobble greasy croissants with extra mayo and wear rumpled Comme des Garçons shirts with sooty black rings around the wrists and collar. In all the time I'd known him, it never looked like he'd recently showered, even when he'd just gotten out of the bath.

On the night he asked me to be his girlfriend, we had this conversation at Little Joy, a dive bar in Echo Park with wood-paneled walls, cans of Pabst Blue Ribbon, a scratched-up pool table, and a perfect date jukebox. I wasn't ready to be his girlfriend. He and I had just started dating, and I'd just broken up with my husband about a month before. *Husband* is too strong a word for what my ex and I were, though the term is technically accurate. Basically we'd been boyfriend and girlfriend in London with little in common but that we were young when we met and both liked Nick Cave. I wanted to be able to work in London, and he'd always wanted a green card for the U.S., so...we got married one afternoon at the Home Office and didn't tell anyone we'd done it for six months. But even though we weren't husband and wife in the "I swear in front of everyone I know to honor and love you until death" kind of way, we'd still been serious about each other, and we still had a painful breakup.

The night my demon lover took me to Little Joy, it was about two months into us dating each other. Give or take a bit. He'd accidentally "lost my number at a carwash" after the first time we made out, so I was naturally skeptical. But at some point he'd had a change of heart. He wanted me to be his girlfriend. I was trying to explain why I didn't feel ready to commit yet when this drunk couple came and sat next to us. "She's too hot for you," the woman blurted as soon as she sat down. I was embarrassed. It was exactly the wrong thing to say at that moment; he was already feeling vulnerable. He threw up his hands like, "I give up." I went outside for a cigarette and saw a pedestrian killed by a drunk driver.

I was in my second year of grad school, tackling two MFAs simultaneously. One in Writing/Critical Theory and the other in Film and Video. Scrambling to complete all my coursework, I also had thesis projects and teaching assistantships for both departments. In grad school I made angry work. Work about women in peril. Women's images plastered to the sides of telephone booths, legs spread like an advertisement for a hooker, only with the words *I want your commitment*. Or, *You make me want to have children. Let's get started*. Women drowning in a bathtub. Women trapped inside peep show booths inflicting self-harm to shame the male gaze. I looked out at the world and saw all the wrong. I wanted to point all the wrongness out to everyone. I wanted someone to do something about it.

Despite the fact that I was angry, this period was the first time in my life when I could just concentrate on being an artist. On "living my purpose," as I saw it. I was not on medication or in need of a psychiatrist, not dating a drug dealer, taking drugs, or risking my life as a sex worker. I had enough money (with student loans, two TA-ships, and a side job at a boutique in Larchmont) to support myself.

I was free. My teachers expected big things from me; my dance film, letters of recommendation, and my writing samples had all been strong. I was the first student in the history of the school to be accepted into both the writing and the film and video program simultaneously. I meant to make good on my artistic promise.

So, of course, according to the structure of any good myth, it is at exactly this time, when things were going so well, that I would meet my adversary.

My therapist at the time, a Zen Buddhist, and one of the best therapists I've ever had, told me that Nosferatu was my nemesis because, even though I had everything I needed to create the life I wanted for *myself*, for some reason I thought that *he* was the guardian at the gates of my happiness. In other words, I thought I needed him in order to get the life that I wanted. I took all my talents and skills and life force and laid them before him, prostrating myself at his feet, pleading for his mercy. I knew my therapist was a good one when, during our first session together, I lamented a separate situation where a male teacher I knew was behaving badly, having affairs with students and then punishing them for it if it didn't go his way. The students suffered, while the teacher paid no consequences. "You're talking about the problem of evil," my therapist said, reframing my frustration to see the larger picture. "Why do good people often suffer, while those who do bad get rewarded? It's a problem humanity has been wrestling with for thousands of years." Because, who are "good people" really, and what or whom is the root cause of our suffering?

Nosferatu is an obvious title for a demon lover, but that is not the only nickname I had for him. His second name was Buckets. It sounds like a friendly donkey in a Wild West cartoon, but Buckets was an abbreviation for "Buckets of Tears." Somehow, I was always making my demon lover cry. He cried when, after an argument about what, I can't remember, I ran off in the rain and he tried to get me to get back in the car but I went to my friend's house and stood throwing rocks outside her window instead.

He cried for good reasons sometimes. He cried because I wasn't ready to commit. I've cried for similar reasons myself. He cried because I said in front of his friends that I thought it was okay to cheat if your partner doesn't find out, which embarrassed him because he said it made him look bad. Later I retracted the comment and apologized. It's actually a ridiculous thing to say. In my defense, post-marriage-breakup, I had come to the conclusion that I was faithful to a fault, giving my loyalty to people who didn't deserve it. I don't blame my demon lover for being upset, but later, his upsetness and indignation would prove to be a real mind-fuck.

One day, cuddling with him in his bed, I told Nosferatu about an experience I'd had at Unitarian summer camp when I was about fifteen. I had a twenty-one-year-old boyfriend at the time, who did not attend the camp with me. I'd gone to the camp with my family right before the crisis hit, before my parents' divorce and my moving out, my stepfather's fury, my mother's depression, my call to the underworld. Though my boyfriend at the time was cool, an Italian-American artist who liked to draw cigarette-smoking comic book heroes, play pool, and quote *Scarface*, I'd pretty much outgrown him. But we were still together while I was at the camp where I met this beautiful boy who worked on staff. The staff kids were in their late teens and held a special romantic allure of freedom and non-family fun. They were known to do acid and skinny-dip in the hot tub. This late-teen staffer had soulful blue eyes and black hair, and like every good Anne Rice–loving teenager, I was into his vampire good looks and shy mystery. We spent the night talking in the main hall, drinking Good Earth tea out of hippie mugs and listening to *Dark Side of the Moon*. He tried to kiss me, but I said no, because I had a boyfriend. Since my boyfriend and I broke up a few months later, I always regretted not saying yes to that kiss.

As I told my demon lover this story, he sat up in bed, righteous as the Grand Inquisitioner, preaching, "You shouldn't regret that! You should be *proud* of that. Proud that you chose to act with integrity instead of on base impulse." Civilization, he informed me, was based on people controlling their lower impulses and choosing to act on their ideals instead. Nosferatu had been brought up in a born-again Christian household, and though he wasn't a believer, he still made claims to piety.

I must confess it had never occurred to me *not* to regret my abstinence with that gorgeous camp staffer, who is now probably a vampire living in a decaying mansion in New Orleans. To be proud of passing up the chance of kissing those naturally blood-flushed lips was completely outside the realm of my imagination. But now, the conversation with Nosferatu had made me question my integrity, and in so doing, to unravel the code by which, up to that point, I'd lived: one should live to the fullest, should seize every opportunity, should carpe diem, should be an actor despite parental disapproval, should dance like no one was watching…even at a strip club. Up until this point in my life, I believed that one should live by one's own rules. And my main rule was that I should always follow my passions regardless of the consequences.

But if that weren't true, then not only did I not really know how to live anymore, but also, my entire life had just been one horrendous, horrifying mistake after another.

Nosferatu's impassioned speech about the civilizing force of integrity was like a little, strategically laid explosive that, when the main building of our relationship began to crumble, demolished every last structure of myself that remained standing.

Nosferatu and I only dated for four months. During that time, he told me that he loved me; that the moment he saw me at the orientation event at our grad school he knew I was "the one"; that he believed in love and marriage and wanted to have children and live an intellectual, creative, morally rigorous life.

But I was still getting drunk with my grad school friends on Thursday nights when the art students would have open studios. He was twelve years older than I and wanted more than I was capable of giving him. He seemed unhappy with our relationship, too, constantly upset and emotional over it. So one night, in an Irish pub just off campus, we amicably broke up.

But then, when he was driving me back to my car, I suggested that we have one last night together, and then we'd go our separate ways. Suddenly, he changed, whip panning from Buckets of Tears to vengeful Nosferatu. His teeth grew long and foul. "No fucking way," he spat as if the words were poison he was spitting on a whore. In the dappled half-light of the car, he looked at me as if I were a seething pile of maggots. Totally disgusted, he waved his hand and said, "Get out of the car."

I don't know exactly how it happened, but in that moment his spirit possessed me. I became his minion, like one of the gaping, wide-eyed slave automatons of his namesake. My eyes grew wide, my voice high and shrill; every fiber in my body, every single cell, was possessed by a need to be his partner that went beyond human desire. I had never felt anything like that before, and I've never felt anything like it since. It was supernatural. My need gripped me by the throat so that I could barely speak. If he would have commanded me in that moment to get back into the car and drive with him to Vegas and pledge my soul to him until death, to infinity and beyond, I would've done it in a heartbeat. But he didn't. He drove away and he didn't look back.

Never underestimate how much a Pisces can fuck you up.

In the months that followed, I did everything I could think of to get him back. I wrote elaborate letters of apology, I tried to explain, I started going to therapy. For the most part, he remained unmoved. Except for one night when he came over drunk after a night out with some mutual friends. We had sex and he kept saying, "I loved you so much. Why didn't you just let me love you?" He kissed me all over and begged me, "Just let me, let me love you, please, let me. Let me love you." I was thrilled. I wanted to let him love me. I couldn't wait! I'd seen the error of my wanton ways and I was ready to change.

But then, the next morning, he got up and left without even saying goodbye, and when I cornered him for an explanation a few weeks later, he told me that it would never work between us because *I didn't believe in love.*

Something about that idea, that I didn't believe in love, cut into the center of my being. The bombs exploded. My building fell. Whoever Amanda had been crashed to the earth in a chalky gray cloud. Amanda was no more.

I spent my final year of grad school trying to pick up the pieces. Demon lovers are known to cause their victims to deteriorate. I broke out in hives and started losing my hair. I cried every day. People would tell me that when I was around him I totally changed, like I was hypnotized. It seemed like I was "dangling on a precipice" one friend said. I couldn't stop thinking about him.

My mind circled on him like a black hole with a gravitational pull from which I could never escape. I tried taking medication after my friends begged me to do something. They were worried I'd harm myself. But the medication only made me tired. I couldn't cure my obsession and I didn't know what to do.

Growing up in the '90s, obsession seemed like a romantic idea. Kate Moss and anonymous boy model careening through a white corridor, in a hungry pursuit only a malnourished waif could understand. But I hated being obsessed. Hated feeling like my mind was not my own, and that essentially I was his unwilling slave.

To the degree that I was diminished, his power seemed to increase, not just to me, but to everyone around us. Other women wondered what all the fuss was about him and became curious; he started taking on young men as protégés. My obsession only advanced his reputation.

And reputation he had. In the year and a half of suffering that followed our breakup, I learned quite a bit about his reputation. There were countless girls obsessed with him. One who told me they'd dated when she was young. He took her virginity and then lost interest. He ghosted. His pattern was to find women at vulnerable points in their lives, young, or just post-breakup, or grieving, and immediately try to make them his girlfriend. When the girl balked and said it was too soon or seemed confused, he'd drop her and then act like she'd broken his heart. The girl would start doubting herself and her integrity. She'd keep going back to him like a rat to a cocaine bottle, trying to get herself fixed.

"It's called intermittent reinforcement," my Zen therapist told me. "CIA agents use it during interrogations because it's so effective."

He knew what he was doing. I know because he counseled other young men at the school to come on strong, then turn away, because it "gets them every time." A young male spy of mine told me that my demon lover had instructed him quite explicitly: *If you make a woman think there's something wrong with her, she'll always come running back for more. She'll want you to take her pain away and then you can do what you like with her.*

To discover that he had a technique, and that I had fallen for it, was totally humiliating.

To make matters worse, a few months after we broke up, he started dating an eighteen-year-old undergrad from some double-digit population town in the Midwest who dressed like her mother sewed her clothes based on fashion advice from Laura Ingalls Wilder. I liked this girl; she seemed innocent and earnest and kind. She came from a conservative Christian family, and seemed a bit overwhelmed by the debaucherous atmosphere of CalArts. Everyone knew he cheated on her constantly. One of his many scorned lovers had graffitied his name on the stall of a girls' bathroom in the basement: *he's an asshole who will fuck you over if he gets the chance.* I didn't write it, but I may as well have. I lived it. But still, I couldn't shake it.

There was some kind of strange relief in Nosferatu's accusation that I didn't believe in love, that somehow my love light had grown dim, or even blown out. It was a relief like getting a medical diagnosis that, though perhaps unwelcome, at least explains why you've been feeling so sick. Before he and I met, I hadn't recognized how cynical and angry I'd become. My adventures in the underworld and beyond were empty if there was no North Star of Love to guide me, no ultimate goal but simply "more experience." More experience to what purpose? Adventure, to what purpose? Even art to what purpose? Without love, what was the point of doing any of it? But then, what did Love even mean?

Searching within myself, I seized on Love as if it were a rope, the only thing I had to hold on to if I were to navigate myself out of my deep dark lostness. Above my bed in pink Sharpie I scrawled a text culled from Trinie Dalton's compendium on werewolves, a testimony by the poet Amy Gerstler:thius

I believe in the glory and despair of requited and unrequited love, fucked up love, hopeless love, love that goes for the throat, waning and waxing love, love that prowls at night, untouchable loves, earthly loves, groveling love, snarling jealous love, never revealed love ripening like aging wine in oak casks in a chilly, dripping cave near the top of an almost inaccessible mountain. I believe in love as holy stubbornness, as duty and surprise and privilege and miracle and ethical stance and whetstone and elating shame and goad and secret power source. As scourge and blessing. As the steel wool of emotions—a real soul scourer—remover of some of the rust from our patina-ed psyches. And I believe that love or trust or deep emotional connectedness does occur between willing humans and other animals—animals we once were, still are, and have ambitions to re-inhabit and know ferociously—to read from the outside in and the inside out.

I was going to prove my demon lover wrong about me. I *did* believe in love. My experiences in the underworld had not taken that from me. I wasn't permanently corrupted by them. Love gave me something to believe in when I didn't know I *needed* anything to believe in.

Trouble was, the more I found out about my demon lover, the more difficult it became to believe that love meant anything to him. He left a trail of devastation wherever he went. Grieving, hallow, haunted women, pining like wraiths in a cave, followed him everywhere. He'd lied about everything: where his money came from, his previous career. He'd convinced most of the faculty that he was a genius of the first order, mainly by critiquing the work of other students, until they realized...he never made any work himself. He was faithless. He cheated. He aimed to destroy. But his convictions about love had caused me to change my entire system of belief.

One time he and I were looking at a photograph of some Jonestown-esque massacre, with everyone lying there dead. Women, children. Strewn about their jungle compound. And he said, "It's just so beautiful." And I was like, "What do you mean? They're dead. It's horrible." And he said, "Yeah, but aesthetically it's powerful. Look. They're all wearing the same Nikes." He was like a cult leader, convincing people salvation was at hand, if only they would commit mass suicide.

231

At the time, there was some documentary out on the girls of the Manson Family, and I remember realizing with horror that I understood now how they had been seduced. Before my experience with my demon lover, it would've been impossible for me to understand someone allowing their mind to be controlled by some bushy weirdo creeping around on Venice Beach. But after Nosferatu, I had more compassion. I saw how easy it is. All your demon lover has to do to possess you is find your deepest wound, the one you don't even know you have, and squeeze.

My wound was a father wound, of course. Both my biological father and my stepfather had lost interest in me when they had sons. For my stepfather, I had simply been an extra mouth to feed. My father claimed to love me, but his love was confusing and conditional, liable to be withdrawn at any moment if I didn't concede to his demands or tolerate his frequent insults. He'd written me songs and adoring letters, praised my creativity, took me camping, made me poached eggs on toast, and bought me bouquets of flowers on every birthday, and before I'd ever even had sex, he'd yelled in my face that I was a slut and an embarrassment to the family. He told me he'd pay for my brother's college education but not mine, then acted surprised at the hurt look on my face, even though at the time I was putting myself through school as a sex worker. When my brother turned out to be gay, he beat him to the floor and my brother ended up in foster care and worse. By my late twenties, I'd stopped expecting my father's approval or even his love, but the wound was still there, whetstone and elating shame, a ferocious, needy animal scratching in the basement of my consciousness.

Perhaps the most troubling thing about my experience of possession, the thing that caused me the most anguish, was that even after I knew, consciously, intellectually, what was happening, even though I knew my feelings for my demon lover were projections, and even though I knew Nosferatu was duplicitous, manipulative, and cruel, I couldn't make my heart stop hurting. I couldn't make myself stop wanting him.

I tried medication, therapy, new relationships, throwing myself into my work. By the time I graduated, a year and a half had passed since my demon lover and I had broken up and it still hurt like the first day. On the verge of losing all hope, I worried my obsessive grief would never end. That he'd captured my heart forever and would keep it as a talisman to empower him until the end of time. After he died, he would keep my wounded heart in his crypt and people would find it a thousand years later and curse themselves.

My mind was not my own, and as a last resort before throwing myself off a cliff, I decided to try meditation. The most essential practice for any witch, meditation is the first step in any how-to magic book; it was what my ballet teacher had recommended to me over five years before, and my Zen therapist had been only too happy to recommend again.

In magical practice there's a thing called a *pharmakon*, an ancient Greek term that can mean medicine or poison, depending on the quantity and quality of the dose. According to the practices of Elemental Magic, my dis-ease was an excess in the pharmakons of water and air. The knife in my chest was a problem of water, a problem of emotion and relationship, a disease of the West (the absence of compassion). Whereas my obsession was a problem of the air, of the East, it was a problem of mind. My mind was out of control and could not be still; it kept circling back to land on and be tethered to the armored arm of my demon lover. If I wanted to heal my obsession, I had to administer to myself a dose of healthy mind. I had to turn my poison into medicine.

The summer after graduation, I checked myself into a Zen monastery in upstate New York. Deep in the Catskills, we novices would wake up before dawn, meditate for hours, chant, meditate some more, spend the rest of the morning performing labors like moving the wood pile or scrubbing floors, afternoons writing haiku or practicing calligraphy, then we'd meditate again until bedtime at nine. The final week was called Sesshin, a full week meditating over eight hours a day, looking no one in the eye, speaking to no one, in effort to gain total intimacy with the self and, thus, the universe. By the end of my summer at the monastery, I'd cleared away most of the sediment that'd been muddying my view of the world. But my head was still cut off from my heart, and my heart was still locked away in Nosferatu's closet. And that heart, stolen and locked away, still hurt.

Nevertheless, in the final days of the Sesshin, my mind had grown increasingly still. With the silt of my aggravation and anxiety settling, the world had taken on a luminous quality, ecstatic and sharp, like Gustave Doré's angels ascending in a spiral toward my own personal Paradiso. I could hear monks chanting all through the woods, day and night, their voices hanging in air fragrant with balsam fir and maple. Incanting the Heart Sutra:

*Avalokitesvara Bodhisattva, doing deep prajna paramita, clearly
saw the emptiness of all five conditions, thus completely reliev-
ing misfortune and pain...*

On the day the Sesshin ended and we novices could finally
speak, I remarked to one of the residents of the monastery how
beautiful the chanting of the monks had been in the forest. He
looked at me with barely disguised displeasure. "There were no
monks chanting in the forest," he told me.

"But there were," I protested, surprised.

He shook his head. "They were all in the Buddha hall the whole
time."

I couldn't believe it. "I heard them plainly, same as I hear you
right now."

"It's called a makyō, a hallucination brought about by meditation. We're supposed to ignore them. I've been here two years and
I haven't had one." He seemed disappointed, and yet we both knew
that in Zen you're not supposed to want auditory or any other
kind of hallucinations, which are delusions of the imagination.
You're not even supposed to pay attention to your dreams. Zen is
about clearing your mind, not indulging its fantasies; that's why
in many forms of Zen you're supposed to meditate with your eyes
open so that you *don't* have visions. "Don't go to sleep!" the monks
would frequently admonish us. Don't have visions. Pay attention
only to what is.

I had heard the chanting throughout the entire second half of
the Sesshin, not just when I was meditating, but also when I was
walking up to the cabins, during my work practice, and at night as

235

I was falling to sleep. It was hard for me to believe the chanting wasn't real.

Having a natural connection to the spirit world can be dangerous, making you prone to all sorts of fancies and persecutions. But it can also provide you with great insight…if you're grounded enough to receive, interpret, and then act on it. The summer I spent meditating had provided me with that grounding and discipline. So though my time at the monastery was ending, and my heart still hurt, on the second to last day there I received a flash of insight: a recipe for an exorcism.

The monastery was at the base of a mountain, at the convergence of two rivers, one muddy and slow, the other fast and fresh. I gathered a treasury of river stones, stopping only when the stones grew too heavy for me to carry. I lugged them, step by woeful step, to the place where the rivers met and set them up in a pile, a lingam, representing the male polarity within myself that needed to be healed, restored, and regenerated.

Stones are the memory cells of the earth. They hold on to everything. Many of them were formed before the time of the dinosaurs, certainly long before humans showed up. Stones connect us to the earth, to history, to the history we store in our bodies. In *How to Know Higher Worlds*, Rudolf Steiner talks about how everything in existence lives; we just live in different ways. Animals, like humans, have agency; they act upon the world. But stones are receivers. Every arc of wind, every sluice of water slowly dialogues with the stone and changes its shape. Stone can teach us to receive, too, to yield with strength and to give us the patience to heal our own history.

Witches work with the elements, the spirits of nature. I'd spent the summer honoring and celebrating the spirits of the plants and trees and rivers on this mountain and now I summoned them in humble request of their assistance. I named all the goddesses I knew, called upon the spirits of the water to heal my heart, the powers of the earth to regenerate my life force, the powers of fire to cauterize my wounds, the powers of air to restore my mental clarity. I didn't follow all, or really any, ceremonial protocols. No circle was cast. No incense lit. No pentacles inscribed in the air in blue flame. Just me and the rivers, the mountains and stones; I could feel their power and their presence. I knew that was all I needed.

I picked up the stones from my pile one by one. To each stone, I whispered a memory I had of my demon lover. I named it: "How he loved to call me Panda and I thought he was trying to belittle me. And he seemed so hurt that I tormented myself for months about it. I should have let him call me Panda. I should have *loved* that he called me Panda. My defensiveness ruined everything..." I asked this stone to carry my memory to a place where it could be healed. I threw the stone across my body, sending it out in the river, to be taken by the currents, gulped away into the rapids' grinding foam. I proceeded this way until my pile of stones was no more; then I said his full name, shouted it into the wind, and declared with total conviction and authority: "I banish you, I release you, I sacrifice you for the greatest good of all concerned. Go with honor, go with love, be gone! Be gone! Be gone!"

It was the phrase for banishing rituals that my mother had taught me.

At the place where the two rivers converged, I baptized myself anew, beginning in the mud and muck and emerging where the currents ran clear. When I rose from the water, I thanked the spirits and walked away. I didn't look back.

That night, as I lay in bed for my final night's rest in the bottom bunk of my monastery bed, I felt a snap in the front of my skull and saw a flash of light. I felt a rush, like water draining from one side of my brain to the other. When I woke up the next morning, my heartache was gone. My haunting had ended. My demon lover, vanished. My river rites had drawn the knife from my chest. In place of that wound was a calm understanding that I had learned what I needed from my demon lover and that I had moved on. Love meant something to me again, and if it had taken a years-long heartbreak to awaken me to that, then so be it.

Chapter 11

c c c

SATURN RETURNS

Did I escape, I wonder?

Sylvia Plath, "Medusa"

I used to worry I would fail my Saturn Return. As if my Saturn Return was a test: pass and graduate into my adult life, or fail and be kept back a year...or a decade. Saturn is the planet each of us has to wrestle in order to enter into adulthood. Everyone gets a Saturn Return; for each of us it begins somewhere between the ages of twenty-eight and thirty, when Saturn, the planet of karma, of hard lessons and boundaries, makes a full circle around the sun and then crosses the threshold back into the sign it was in at the moment of your birth. It takes Saturn two and a half years to make this transit through your natal sign. And during that period, as the astrological theory goes, Saturn, "the great taskmaster," lets you know whether or not you're on the right track in life. If you're on the wrong track, things will fall apart. Your relationship will break up. You'll get sick. You'll quit school or your job, or whatever it was you were so attached to, and decide to move across country and start over. Things like that. Many people experience their Saturn Return as painful. Saturn interrogates: "Are you sure this is what you want to be doing with your precious, fleeting life?" Oftentimes, the answer is no.

Saturn is known as the *Sun of Night*. Whereas the sun is large, bright, and life-affirming, Saturn is dim, a pale cold ghost plowing through the black spheres of outer space, blinking his milky geriatric eye, reminding us of how quickly we'll be gone. Saturn is an old man, a grandfather. In the NASA recordings, Saturn sounds like static electricity crackling along the edges of lead. Ringed in ice dust 40,000 miles across, the plains of Saturn are the wasteland we must cross to make it to adulthood.

Medieval astrologers called Saturn "the Greater Malefic," *the big bad*. In mythology, Saturn began as Cronos, the Titan who devoured his children. In another version he was Kronos with a *K*, the father of time. Saturn's female incarnation is a familiar figure to us witches—Hecate, Guardian of the Crossroads. No matter how the great gas giant appears to us, Saturn is the planet of initiation.

Part of what makes Saturn's initiations so painful is that they're all bound up in our karma. Our Saturn Return is a life review, and if there's been a pattern to your choices, you're going to start seeing it. But this review is not just of *your* karma, but also your family's. Karma isn't just the consequences of your own deeds; it's the consequences of the actions and beliefs of your ancestors. Karma is DNA.

* * *

My Saturn Return reached its zenith in a double-wide trailer in Ojai with wood panel walls and beige carpet. A boomerang child, after the Zen monastery and grad school, I moved back in with my mother, while Saturn was transiting the sign of Leo. Follow Highway 150 from the Pacific Ocean and wind your way east, through the Topatopa Mountains, past family farms with hand-painted signs for marmalade and strawberries, past places with gingham curtains in the kitchen and goats in the yard, and you'll find the little town of Ojai. I hadn't spent much time with my mother since a few summers previous. She was living in a trailer then, too, in the eucalyptus groves and tar sands of Elwood Beach near Santa Barbara. That mobile home park was the only place she could afford, and then only because her income from her administrative job at the local university was supplemented by the treasury of Pete, a man twenty years her senior whom I loathed. A wealthy retired Boy Scout official from Santa Fe with a long white ponytail, he'd never had any children of his own and couldn't understand why my mother tried so hard to forge a good relationship with me, her prickly, wayward daughter.

My mother wasn't the only woman Pete was "helping." I don't think my mother even liked Pete, even though she tried hard to convince herself that she did. Whenever I asked her what she saw in him, she always told me she was *grateful* to him. When she first got divorced, he'd offered to let her stay with him for free in his condo at Leisure World, the retirement community in Long Beach where my great-grandmother had lived when I was a kid, with her beanbag frog and Andes mint candy. Later,

241

he paid the ridiculously expensive space rental on my mother's Elwood mobile home.

Never having fully recovered from her divorce, my mother had a hacking cough at that place. There'd been an electrical fire in the walls while she was sleeping, from which she'd narrowly escaped with her life. After the firemen came and sprayed the house with fuzzy green chemicals, she was too tired and too depressed to clean the mess away. I arrived months later to find her sitting in a pool of chemical cancer spores, willing herself to get a long, slow kick off Kyriarchy Island. Every time she coughed, it was as if she drove a spike into my hand—it pained me that much. I wanted her to take care of herself and she refused. It was like it just wasn't important to her.

Witches need to keep practicing witchcraft, even if we're busy, even if we're depressed. When witches stop practicing witchcraft, we languish. My mother was pasty white and swollen then. Her witch practice at that time had dwindled to the point where it was mainly conceptual. She *thought* about the Goddess still, reading books like Merlin Stone's *Ancient Mirrors of Womanhood*, but she no longer made braids of cardamom-infused Lammas bread or held monthly full-moon ceremonies with her moon group. Her best friend and moon groupie, Ginny, lived in the trailer across the way, but she, too, was busy working all the time, three jobs, two demanding sons. Both she and my mother were too exhausted to do much more than sit on the couch together and commiserate.

During my childhood, they'd planned rituals together, with my mother leading and Ginny organizing. They held ceremony at public parks and at the bedsides of dying friends. They'd read each

242

other's tarot cards and sip wine from red glass goblets, giving each other goddess figurines as birthday gifts: a smiling green Gaia with an earth in her belly; a prehistoric sandstone goddess, fat and reclining with her hand on her hip. "Yes, yes, yes!" They would squeal as they unwrapped their gifts and planned their future altars.

The Santa Barbara Elwood trailer had an enclosed porch out back we called the sunroom. The Sunroom of Night. It was stuffed with boxes of Christmas lights and old spelling tests, ripped trash bags full of clothes to give away. Boxes of my stuff, my old letters and notebooks I'd made my mother hold on to when I went away to London, and boxes of notes for her own book about the fall of matriarchy that she'd abandoned years before. She was carrying a lot in that room. A blender she'd had for almost thirty years that she got as a wedding gift when she married my father. It broke the first time she used it. She'd carried it with her for decades. The idea was that at some point she was going to fix that blender. She took comfort in the idea that, if she held on to those broken things long enough, somehow, by some magic, she'd find a way to fix them.

Though the Sunroom of Night actually got a lot of light, it always made me depressed. In the middle of the room, jammed between all the boxes, was a hot tub Pete insisted my mother get. I don't want to know why. Anyway, it was in disuse, puddled with a brackish green slime that splashed in my mouth when I tried to siphon it out so we could get rid of the damn thing. My mother was grateful for my willingness to wrestle with that slimy hydra; she wanted that hot tub gone the moment she and Pete broke up.

But that was the only piece of Saturnine ballast in that room she wanted me to touch. My renovations went too far when I threw away her herbs one day while she was at work.

When I was a child, my mother had a little room she called her apothecary, filled with glass bottles of herbs and powders and potions all made or ground by hand. She'd use them to make medicinal teas and poultices. She wrote in her Book of Shadows, the book where witches record their spells, all about the properties of the plants: oil of clove eased the pain of toothache; damiana was sweet enough for healing baths and love spells; belladonna could be used as a pain reliever, but only with extreme caution—too much and the nightshade became a poison. By the time my mother reached her Elwood Trailer period, her apothecary had become the Sunroom of Night and fallen into disuse. The chamomile had turned to powder, coating the bottom of the jar like old mustard; the valerian was spindled in fuzzy gray mold. In my mind, every time my mother walked past these mummified medicinal relics, she'd beat herself up about how she wasn't doing enough and all the things she'd lost. I saw these dead medicines as a toxic form of bloodletting, leeches sucking at her confidence, just another piece of evidence that she was no longer the woman she wanted to be. But when I threw them away, she was furious.

It was as if by throwing away her herbs I'd thrown away any chance she had at rebirthing her witchcraft. I understood, but I couldn't concede. The herbs were old, mostly dust; they were unusable. When you get the Death card in tarot, the best thing you can do is pull the plug on whatever it is in your life you're keeping on life support. If you don't let it go, it will suck all your energy.

Rebirth will be impossible. My mother had taught me that herself. But rather than seeing my intervention as help, she saw it as a violation. The herbs were an extension of her body, their rhizomatic roots reaching back into her earth, her history. To have someone take them from her without permission was to have someone destroy a piece of her and violate a boundary she didn't want crossed. And yet, I'd thought I was protecting her. Funny how protection and violation are often two words for the same action.

Saturn is the planet of boundaries. In my sessions with my witch clients now, I often tell them that Saturn's boundaries are like the walls of your house. Without the walls, your house would be useless. We need boundaries; we need structure and security. Saturn gets a bad reputation. He was once the god of the harvest. His festival, Saturnalia, inaugurated winter with the fruits of fall laid out in a cornucopia upon the table. It was a time of reversals. On that day the slave would be master and the master, slave. Like many goddesses before him, Saturn was the god of grain, threshed into the soil, sprouted and grown, turned into bread, into body, into earth. Saturn was death and resurrection.

Because of the fight years before over the thrown-out herbs, and many other things, I'm not sure my mother wanted me to live with her in her trailer in Ojai. I think she was worried about it. But, to me, the move seemed like an ideal solution: I could live in the orange groves of Ojai rent-free, job-free, and focus on my writing. I was grateful for the opportunity to have some rest. I knew I was deep in my Saturn Return. I knew my Saturn was in the sign of Leo, the sign of creative self-expression. I was writing a pilot about a haunted plantation off the coast of Georgia that calls its descendants back to deal with their ancestral history. I was blind to the fact that I was working on my own.

When I moved in, my alliance with my mother was loving, though uneasy. It was a difficult time for my mother then, still. I visited her a few times in her cubicle at work. Poked and prodded as she was by the Machiavellian tactics of her bosses, she nevertheless kept a goddess figurine on her desk below a picture of her brother and his partner pinned to the partition wall. My uncle had died a few months before, after a decades-long battle with HIV. His partner of twenty years shot himself in the head out of grief three months later. We spread their ashes in the desert. My uncle had lived with my mother at the mobile home in Ojai, too, because he'd needed her care, but like me he also hadn't paid rent. Saturn is the planet of boundaries and it's always toiling to teach the women in my bloodline to have better ones. Still, my mother was proud to be able to offer us refuge, and to be able to buy the place outright with no mortgage, even though it meant a two-and-a-half-hour commute to work and back each day. And she was excited because behind the double-wide, there was space for a little garden. There she grew the vegetables we ate in our dinner salads and worked on her medicinal herbs. Somehow, in all the difficulty and stress, she'd managed to eke out a small lifeline for herself by resurrecting her connection with her plants.

Wanting me to feel welcome, my mother insisted I take her bedroom, while she slept on the trundle bed in the spare. Mornings

246

I'd wake up at 6:00 a.m. and meditate, then do chores until she woke up, unable to write if I knew at any moment she might come in and talk. To make her morning commute bearable, she'd wait out the traffic at her computer, glued to the Democratic Underground, an alt-left website with which she was on an intimate acronym basis: DU. My mother's task was to hold up the pillars of DU. She tracked the stories, learning the names of the wrong-doers, noting in which news stories they made an appearance, making connections. I'd make her poached eggs on sourdough and serve it to her at her desk, where she'd sit, saturating herself with the misdeeds of those in power. They really were as horrifying as she'd suspected all along. Her Democratic Underground was the home of rabbits, thumping out the approach of men like her father, evil men, lurking in back rooms, smoking cigars, plotting 9/11 from the inside, hatching schemes on how to betray the vulnerable, persecute women, enslave people of color, destroy the environment, and undermine democracy. *Thump thump thump*, went the listserve. Like the rabbits of *Watership Down*, saying, "There's terrible evil in the world."

When she left for the day, I'd write. I'd walk to a nearby café and sit beneath the oak trees, writing out my TV scripts by hand or working on completing my novel about Persephone's escape from the underworld. I'd write for hours, as long as I could, then return to my mother's wood-paneled chamber and fend off the tentacles of the Internet that devoured her each morning.

In the evenings, when my mother and I were calm, sometimes we'd go through a box of old photographs sent by my grandmother and write the stories we could remember on the back of each one. Most of the women we now identify as witches wouldn't have called themselves that for the past thousand years or so. Many would have considered themselves Christians, Protestants, or Catholics, but they practiced the techniques of witchcraft, speaking to spirits, using herbs, finding lost objects. The roots of my family lineage go back deep into the land, by the standards of European Americans at least; we were here since before the Civil War, since before California even became a state. Images of women in high-necked Victorian dresses wearing gloves of hand-crocheted lace, standing before a clapboard shack in an oil field in Culver City. "I think that's your great-grandmother, Grandma Een," my mother told me. "She always wore her hair piled on top of her head like that." The woman in the photograph was too glamorous for that oil field; children with dirt streaked on their faces played with an old tin can at her feet. My mother had a special interest in the women in my family, though mainly it was the men who were recorded in history. I'm a direct descendent of Daniel Boone, frontiersman and coonskin cap wearer. Also, John Hart, signer of the Declaration of Independence for New Jersey. The men in my family came to California for the oil, the black gold pooling in underground oceans beneath the dry earth. And some came for the metals, the yellow gold, the silver. But the stories of these men's wives and daughters weren't written down. The only stories we know of my ancestresses are those within living memory, many truncated to just a footnote.

After her husband died, my grief-stricken great-great-aunt Meta left her daughters on the steps of a whorehouse in Anaheim as punishment for ingratitude. The girls sat on the steps until eventually my great-great-grandmother Marianna came to rescue them, back when there was no Disneyland, no I-5, just orange groves and jackrabbits for days. I loved the picture of my great-great-grandmother Marianna. In it she wore an embroidered bolero jacket I still have hanging on the wall in the room where I practice my magic, a maroon velvet jacket lined in gold silk, with scratchy gold embroidery and stained glass beads. As the witchiest of my kin, Marianna wore that jacket in the circus. My grandmother tells me she was a feisty woman, with a monkey that bit. She smoked cigars and drank whiskey and scandalized Southern California when she insisted on wearing pants so that she could straddle her horse. Her saddle is still in the Anaheim museum today. But, as the story goes, she always had to have a man. As soon as one would leave, she'd dig around in the earth until she could find another to take his place. My great-great-great-great-grandmother went by Lady Dean. My mother is convinced she was a noble, though I have my doubts. On her way from England, she died in childbirth while sailing around the cape to the port of San Francisco, where her seven surviving children would seek their fortune in the Gold Rush.

In the box was a picture of my grandmother from the early '50s, all blond and coquettish, with her pointy bra, modeling for a catalogue. Standing beneath the studio backdrop, leaning her weight jauntily on the tip of her umbrella, she tilted her chin up toward the spotlight. She must have been about eighteen in that photo, before she married my grandfather the demon, then contracted polio. Once divorced, as a single mother, eventually she fought her way into a position selling ads at the *Morro Bay Tribune*, and worked her way up, from secretary to editor, until she was thrown out via patriarchal coup d'état. She was born at the exact moment of a great earthquake. An ornamental plate fell to the ground and cracked; it still hangs upon the wall in her house in Northern California. A sign that the goddess Persephone ruled our family line, the earth shook, and Hades rose from the chasm to claim his underworld bride.

In that same box was a photograph of my mother from my early teen years when she was at the height of her witchy powers. Her hair long, she's draped in fabrics the color of stone and wine and blood. She holds a power amulet between her fingers and stares out at the viewer with an arched brow and narrowed eyes, as if staring in the face of some medieval prosecutor with an expression like, "I see you. You're a hypocrite and you have no power over me." That picture always scared me, because I knew the inquisitors, hypocrites though they may be, did in fact have power. They controlled the planet. They certainly controlled my mother. When she divorced my stepfather, she had nothing. The powers that be offered her a choice: submit, and scratch out a life beneath our rule, or be destroyed. And in fact, we might destroy you anyway, just for pleasure. What good could candle spells and moon goddesses be in the face of that?

We kept all these pictures in a heavy folding box, its slick red cardboard suggesting it'd once been used for Christmas sweaters. One evening, after a few hours of weeding through the stack of photos, I looked down and saw a little girl, strawberry blond and awkward, her face swollen with allergies and asthma, and I realized it was me. My image, on top of this huge stack of other images, women from my family, stories of love and longing and struggle, and the time would pass, and other faces would come after mine, and on the back of my photo there'd be one line of penciled text to sum up my life: *She once lived in a garden shed in Santa Barbara. She was once the Oracle of Los Angeles,* though I didn't know at the time that's who I would become.

Some of my ancestors emigrated from France as Huguenots, Protestants who escaped Catholic persecution and fled to America. In French, there's a word used to discuss the provenance of wine: *terroir. Terroir* refers to all the things that affect the spirit of a grape and influence the flavor of the wine. Technically, *terroir* is the land, but more it's the spirit of the world the grape grows in. The temperature of the briny air as it gusts off the winter sea, the mineral salts in the nearby creek, the veins of copper running through the fields and the pine sap soaking the hills nearby. For me, Saturn didn't just represent my walls, the ones I'd built for myself; it lived in my foundation, my family, my *terroir.*

My mother would often joke that I had moved to Europe to get as far away as I could from the story of my family. But in Europe I learned that wherever you go, you take your stories with you. Saturn permits no escape. One night, my mother and I had an argument. A common one for us. Our arguments would drag us into the dark, and down at the bottom I'd find a piece of my mother I didn't want to see. A piece that terrified me.

In her depression she no longer seemed to inhabit her body. Her hair, once her glory, white and thick down to her waist, she now wore up in a schoolmarmish bun like Mrs. Claus, if the jolly elf had her rosy cheeks sucked gray by a vampire. In her most active witch years, my mother had worn long drapes of fabric in mustard ochre or russet batik. I'd always admired her necklace collection: Yoruban palm beads and turquoise squash blossoms and a silver moonstone pentacle she'd bought near a sacred well in Glastonbury. But she rarely wore jewelry anymore, with the exception of a silver ring with a symbol for balance that her finger had grown too swollen to take off.

By her own admission, my mother was just waiting to die. She told me so herself. The only reason she kept going was me and my brother. She went over her past relationships again and again, like a river over a stone, wearing the memories smooth, polishing them and holding them up to the light. "Why didn't they love me?" she'd ask again and again, about her father, about my father, about my stepfather, about Pete. "What is it about me that makes me so unlovable? I try to figure it out, I try to do everything right, and I just can't figure it out. Why didn't they love me?"

My mother's sorrow, her pain and self-criticism, her lack of self-love provoked in me an irrational fury that I would never extend to anyone else. I didn't know where it came from, or why I felt it, but it was something about how our stories were blended together. Something about how her struggles were tangled with my own. And even though I could name this fury, and reason against it, I felt what I felt, and my feelings could not be banished. Starting at my heart, when she'd say these things, my blood would catch fire. I'd want to tear down our house and stomp on the walls. "It's not that you're unlovable," I'd howl at my mother, wanting to scream it in her face and shake her. "They couldn't love! They couldn't love you; they couldn't love anyone!"

In the lonely afternoons, after I'd finished my work for the day, I'd take long walks along the backroads of Ojai, spiritual mecca of late nineteenth-century theosophical societies and yoga gurus, nestled between two mountains in groves of citrus and avocado. California! Land of my birth. A golden land with a golden hour, right before sunset warm light would shoot streaks of pink along the leaves and fill the air with monarch butterflies. That golden light caresses your face; anyone whom it touches takes on the shine of love. It troubled me that my mother felt herself unworthy of it. I'd never, never once in my life, ever seen my mother be mean. Even at her most wounded and depressed, she always had love to offer the world. She fought for the rights of the vulnerable; she knew the goddesses' names. She craved simplicity; she loved to watch the plants grow and learn their habits and protect them. She'd read everything, and even though she hadn't graduated from college, she still had perfect grammar and spelling, and beautiful handwriting in loops and swirls.

One of my favorite things about my mother is her ability to love what other people love. As a child, my brother loved blocks, and my mother could play blocks with him endlessly, just because she loved to watch him love them so much. I loved contemporary dance, and my mother could talk about dance with me endlessly, even though she didn't know anything about it, because she appreciated love wherever she saw it. If someone loved something, she wanted to celebrate that love; she would be a devotee kneeling at the altar of that love, even if she never felt like she would get any of it in return. Even if it was doled out to her in scraps that barely kept her alive, my mother's hunger just made her appreciate love more.

As a young witch, my mother understood the power of naming. She named me Amanda, meaning *worthy of love,* because she wanted me to always know that I was valuable and worthy. She wanted to give me the thing she never felt like she could get for herself.

I was a couple miles from home by this point in my walk, and I came upon a junk heap on the side of the road. Rusted metal things that looked like they once lived in a tractor, diseased children's toys matted with mud, a mattress and a dresser drawer and an old lamp with its guts pulled out and…a goddess about three and a half feet high. Venus, Goddess of Love, with coils of hair falling below her waist, made of white cement and stained at the foot, as if she'd been half buried in the earth for decades. Chipped around the edges, she was still intact, though heavy when I tried to lift her. For most of the two miles home, I carried her on my hip like a child, though she kept sliding down, and sometimes I'd have to flip her around and carry her on my back, like an eighteenth-century peasant carrying bushels of hay.

In the little plot of land behind her trailer in Ojai, my mother's *terroir* was imperfect, but still beautiful. She'd made a strong effort to grow things in it. Even though it was difficult, her earth packed hard like a dirt parking lot, she grew pumpkin and squash, corn and beans. She could conjure the plants up from the earth with the gentleness of her voice. She didn't like pesticides and had long been a follower of permaculture, a witchy system that looks for ways to encourage mutual benefit and collaboration between animals, plants, and people. She grew herbs on a spiraling mound, with the rosemary and lavender at the top so they could grow their roots deep, with the thirsty mint and skullcap at the bottom so they could drink the water as it drained away.

I put the goddess near the squash. There she stood in the wide wrinkled blossoms, reclining upright against my mother's herb shed, surrounded in vines, serenaded by the burbling of our electric fountain. She could gaze at the little tabby tiger sleeping in the crook of our neighbor's lemon tree. Each night when my mother got home, even after eight hours in her cubicle and several hours of traffic, she still made an effort to spend time in her garden. And so that night, when she stepped into its blue shadows, I ran to the back bathroom and listened at the window screen. "Oh!" my mother exclaimed, delighted. "There's a goddess in my garden." From behind lace drapes crocheted by my ancestors, I watched my mother caress the Venus's face and smile. She never asked me how the statue got there. I believe, secretly, my mother always knew the Goddess of Love would find her.

Soon after the goddess appeared, I went to visit my friend Milly in Georgia. Milly and I were collaborating on the screenplay about the haunted plantation, and I wanted to do a little reconnaissance. Writing the script, I surrounded myself with the muses of the South, field recordings by Alan Lomax, Atlanta crunk, Will Oldham's Palace Brothers, Cat Power, and the songs of a rising star of New Weird American folk, who lived in Athens, Georgia, and wrote hymns of such simplicity, humility, and beauty that I immediately fell in love. I'd listened to this musician over and over again while I was in grad school, trying to break the curse of Nosferatu. His music kept me company while I was crying in my bed, or marveling at the stars from the desert hilltops, willing myself forever up and out into the starlight. I'd look at pictures of him on Myspace, sitting on his front porch in the Southern twilight: a blond-bearded frontman with a Southern drawl, a swashbuckling swagger, and a way about him that said he loved the world so much he could eat it, if it didn't kill him with heartbreak first. I messaged him to see if he would be playing a show during my visit to Georgia. His response was swift. No shows, but if I was in town we should get a drink anyway.

We rendezvoused at a bar. He kept his pink baseball cap pulled low over his blond curls. Worried who would see him, he wanted to sit in the back. His ex-girlfriend was on a heartbreak rampage. Soon we were at his house. A little farmhouse out on Nowhere Road nearly devoured by kudzu and pine, golden cows lowing in the fields nearby. On the ride over, the musician worried that he couldn't be consistent emotionally. He'd left his ex-girlfriend in the underworld. He loved her but it was this whole big wild world up in the sunshine he needed to explore. "I'm a dick sometimes," he told me alluringly.

In his living room, he turned on the fairy lights swaddling a naked doll with blue blinking mechanical eyes. A phone number was inscribed in black Sharpie across the belly. I suspected that if I inspected the house closely, I'd find many phone numbers. A drum set, an old couch, a drawing of the winged lion Abrasax (the god

256

who blesses the couple in tarot's Lovers card) taped to the wall over one of two upright pianos. In the kitchen, a handwritten note was pinned beneath a magnet: "Fridge is off. Turn her on."

We sat shoulder to shoulder on a piano bench, my head tilted onto his shoulder, his fingers slowly, sadly peddling the ivory keys. "Play me one of your songs," I asked him, and named my favorite one.

"You like that one, huh?" He smiled. He loved applause; he was a Leo with a Leo rising.

I nodded. The song was a dirge, emerging from the pond of memory, dripping plaintive wet, surrounded by fireflies and smelling of a lost childhood.

"The chorus especially, where you say, *Please, I've waited*, again and again," I told him.

"Okay, then," he said.

His voice trembled and broke as he sang. I could smell him all salt and beer and sadness and poetry, and I placed my fingers on his beer-colored wrist. And he finished the song and turned to me and curled his fingers in my hair and the breath was sucked out of me and he said, right before he kissed me, "Just for tonight, can we be madly in love?" And I said yes with everything I had. Yes, a thousand times yes. Even though I knew that one night wouldn't be nearly enough for me.

Totally a creature of his environment, he emerged from the mean farms of Alabama, where people will take a shotgun to you for standing on their driveway. He was country gospel sung in a field by starlight; he was owls, majestic and fierce, trapped in a cage at a country zoo; he was a teenager practicing on his acoustic guitar to drown his father's rage as he yelled at his mother in the living room for not stirring the coffee right; he was days spent shirtless shunting tourists in inner tubes down a lazy river; and cocaine-fueled all-nighters recording with a ten-piece band of un-shaved womanizers. When he was a child, he had a book about lambs that he loved; he'd read it over and over. One day his parents came in to find him reading the book and crying. When they asked him why, he said, "Because the lambs are so beautiful." They took the book away from him, saying no boy should be crying like that. He told me his seventh-grade English teacher fell in love with him because he had a poet's eyes. She was right. He had a poet's everything. A poet's voice, a poet's woundedness, a poet's ability to recognize beauty, and a poet's love of wine, women, and song. If wine were beer and Adderall. I returned to California ad-dicted. But the planet Saturn favors sobriety. Saturn's energy is slow and methodical. True Saturnine work is often plodding and unglamorous. Intoxicants are just a distraction.

My mother, too, was in love when I returned home. Will, a family friend who would often visit our house with his wife when I was a kid, was getting a divorce. As a child, I remember my mother saying that Will was the only man she ever met whom she could trust. I always knew they had a great fondness for one another, but their relationship had never seemed inappropriate, their inter-actions never veering beyond anything but friendly. Then his wife had an affair. As a little girl, I had always loved his wife. She'd worked with my mother at Hearst Castle as a tour guide and had long hair down to her waist and sang opera and seemed in fact to be a creature *from* an opera, petite and fairylike, cooking elaborate French meals and letting me play dress-up in her silk slips and lace dressing gowns. Eventually she grew to feel that Will, my mother's new suitor, was not glamorous enough for her. He loved model trains and WWII books and B movies from the '50s with bad special effects. Will's ex fell in love with a curator from the Smithsonian. But then, after she filed for divorce, after a heart-broken Will contacted my mother and asked her if she might be willing to go with him to the county fair, his ex got cancer. Will rushed in to take care of her. My mother and I worried that all his ex would have to do is crook her finger and he'd go running back to her. But in the meantime, my mother was so happy. *She'd* talk with him about his love of model trains for days if he wanted. She took down her bun and started wearing her jewelry again. In the morning she'd get up, and instead of shooting up an adrenaline shot of DU, she'd play her "Goddess Workout" tape on the VCR and belly dance. Hips swinging, coined scarves jingling around her waist.

One day, when they returned from an outing to the model train show, I asked her how it was, and she said, "Wonderful. Just perfect," all aglow and happy, cheeks pink as cotton candy.

"Maybe you'll fall in love and live happily ever after," I said, but the way I said it made it sound like I didn't want it to happen. I was shuffling boxes around in the cupboards, slamming food onto the table. My mother came up and touched my arm. Will stood at the edge of the kitchen, silent and still, as if watching a wounded animal that at any moment could leap out and bite.

"Leave me alone and stop patronizing me!" I shouted, instantly transformed into a sullen teenager by the magic wand of my mother's happiness. I ran into my room and grabbed my paper and pen, scuttling out to the front porch, letting the screen door slam shut behind me.

My mother was falling in love and it felt like the apocalypse. She wanted love, she'd always wanted love, and she'd believed she could never have it, and now it was upon her and whenever I saw them together I had to fight the urge to draw my sword and heave a battle cry. I was terrified that we would be betrayed. Some crisis would come and drop my mother back into her underworld, a dry well she'd claw at until her fingers were raw and bloody and she didn't have the strength to pull herself out again. If this love failed, I was afraid it would kill her.

It was late summer, the hottest time of the year, but it smelled like Yule, the pagan holiday where the Holly King slays the Oak King and winter stills the land. It smelled like roasting chestnuts and bonfires; the trailer park was covered in what looked like snow. Except the air was hot as Hades, and the flakes hushing in the leaves were ashes from fires surrounding us on all sides. In the heaving red sky, you could look straight at the sun for as long as you liked, the Sun of Night. You could see the precise disk of it, hovering and smoldering, over a darkened alien world hurtling toward its end. Who knew the end of the world would be so beautiful? I sat on the front porch and allowed myself to turn to stone, covered in ashes. A grasshopper I'd spent weeks watching as it molted from small electric green nymph to a meaty camouflage locust was slowly, loudly chomping a delicate flower down to the nub. I sat on the porch and cried and felt like a brat, out of control and caught up in a river of dread and anxiety that seeped up from some hole deep inside me where I couldn't see the opening.

From the mountains came a black road, unfurling across the sky. Thousands and thousands of vultures flying in an endless ribbon. It seemed impossible. Black winged, red gelatinous heads jangling, hissing and grunting, coasting on wings a full man across. I'd never seen anything like it before. I'd never even seen a vulture in Ojai before, and now here they were by the thousands, flying toward the fire rim, toward what I imagined was a battle-field of burnt carcasses.

In Vedic astrology, Saturn corresponds to the god Shani, Lord of Karma and Justice. According to Hindu scholar Subhamoy Das, Shani "governs the dungeons of the human heart and the dangers that lurk there." Astride a vulture, Shani rides his way through our astrological houses, herding us like a sheepdog. Our work is to ride that vulture with him, into whichever house Saturn appears in our birth chart and do our work there. Our work is liberation. Our work is always liberation. Saturn commands us to storm the Bastille in the house where he dwells and free the karmic prisoners languishing inside. But unlike Mars, the planet of aggression, Saturn's battles for liberation are not all fireworks and glory. Saturn's fight is a war of attrition. To achieve Saturn's agenda—ultimate liberation in the spirit of Love—we must demonstrate endurance, patience, diligence, and discipline. We must be willing to delay our immediate gratification for future rewards. But those rewards are far reaching; they extend deep into future generations.

* * *

In the tarot, Saturn corresponds to Major Arcana XXI, the World card, the last of the archetypal cards of the major arcana. The World card signifies the completion of a long journey. But that completion is actually a new beginning. As you begin again, you show up not inexperienced and naïve like a newborn, like the Fool, but wise and engaged, like the Anima Mundi, the dancing angel in the World card. When the World card shows up in a reading, you know you are on the right path, the path toward wholeness, the path toward self-realization.

To know where in our lives our Saturnine battle of liberation must be waged, we look to our natal charts, the circular drawing that describes where the planets were at the moment of your birth. Wherever we find Saturn, there we will find our Bastille. The Bastille is the eighteenth-century French prison that held the beggars and debtors; when the paupers of France broke in and liberated it, they launched the French Revolution. My Bastille is in my fourth house: the house of the ancestors, the land, the chthonic, of things buried, of gems and caves and lava and the shades of the underworld. The fourth house is our umbilical cord, spiraling into history, into our DNA. When Saturn dwells in your fourth house, your task is to excavate the stories of your family lineage and heal them. In medieval astrology, the fourth is the house where you'd seek buried treasure. Famed astrologer Liz Greene calls the fourth house a great subterranean river moving beneath the surface of the personality. She says, "Any planet placed in the 4th points to something hidden in the psyche that must be discovered and brought to the surface before it can be dealt with constructively."

262

Not surprisingly, Saturn shares my fourth house with my moon. In astrology, the moon not only represents your moods and patterns in this lifetime, but also your mother and her family line. Each of us are like characters in an epic novel, spanning generations. If we do nothing to change the stories of our ancestors, they play out again and again. My task was to resolve the narrative of my family lineage. I may not like this task, but nevertheless, it was the task that had been given me. In resolving my family's stories, I would generate new ones.

As I sat in stillness, watching the vultures, I could hear my mother and Will returning from their walk. "It's not that she doesn't like you," I heard her whispering to him. "She's afraid. Every time I've ever gotten involved with a man, she ends up getting pushed out of my life. She's trying to push us out first, so she doesn't get hurt."

"I can understand that. But she doesn't have anything to worry about," Will whispered back to her. "I'm here for as long as it takes, for you, for your children. For all of it."

A month passed and I found that, rather than working on my screenplay, or finishing my novel about Persephone, I was writing the musician love letters. Rather than calling him by his given name, I addressed the letters to Orpheus, for the women he'd left in the underworld, and for the bacchantes who'd sidle up to him at his shows, wanting a piece of him. I should've been more careful in my naming. In the myth, Orpheus leaves his true love stranded in the underworld, and the other women in his life? They become so furious with him they tear him limb from limb, leaving only his head to sing in a cave, bobbing in a cauldron of goat's milk.

Anointing myself with oils of rose, dizzy with tinctures of valerian, when my mother was out on date night, I'd whirl myself into trances and call the spirit of Orpheus into my candlelit room, visualizing sigils traced on the floor in blue flame. In these sessions I'd receive visions from Aphrodite and inscribe them into letters I'd send him swollen with flower petals and sealed in the pheromone juices of sex magic. Soon his responses went from being casual and slightly aloof to fevered and poetic, comparing me to a long-limbed, big-eyed doe. After another month or two of love spells, letters, and phone calls, he called for me to join him on his upcoming tour. Mission accomplished. Goodbye, screenplay. Goodbye, novel. I promised I'd write them from the road.

On the tour, Orpheus and I were so in love. By night he played Baltimore, Boston, DC. In the day we went to the museum, saw dire wolves and mammoths and saber-toothed tigers and other beasts long since extinct. I smiled at the man next to us, holding his daughter up to see the animals frozen in their amber tableaux. Suddenly Orpheus was upset, walking into the sculpture garden. I couldn't get him to talk. "What is it? What is it?" I asked him, but he just shook his head. Eventually he said, almost with dismay, "I'm so in love, I don't know what's happening to me." He looked up at me. "I don't know if I'm cut out to love. Love churns up petty emotions in me. Jealousy. Melancholy." But his storm soon passed and we were back on the road again, traveling through Pennsylvania, Ohio, Illinois, unable to stop touching each other, unable to be out of each other's sight for even a few minutes, having sex in bathroom stalls and greenrooms and the back seat of the van. And then he'd get onstage and he'd sing, in cavernous crowded clubs or tiny backwater roadhouses, with women swooning in the audience and batting their eyelashes. Every night, it was as if he were singing just to me. If we were across the room or across the universe from each other, our molecules were bound; if he turned, so would I.

Simultaneously, everything was a miserable disappointment. Orpheus had warned me that touring wasn't glamorous, and he was right. We rarely slept in hotels. Instead we slept on the cat fur floors of some bouncer's studio, frequently without blankets or pillows, having to drink ourselves silly so that we could pass out or risk facing a night of snores and hallway drafts and sirens from the street. Every day the van accumulated trash: wrappers, boy sweat, damp jackets and socks, over-brimming with gear. When we got out at a gas station, I'd stand looking in the open door of the van: a whale cut open revealing a ton of plastic in its guts. I couldn't believe I was going to climb back in that thing. Some of his bandmates resented me and the space I was taking up (even though I tried to do what I could, bought a hotel room sometimes, paid for breakfast, tried to be generally amiable). I was taking up precious space in a van that was constantly breaking down. He didn't yet have the tour bus he rides in now. And, like his sad little van, Orpheus was just on the verge of breaking down himself.

While Orpheus focused on receiving his adoration, I spent most of my time waiting for him to be free to be with me. My intention

265

was to write on tour, but it proved impossible in the cramped vans and cacophonous bars. But the tour was short, and when Orpheus invited me to leave Ojai and move in with him in New York, I expected things to change.

We moved into a brownstone in Bed-Stuy, Brooklyn, full of a bunch of other up-and-coming musicians. These musicians were always working. They'd walk in and drop their bags and be playing guitar before their asses hit the sofa. Orpheus would stay in our room, hypnotized by Pro Tools's sacred geometry. He put his drum set in the center of our room, with tambourines and amps and umbilical cables sucking at the walls. The bed was shoved into a corner at a weird angle. I was desperate to rearrange things. He had invited me there, to that house, but it wasn't mine. There was no room for a desk. No place to write in the whole house, where I had all the solitude of an indie rock orchestra pit.

In New York, I worked all the time to make ends meet, first at an art-book publishing company, and then at a restaurant that specialized in fancy margaritas. On a typical day, I'd return home to find the boys from the band crammed into our room, recording equipment strewn around, the boys lazing in their Vans, mustaches, and jeans. They'd be listening to the playback tracks. A brooding piano, a trumpet somewhere, sounding way far off. Orpheus said, "That trumpet sounds pretty wounded back there. I don't know if we want it." They didn't look up when I entered.

When the boys left, Orpheus pulled me into the room to make love. He wanted to go for hours and never stop unless he was playing music. When I said there were other things I wanted to do with my life than just listen to him practice with his band and have sex all the time, he said, "We don't have sex all the time."

"Yes, we do," I told him. "We have sex like five times a day."

"Five times a day is not a lot," he said, pulling me close again.

One night he played the Cake Shop. After load-in but before the show, everyone lounged around. The boys were quiet. They flicked matches at each other and talked about record labels and kinds of amps and places they've toured: musicians' standard discourse. Orpheus and I sat together uneasily. After one of our biggest fights, I tore off to go write and he stayed home and wrote a song. Both of our pieces were about wolves, their muzzles bloody in the snow. We were connected in the realms of magic like that. But after about six months I realized that though we were in the spirit world together, I was becoming a ghost. I was not Amanda, writer and witch. I was Eurydice, Orpheus's girlfriend. We'd made love all afternoon but it ended in a fight. He wanted to know where I'd been while he was rehearsing. Whenever I went out, he'd quiz me on what I did, who I was with, where I sat.

"I thought you were sitting by the window."

"I was, I moved."

"Why'd you move?"

"It was too noisy by the window."

"Was anyone with you?"

"No."

"You didn't know anyone there?"

"No. No one. I was just writing."

"Did you move to sit next to someone?"

"No."

He was suspicious of me; he constantly worried that I would cheat on him. He felt threatened by my sexual history. But I knew his jealousy was not because I was unfaithful, but because he was. He worried that I would do the same to him as he had done to me on all the little tours he took when I had to stay home and work. *I want to lock you in a tower until I'm ready to be the man you need,* he told me. We fought constantly, and I would be this close to leaving, but then he'd have a show, and I'd see him onstage, celebrant, priest, consort of my same goddess, and I couldn't bear to leave him.

That night at the Cake Shop was the same as every night. Our lovemaking, our fighting, our silence and sullenness. He went onstage, looking tired and half drunk. But then the club lights dimmed, and the mic turned on, and there he was, in all his glory. As if he'd called the gods to enter him, he came alive. As if his life offstage were just a waiting period, an elevator ride, until the music started and he came to true form. Orpheus awakened, a sleeping beauty kissed back to life by the music singing through him. That night, I saw him onstage and I knew, he was in love with the Muse, husband to the magic bride. If I stayed, I would always and only ever be his plus one.

When Saturn departs the house of your return, if you were a good student and mastered his lessons, he will leave you with a gift. When I returned, alone, to Los Angeles, the gifts I received were abundant. A few months after my return to my native land, I decided to hold an official witch ceremony on my birthday. It was to be the first time that I would officiate a ritual as priestess.

In New York, I'd felt rootless, severed from my connections. I needed a way to touch ground. I returned to Los Angeles, eager to reconnect with my friends and my community. I moved to Echo Park, into a bright yellow cottage with an opuntia cactus scratching up against the white picket fence and heirloom tomatoes climbing joyously up the wall. I shared the place with my friend Milly, the writing partner I'd gone to Georgia to visit before I got sidetracked in the erotic underworld with Orpheus.

Uncertain how to hold a formal ritual, I called my mother and asked her how she did it. It was the first time that I'd asked for her ceremonial help as an adult. By then she had moved in with her new love, quit her hateful job, and enrolled back in college where eventually she would go on to complete her BA, and then her master's degree. Speaking with her on the phone, it was as if she were singing. It had been years since I'd heard that lightness in her voice, and my decision to return to the craft only increased her ebullience.

She reminded me of the steps I'd seen her perform so many times when I was growing up: ground and center, cast a circle, call in the guardians, invoke the Goddess, do the working, give offerings, thank and release the spirits, ground again.

I held the ceremony on the living room floor around a temporary altar I'd constructed on coils of lace my ancestors had woven and bowers of juniper from our front yard. It was an intimate ceremony, formal and fumbling. Since it was the first time I'd done it, I felt like I had to follow a strict formula. I spent days collecting items for the altar; they had to be just right. It took me hours to decide between a smoky quartz to represent the spirit of the North or a chunk of black tourmaline. I spent days writing out the procedure, borrowing chants from my mother and the books I'd "borrowed" from her library. I had to read from the printout as I did the ceremony.

After we grounded and called in the Guardians, I used a traditional chant made famous by British twentieth-century Wiccans Janet and Stewart Farrar, which they learned from the witch Doreen Valiente, and she in turn from her witch grandfather Gerald Gardner, who, I believe, assembled it from a variety of sources: an eighteenth-century French text and an obscure magazine article called "The Black Arts."

> *Eko Eko Azarak*
> *Eko Eko Zomelak*
> *Zod ru koz e zod ru koo*
> *Zod ru goz e goo ru moo*
> *Eeo Eeo hoo hoo hoo!*

It's a chant that basically means nothing, which is true of chants in many magical traditions throughout the world. Like a sound poem, the words are less important than the power you feel when you say them. None of my friends were brought up in witchcraft, and so I think initially they felt a little silly chanting this meaningless rhyme, but after a few rounds they started to get into the groove, giving themselves over to the spooky, crackly rhythm of it. In that sense, the chant did exactly what it was supposed to do.

It was a small gathering. I chose eight of my closest friends for the celebration, plus me making nine, a good number for a coven. Each of the people present represented a different quality I wanted to honor and embrace. To each member of the group, I gave a commitment for the coming year: "As you are my witnesses, I vow to you, in service of the greatest good for all concerned and the greatest good for all beings, I commit myself to…" I went around the group. For health, I'd invited Lauren. She who never eats sugar, has never in her life smoked pot, and will drive across town at rush hour (something every Angelino understands as true commitment) to get pastured eggs from a lady who raises the chickens in her organic backyard garden. For abundance, I'd invited Jade, a friend who always inspires me because she expects to be valued for her work. The first in my friend group to set up a retirement account, Jade asks for raises and she gets them, *and* she always contributes back to the world, raising money for battered women's shelters and volunteering on Get Out the Vote campaigns. For wisdom, I invited Jordan, a social worker with the homeless and a double Cancer; she always places her connections with others before anything else; she helps me understand that it is by cultivating community that we create our greatest strength.

Something powerful happens when you call your friends together to help you achieve specific intention. You recognize them; you honor them. You say, "You matter to me," and they echo the same back to you. It creates a web of power, a trampoline, and in my case, it bounced me up, a little bit closer toward finding my true purpose in this world.

Each person brought me a memory of something we'd done together; each person brought me an object that represented a wish, something they hoped would grow in their own lives and in mine and in the world around us. It was fun to see all my friends by candlelight, to sing the songs I'd remembered from my childhood. As each person added their wish, we threaded together a web of connections. I read the Charge of the Star Goddess:

> *I Who am the beauty of the green earth and the white moon*
> *among the stars and the mysteries of the waters,*
> *I call upon your soul to arise and come unto me.*

I wasn't yet the Oracle of Los Angeles when I did this ceremony, much less a professional witch; nevertheless the ceremony fulfilled its purpose. It reconnected me with my roots, my people. Saturn had led me back to the earth. To touch ground on what in my life was real and of true value. The ceremony was imperfect. I have a stronger sense of each section of a ritual now; it's important to know why you do each part, and to develop your own relationship to it. But even though it may have been a bit clumsy, after the ceremony I felt a sense of rightness.

On the night of my first ceremony, I realized that nothing could give me the satisfaction of witchcraft. No lover, no job, no money or career success. Witchcraft was love; it was engagement with life. Witchcraft marked the X on the spot where I realized I wasn't at the mercy of the world, but that I could create the world I wanted, together with my friends. This power was something unassailable and true, something that could never be taken away nor doubted. I knew this was a place I could always return to, my root, my fourth house, my *terroir*.

272

Chapter 12

ɔ ɔ ɔ

HOW TO TRAVEL THROUGH THE UNDERWORLD AND MAKE IT HOME ALIVE

Can we imagine reconstructing our lives around a communing of our relations with others, including animals, waters, plants and mountains...not the promise of an impossible return to the past but the possibility of recovering the power of collectively deciding our fate on this earth. This is what I call re-enchanting the world.

Silvia Federici, *Re-enchanting the World*

The cavernous gallery space was empty but I could hear crowds gathering outside the front doors. Inside was quiet, an aquarium of flickering light cast by a video projection on the wall behind me. There were at least ten other artists showing at Human Resources that night. The entire office space upstairs was ankle-deep in chalky red clay. Downstairs in the main gallery, I crouched in a box about the size of a refrigerator on its side, a cardboard temple I'd made myself. I'd spent the day of the opening reassembling it in the gallery, laying its floors with geometric woven carpets in maroon and indigo, sheepskin blankets and plush pillows. In a few moments, the curator would open the front doors to a stampede of art audience: artists, writers, collectors, college professors. It was in this cardboard temple box that I would make my first appearance as the Oracle of Los Angeles.

It had been several years since I'd performed that first formal ritual with my friends. After that first ceremony on my thirtieth birthday, my mother gave me her Book of Shadows, and under her tutelage I started studying from the rites and rituals she'd written there. I pulled out all her old witch books and began a rigorous daily practice on my own. I took classes with healers, witch elders, and shamans. I made a commitment to the Goddess, to the life force in all its raw beauty and power, that I would place Her at the center of my life.

Since my birthday ceremony, I'd led personal rituals and workshops for small groups. But that night at Human Resources was to be the first time I performed a magical act publicly, with people who hadn't actively sought me out with the intention of practicing magic together, people who didn't know anything about what I was doing. I willed myself to breathe slowly, closing my eyes and letting my vision adjust to the dim filtering through the dozens of one-inch windows I'd carved into the cardboard walls with a box cutter on my back lawn. It had taken me days to fashion my little oracle booth, the structure flapping and falling over in the wind as I labored to make it stand with sandbags and duct tape. Now reconstructed in the gallery space, I kneeled inside it, behind an altar of electric candles, a rattle, a little pile of bones, and other tools of divination. Gulping the scent of frankincense essential oil off my palms, I tried to soothe my nerves and ground into my intuition.

My homemade oracle booth was a replica of Los Angeles City Hall, which stood in real life less than a mile away, a bone-white Art Deco erection of the 1920s, its tiered tower jutting thirty-two stories high. From its halls the city's authorities—the mayor, the lawyers, the judges, the administrators—make decisions about who goes to jail, which kids get funding for their schools, who gets access to health care, which homes get bulldozed to make a freeway. If you climb to the top of the tower and survey the streets below, a few blocks away you might catch a glimpse of Skid Row. Tents and cardboard homes that sprout up at night, padded with rags and newspaper, a whole second city in the heart of this one, with its own systems of authority and social order. Every morning a patrol comes through with a bullhorn, demanding the structures be demolished so tourists don't get the wrong idea, that the city doesn't care about the homeless, a Sisyphean task commanded by the despotic gods of capital. There are no natural borders corralling people in to Skid Row. No rivers, no deserts, no mountain ranges; the streets are porous and can be crossed. Technically, the people who live there can leave anytime. But invisible walls trap them on those streets, the forces of racism, trauma, addiction, poverty, white supremacy, capitalism. The story our civilization tells itself is that this suffering is a sad but inevitable fact of life, that there's nothing that can be done. There will always be winners and losers. We tell ourselves this story, but it isn't true. We can change the way the story goes.

On the night I became the Oracle, I was thinking about the city as a living organism that communicates to itself, that is constantly speaking its pleasure and its need, an organism changing, evolving, living, and dying, but also that is, essentially, immortal. Each of us makes up a cell in this being; each cell participates, performs its labors, proclaims its values. My plan that night was to open myself to the voice of the city itself and let it speak through me. To let new stories be told.

"Opening now," the curator, Brian, shouted as he walked to the front door, jingling his keys. I sat inside my booth, visualizing roots reaching from my spine into the tar soil and fossils beneath me, rooting between the tectonic plates, as the chatter of gallery goers, single-channel video installations, and car alarms from outside rose in a tide around me. I listened for the Queen of the Angels, the Spirit of the City of Los Angeles, the Spirit of the land before the city was born, the voices of the settlers, the voices of the Tongva and Chumash who lived here long before any European settlers arrived and who are still living here, the voices of the saber-toothed tigers and mastodons who were here long before humans of any kind. The Spirit of this city is an egregore created by all the beings who have ever walked this land, who have contributed their stories to this dynamic, clanging beast, sprawling across what was once chaparral and riparian woodland, and before that, ocean, and before that, stardust. I listened for Spirit, the Spirit of the Earth, the Anima Mundi, the life force that reaches across the world, beyond history and culture. And, as the first gallery goer came and kneeled before my little cardboard temple and peered inside, I found I could hear the Anima Mundi speaking.

The voice was low at first, the rumbling of an elephant. As soon as the doors of the gallery opened, people lined up outside my little cardboard City Hall. One by one, on their knees, they climbed inside to consult with the Oracle and placed their palms on mine, shining their eyes at me. The fact that they had to enter on their knees was important. In order to enter a ritual space, a space between the worlds, you need to cross a threshold; even if it's subtle, something has to happen that signals something outside the ordinary is about to happen. Changing the way our body moves through space can initiate a change in consciousness.

My first visitor was Liz, a girl I knew from grad school four years before. We weren't close, but we'd had plenty of nights together chatting at openings, discussing our course assignments, or joking about our hangovers. She knew me, but she entered my cardboard temple with wide eyes, hovering, her thumbnail scratching a nub of cardboard until she conjured up the nerve to enter. Slowly, nervously, she crawled toward me along the carpets, then folding herself cross-legged, held her hands out to me palms up, her head bowed. Her hands were petite, silky. I smiled at her. "The Spirit of the City welcomes you. Do you have a question?"

I could feel her hands grow damp. Someone stumbled by, jostling the box, but Liz remained steadfast. She leaned closer. "A few months ago, I had a miscarriage," she whispered. "Will I ever be able to have children?"

For a moment I froze. I hadn't expected the first question of the night to be something so personal. Liz waited in stillness, eyes troubled with tears. Through the little windows cut into the walls, I could see a line had formed across the room and all the way to

277

the street. Impatient people crouched down to peer inside, gauging how long they would have to wait. I shook off their urgency and willed myself to focus, tuning in to the heat inside my little enclosure, the feeling of the air on my skin, my breath expanding between my shoulder blades. I felt my weight resting on the earth beneath me, my roots pushing through the gravel. *Listen*, I thought to myself. *Open your heart and listen.* An image of the Empress tarot card flashed in my mind. I could hear the whispering of vines as they grew around us, leopards clawing and the screech of parrots as they flocked over the rivers of the Amazon. The Empress is the jungle teeming with life, is unbridled creativity; the ultimate mother, the Empress is fertility itself. I saw the Empress slink up to Liz and slip inside her; flowers and water dripped from her fingertips. I heard the Empress whisper to me, "Your body is not your enemy." A message I passed on to Liz. She acknowledged that with her fertility treatments, she'd begun to see her body as a rebellious animal she'd been trying to subdue by force, an animal made to mate in a cage. She wanted to return to the wild. She had an abundance of passion, an abundance of fertility that needed to be expressed. She needed to recognize her body not just as a machine of creation, but as a site of passion and pleasure. "Make space in your life for creativity of all kinds. Start creating for pleasure again, and the children will follow," I said, seeing her in a field surrounded by cubs. Liz cupped my hands in hers, squeezing, pressing her forehead to my fingertips. "Thank you," she whispered as she backed out of the arched threshold and was quickly nudged aside by the next person waiting to crawl in and visit the Oracle of Los Angeles.

For each person who entered, I would answer one question. My intention was singular: I wanted to be of service to my community. To show up with everything I had, listen closely to whatever vision or image arose from the wellspring of that listening, then dip my hand into the waters of the unconscious, catch and present the fish that would help them. I wanted to present each person with a gift. Though my magical intentions were sincere, I expected people who visited me in my little cardboard temple to view my piece with aesthetic distance, as an art object, like the other pieces in the show. But that isn't what happened.

Most of the petitioners to the Oracle would grip my hands, look at me earnestly, eyes wide, and whisper, "Tell me when I am going to fall in love," or "What will happen to my father's spirit now that he's died?" and then await my answer, palms sweating, nervously chewing their lips. When the concept of divination was invoked, even people who knew me personally, who didn't seek my opinion in any other context, were hungry for divine messages.

A few people clambered into my sanctuary and immediately folded their arms, declaring, "I don't believe in this kind of stuff." They'd smirk, then ask, "What will Donald Duck have for breakfast tomorrow?" Even though my oracle booth was in a gallery with other artworks, people immediately interpreted me as either a "real" conduit for the divine or as an exploiter of the naïve and the credulous for personal gain. I can't recall a time when I've seen someone look at a piece of art in a museum or gallery and say, "I don't believe in this kind of stuff." They might say they don't like a piece of art, or don't understand it, or feel like it's some kind of elitist trick, but in all those cases, they're dealing with it as an artwork. But to say that they don't *believe* in it would require leaping to a philosophical position few artworks demand: do you believe in art? In this case, the question my piece brought up wasn't "Do you believe in art?" but "Do you believe in magic?" The people who did were hungry for it, so hungry it felt almost like they would grab any enchanted bread roll sitting on the table, no matter how stale, and the people who didn't believe immediately folded their arms and refused to eat before they even looked at the menu. When it comes to magic, for me it's less a question of belief and more a question of value. Magic is a practice, not a belief system. Rather than asking, "Do I believe in this?" I ask myself, "Do I get something out of this? Is it meaningful to me? Is it helpful?" When it comes to magic and witchcraft, most always, my answer is: YES.

A friend told me that while she was mingling at the opening, people kept coming up to her saying things like, "Have you been to visit the Oracle of Los Angeles yet? What she told me just saved my life." I was in my little oracle booth for hours and hours until my voice was hoarse and the flames of my electric candles began to flicker and die. Ultimately I had to turn people away. Somehow visiting the Oracle of Los Angeles had made people's aesthetic distance disappear. They wanted to voyage with me into the unknown; they wanted an opportunity, if only briefly, before they headed back into their lives as art handlers or nonprofit directors or bookkeepers, to enter a realm where anything was possible, where maybe reality could be enchanted after all.

When I first studied philosophy in college, the philosophy of women was patronized as being "the Philosophy of Care." Witchcraft has taught me that care is the most important thing there is. Care is love, and love is what heals us. When my clients come in, I fumigate them with sage and rosemary and lavender that I grow myself in my garden. I say blessings over them and cast out the troublesome spirits that haunt them, sweeping them with a cinnamon broom and ringing koshi bells. I make them moon tea from a recipe my mother taught me as a child with raspberry leaf and lemon balm, peppermint and passionflower. I remind them where they are, in my magical studio. They are safe. "Look around you," I say. "Look at the fresh flowers and the candles and remember to take pleasure in the experience." We lay out tarot cards and look at the pictures, the mythological figures and arcane symbols; we talk about where we can see the Magician or the Empress or the Star card at work in their lives. We light candles and anoint them with oils. We enter the realm of magic, and fresh possibilities for my clients' lives begin to emerge. In magic is comfort and power. Both spring from the fertile earth of care.

In our travels through the underworld, witches become map makers. Culture, art, the mystery religions, these systems of symbols are maps. Somebody has to create them. Our musicians and healers, poets and witches, travel through the corridors of the underworld by torchlight. We were not wrong to descend into these caves, but for our own sakes, for the peace of mind of those we love and for the sake of the planet, we who travel there must not get lost. We can join our lights together and return to the world. We can use our symbols, our stories, our mystical methodologies to forge connections with each other in these underground spaces. Symbols and stories order our world; they create the narratives by which we live. It matters whose stories get told; it matters how we tell them. Imagination matters. Our connections to one another matter, as does the pleasure we take in our experience. Witches stand in solidarity with those already doing this work. Because people have been doing this work since humans first appeared on the surface of the earth. Now we listen to them, we participate, we use techniques of the healer, the poet, the artist, the scholar, the cunning folk, the green men, and the medicine women to heal ourselves and care for our wounded world.

When I think of altars, I think of sacred, ancient cairns where benzoin incense billows from a censer at the center of a circle of stones. Or an altar in the chancel of a cathedral, walls vibrating with Gregorian chants, tinted rose from stained glass, the miracles of the saints shining down upon the adoring masses. I see human hearts sacrificed to the gods upon altars deep in the recesses of an Aztec temple; plumed priests with warrior faces, serious and determined, placating the deities who wind smoke-like through the still, dark air. Altars are the thresholds between the spirit world and our material realm; they reflect the values and desires of the people who make them. When we create our altars, we create our connection to the divine. Our altars function as portholes to our own chosen Valhalla. For witches, our altars are a way to honor the divine here on earth, to recognize as sacred the ground beneath our feet.

I'd made many altars in my lifetime, but when I formally began to dedicate myself as a witch, I understood that the altar is the place where we carve out space for the sacred in our lives and prioritize it. Before I made my first serious altar, out of necessity I'd taken a gig that was only supposed to last a few months, but that ended up stretching into years as an educational administrator in the industrial armpit of Los Angeles. After all my adventures, it looked like I was going to end up trapped by the same system that had ensnared my mother when I was a child. I spent my nine-hour workdays sprawled in my swivel chair, slunk down and splayed out like some exhausted cartoon character, fingering the fuzzy leaves of the African violets next to my Dell monitor, wondering which jungle they came from. I imagined forests dripping with rain, the whoop of monkeys as they soared overhead, mist swirling through the brambles like a nature spirit. I wanted to join them.

This administrative period was after I'd performed in my oracle booth but before I started supporting myself as a professional witch. During one of the weekend workshops I was constantly taking to increase my understanding of the craft, I had an epiphany where the Goddess told me I needed to create a space for Her to enter my life. I couldn't just hold her in my mind. I needed to make a place for Her with my own hands. On the night before the full moon in Taurus, I constructed a new altar in honor of Her.

Fumigating my magical studio with the smoke of cedar and juniper, then dousing walls and floor in salt water and oil of white camphor, I cleared the dust from every corner. On my new altar I laid an opalescent violet textile, given to me by one of my mentors in grad school, a feminist who'd always advocated on my behalf. I placed seashells, exposing their slick pink underbellies, and drenched the fabric in strings of pearls. I gave the Goddess hand-dipped beeswax candles, still smelling of honey, and laid out all my ceremonial tools that I'd carried with me since childhood: a blue ceramic cauldron that looked like it was made of sea foam, glazed with dyes made of kelp and purple sea bark; a white soap-stone knife I'd received from a friend after having a vision of it in a dream; a wooden wand carved in geometric shapes, stained red with menstrual blood; a black stone with a secret split that, when pulled apart, would reveal a primordial fossil spiraling in Fibonacci perfection.

Naked, I stood before my new Goddess altar and called in the Spirits. Evening light shone through the tangle of flowers on my sheer curtains. I lit a white candle and whistled for my familiars and my guardians. Shaking my rattle, I danced for them and let them enter my body with the rhythm, blood pulsing hot in my feet. Facing each of the four directions in succession, I visualized a blue flame shooting from my fingers as I traced pentacles in the air.

"Hail, Guardians, Spirits of the North. Watchtowers of the Earth. Guardians of stone and bone and blood. Guardians of life and death. I call you now. Come, witness my rite and charge my spell. Be here with me." I saw them rise in the North, the crystal spirits, the gnomes, the earth watchers, jutting up into the sky. All granite and quartz and tourmaline, smelling of pine sap and damp, loamy earth. With a beckoning gesture I called them into my circle and stomped my right foot, bringing them into the room with a thud. I continued until all of the elemental beings were present: Sylphs, airy guardians of the East; the fire Salamanders of the South; and the Mermaid guardians of the West, dripping salt water and perfuming the room with the scent of orchid and vanilla.

Finally, I called upon the Goddess Herself. I always know when

284

She arrives because I feel tingling along the back of my neck and arms, my heart swells, my flesh flashes hot. I imagine a similar feeling for the astronauts who leave the protective blue gauze of our atmosphere and look back on our planet from outer space. Awe. Humility. Gratitude. Wanting to fall to your knees in the face of so much beauty.

Kneeling before the altar, I presented Her with offerings. Cakes sticky with honey, and handmade cones of incense resin: amber, jasmine, and rose. During this ritual, at my most humble and clear, I spoke my spell in a whisper, "By the powers of the Goddess within me, let me find a way out of this trap; let me find a way to devote my life to beauty and pleasure and love. O, Great Goddess of Love, let me be your servant in this world. Yours and only yours. For the greatest good of all beings. Hail and welcome!"

Three weeks after performing the spell, I was laid off from my horrible office job, which meant I could collect unemployment. A relative unexpectedly sent me a $10,000 check. More and more people started calling me to conduct tarot readings, healing rituals, and spells on their behalf. Invitations to speak about my work at galleries and institutions began to come through. While I'd been slowly, steadily incubating, accruing performances and public rituals and the occasional tarot reading for cash, it wasn't until I performed my simple altar spell that my initiation was complete and the Oracle of Los Angeles took her first steps. But the Goddess had made it clear that the work wasn't just to please myself; my work in this world was to find a way to be of benefit to my community.

* * *

285

Persephone, the goddess of my grad school thesis, was perpetually trying to escape the underworld. But every time she thought she'd made it out, she'd eventually discover she was still inside. The underworld was a labyrinth with no exit. Success doesn't lead you out. That's part of the trick; success is just another one of the mirrors that make up the walls of the fun house. I'm a professional witch now, supporting myself doing something I love, no longer drawn toward things that harm me, but I still haven't escaped the underworld. Nevertheless, I've made my peace with this.

I charge for my services. My work takes a lot of time and energy, and I saw what not getting paid for her labor did to my mother. It exhausted her and drained her resources. Living even modestly in Los Angeles is not cheap. My rent has doubled in the past five years. I have student loan debt, health care costs, car payments, car insurance, gas and electric, the bills we all have to pay. It's only been in the last few years of working as a witch that I've been able to max out my yearly limit on my Roth IRA. Even though I'd prefer to focus all my time working at my altar, developing new rituals for my clients, and making new healing teas out in the desert, those things don't pay my rent. I still have to think about my work like a business, because I still live in a world where eight super-rich men hoard as much wealth as half the human race; I still live in a world where people like them make the laws and control the narrative.

My initiations have taught me that there is no escape and nowhere to run. There is no outside capitalism anymore. Capitalism has contacted all of our tribes. There is no persistent, everlasting fairy world where a witch can escape and be safe forevermore.

But as witches, escaping isn't our mission. Once we realize we are witches, we use our magic, not to escape into an enchanted world outside the gates of ordinary reality but to bring forth the magic from within ourselves and pour it into the world around us. Little by little, the witch expands her magic circle to everything she touches, until she can push her circle up against the circle of another enchanted creature, join forces, and find more. This work is not easy. It's confusing, imperfect, and difficult. We are under constant pressure to sacrifice our integrity and are often forced to choose between a multitude of evils. There's no bible to tell us what to do, no grand authority to make our choices for us. But wherever we are, we begin. As witches, our work is to recognize the resources we have, cultivate the tools we need, and midwife our magic back into the world.

Human Resources, the art space, is closing down soon; a real estate developer bought the building and is turning it into a boutique hotel. Capitalism just keeps coming and coming. The last public ritual I performed at Human Resources was called Capitalism Exorcism. It wasn't easy to get the ritual started; I had so little time to prepare. I was scraping price stickers off a herd of glass pillar candles until the very last minute. I worried I'd begin the performance and forget the words. Someone I'd flirted with at a Halloween party caught me upstairs in one of the unisex bathroom stalls, muttering the text of the exorcism over and over again while toilets flushed on both sides. Seeing that I was nervous, the bartender offered me a beer, but I refused, having long since given up performing under the influence.

I entered the dark room and it fell silent. A hundred people stood in a circle around me. My ritual garb was fashioned after a snake priestess of Crete, bare chested, gold skirts cinching my waist and trailing along the floor, black paint fiercing my eyes. Later, a friend told me my hair looked like a living thing, snaky and electric, beneath my crown of rosemary and juniper. Invoking the Goddess, I howled:

> *She who is within us and She who looks back at us*
> *She who births us and She who swallows us*
> *She who knows no sin*
> *She who knows no shame*

> *Spirit of Nature*
> *Earth Air Water Fire*
> *Creator*
> *Preserver*
> *Destroyer*
> *Arise!*

> *Be here with us.*

My voice thundered against the walls. Holding up a censer of dragon's blood incense, I circled the room, filling it with smoke. Using a technique drawn from the Goetic workings of Elizabethan magician John Dee, I inscribed demon-catching symbols on the center of the gallery floor in red chalk. A five-pointed star encompassed by a circle, only rather than invoking a hierarchy of the Lord's angels, inside I inscribed the names of goddesses and fierce female artists to form a cauldron of power at the center of the room. Nearby, I inscribed a smaller sigil stamped with a banishing rune I'd created out of a dollar sign and the phrase *Capitalism, we banish you.*

I unfurled nine red cords from the capitalism sigil on the floor into the crowd around me, so that people could hold the reins and control the demon. People I knew, pale blue light shining off their glasses, wet cans of Tecate sweating from their hands onto the floor, shifted foot to foot, nervous, excited, gathering closer as waves of intention spiraled, joining our forces to cast the demon out.

We reject capitalism because it is abusive. Because it's a system that argues: as long as the oligarchy is profiting, no atrocity is too grave, no violation too gross. Slavery, genocide, atomic war, swamps drained, forests burned, animals brought to extinction. Nothing is out of bounds and there are always plenty of reasons why it has to be this way...free market, forked tongue. To be fair, it isn't just capitalism. Before capitalism, before empire, there was still bloodlust, born at the moment of the first rape. An egregore that became stronger the first time a human roped a bull and commanded it to till the soil against its will. Every time a child's food was stolen to stuff the belly of a king, the power of the egregore grew. But my purpose was no longer just to point out what was wrong and then hide in the wilderness hoping the demon wouldn't come for me. Capitalism is the system we have now, and so this is where I make my stand.

It was time for the exorcism. The room was still. Silent. We could feel the egregore of capitalism pressing in on us from all sides. Humming in off the 110 freeway to the north, the first free-way ever, slicing neighborhoods in half; a black cloud of fumes blowing in from the industrial warehouses and toxic factories to the south; and from the east the temperatures rising and from the west the cost of rent rising; rising on all sides. We were ocean beasts, weird and glowing beneath the pressure of the kyriarchi-cal demiurge: that colonizing force, melting our icebergs, gripping our guts, eating its way out, gobbling our bodies, our planet. I called out:

> *O Spirit of Capitalism!*
> *You who value profit above all*
> *You who determine that only the rich shall be saved*
> *Destroyer of Relationships*
> *Destroyer of the Environment*
> *Promoter of War*
> *Exploiter of Shame*
> *Settler of the World*
> *And*
> *Colonizer of Our Minds*
> *We call you now to appear before us in this circle*
> *By the Power of the Great Goddess,*
> *We command you O! Spirit of Capitalism*
> *appear in this seal*
> *cause no injury, and be bound…*

A sulfurous stench filled the room. I stomped my feet, brought two stones together with a loud crack. I was not a witch alone. My

290

people were with me. I could feel my blood coursing through my wrists, my neck, my heart and theirs, our pulse, going back in an unbroken line, to the beginning of all life on earth. We were sacred beings. Free. We took up the cords and walked widdershins, counterclockwise, against the sun, grinding the genetically modified grain of capitalism backward into dust.

We have never stopped resisting.
We are the children of Lilith
our DNA is that of the primordial goddess
who bends before no man.

O! Spirit of Capitalism
Hear our indictment against you.
Attend to us!

One by one, the people in the crowd stepped forward, naming their grievances. Brothers imprisoned or killed by the police; sisters lured into addiction by the pharmaceutical industry; daughters raped by a coworker at a holiday party; fathers denied a visa; mothers kicked out of their homes so the landlords could build condos. Humans spending their lives in cubicles, destroying their bodies, wasting their time to generate capital for faceless corporate overlords. Knees bent in grief watching their world swallowed in fire, coated in oil, sucked lifeless by factory farms.

We are witches and rebels and lovers of the earth.
Now, here

291

again and forever
we proclaim our refusal to submit.

As each person stepped forward with their testimony, the crowd responded, echoing back, "We hear you, we see you, we suffer with you." Using a ceremonial athame, I cut the cords binding the Spirit of Capitalism to my community. Our tethers withered to the ground. Banging our drums and stomping our feet, we chanted:

O! Spirit of Capitalism, we created you
And now we destroy you!
In the name of the Goddess of Love we destroy you
We cast you out forever from our minds and hearts
We banish you
We banish you
We banish you
Begone!

It's rare that we get to declare our collective intentions like this—at least it is for my people, the weirdos of the world, the artists, the exiles, the people on the fringe. Most of us don't holler at sports rallies; most of us don't go to church anymore. The tenets of the Abrahamic religions don't resonate: God the father, watching us from on high. Following the laws of the priests and popes of the world, the CEOs and presidents, their laws were not created by or for us, nor their idea that the earth was created for amusement and exploitation by "Man."

And yet, the places where we do find ideas that resonate, the political rally, the university, these places are devoid of ritual and of magic. They have been settled too. But by practicing ritual, we *create* the world we want to find, a world where the imagination is exalted. A world where we priestesses, witches, and weirdos can banish the Spirit of Capitalism together, or at least contribute to the effort. Practicing ritual together strengthens the bonds of our community. We empower each other. We stand together, arm in arm, breath mixing, declaring our support for one another, collectively addressing our grievances, in recognition that we are not alone. We are not just isolated individuals struggling to stay afloat in a system that dictates to us the terms of how we should live and thrive. We are not merely objects acted upon by outside authorities. When we come together, we do more than resist. We *create* connection. We create healthier ways of living together on our planet. We create love.

> *And now, O! People of Los Angeles,*
> *The Spirit of the Goddess is with us.*
> *We create Her.*
> *She is already here.*
> *Through us She is reborn again and again.*
> *Her spirit rises within us*
> *What will we create?*
> *Speak your vision now...*

From the circle, voices rose. A young woman with sharp bangs and dark-rimmed glasses declared: "I create the Spirit of Trust. That we can all trust each other to stand up for one another."

Together, the group of initiates echoed back to her: "We invoke the Spirit of Trust. We create this Spirit with you…" More and more people joined in, calling in the Spirit of Patience, calling in visions of gardens on every street, of compassionate support for people recovering from addiction, for an end to borders, for shared resources, for enthusiastic consent. We all called out:

All acts of Love and Pleasure are Her rituals.

"Anyone who wishes to be initiated into the cult of the Goddess of Love, step forward now," I said. Hundreds of feet advanced. We rise, we fall, we rise again. Like the priestesses of Eleusis two thousand years before me, I raised a sheaf of wheat above my head and chanted:

> *By the powers of the Goddess within us*
> *together we consecrate ourselves.*
> *We are witches*
> *children of the Goddess of Love.*
> *Together we are powerful.*
> *Together we are free.*
> *Together, we are initiated.*
> *Victory to the Goddess!*

"Victory to the Goddess!" a chorus of voices sang back to me.

Epilogue
ʕ ʕ ʕ

Your corner is your corner, comrade and sister, and it's
your turn, as we are here in Zapatista lands. These new
bad governments think that they will easily defeat us,
that we are few and that no one supports us in other
worlds. But no matter what, comrade and sister, even if
only one of us remains, that one will fight to defend our
freedom. And we are not afraid...

Letter from Zapatistas to Women Who Fight
All Over the World, February 2019

When a thing is sacred, it cannot be destroyed.

Chloe Erdman

My mother's body is not comfortable; her hips are sore and
cramped. We've been traveling for fifteen hours already, our tail-
bones bent at odd angles. Catching our connecting flight in
Copenhagen, she had to have a wheelchair meet us at the gate or
we wouldn't have made it across the airport in time. Her feet no

longer respond to her commands; she tries to find a way to adjust them so that they're not tangled in our bags and pinched by the seats, but there's hardly any room. The airplane is so basic it may as well be military.

"Are you nervous?" my mother asks me as I punch the pillow and squirm in my seat, trying to find a way to settle in for the final leg of our journey from LAX to Athens, Greece.

I shrug. "You mean about the tour?" I ask her, and she nods. Though it's not at all clear that's really what she means. I've already been short with her several times on our thirty-plus-hour journey; I think she might really be asking if I'm nervous to spend so much time with her. Three weeks traveling with anyone is a long time, especially if that person is your mother. "I guess I'm nervous about all the other people."

She pulls a blanket up around her shoulders. It's freezing on the plane; you can almost see our breath. "Yes, me too," she murmurs, "I worry what they might think of me."

Even though the women on the tour will all be there to commune with the Goddess, she's still nervous how they might treat us if we call ourselves witches. When she was living in San Luis Obispo, she tells me, after she and my stepdad broke up, she was teaching the Cups for the Queen of Heaven classes about women's spirituality. The local independent newspaper started writing about how she "called herself a witch." Some people in her community didn't like that. They didn't want a weird, eccentric, irrational person teaching classes at the Unitarian congregation or saying she represented them. She felt pushed out, marginalized, like she had to hide.

"But if you're a public person, people are always going to disagree with you and criticize you; that's how you know you're getting successful," I tell her. "The more public you are, the more people are going to wag their finger at you."

"Yes...or kill you." She nods, consistent with her track record of always believing that the worst thing that can happen, will happen.

"I'm more worried about spending all that time with people I don't know and not being able to have time to myself," I say. I never would have chosen to go on a tour on my own; it wouldn't have occurred to me. I like fumbling my way through foreign places, allowing the winds of fate to prevail. But I'm glad my mother invited me to come; I want to get closer to her. I want to try opening myself to my mother's way of doing things, even though I'm not sure I'll be able to do it. "Do you think we'll get a chance to do our own thing ever?"

My mother gives me a look. I know she's worried that I'll behave like I did when I was seven and we took a trip to New York City. We got off the bus and I ran off into the crowds of Times Square before she could even collect our luggage. I can feel her resist the urge to bring that story up; she knows it bothers me when we constantly retell the story of how difficult I was as a child. She pats me on the knee. "I'm sure you'll get your chance to wander, honey."

When, during my Saturn Return, she and her new partner, Will, got together, she was in her fifties. Not only did she fall in love, but also after they got married she returned to school, graduated at the top of her class with both a BA and a master's degree.

After that, she pulled out the book she'd been writing all throughout my childhood and began working on it again. It's the reason for our trip to Crete: research. She loves to go over all the plot points of the book with me. It's an epic trilogy of historical fiction cataloguing the resistance of women throughout the ancient world even through the final triumphs of patriarchy. The series begins in Egypt, travels west to Libya, and ends where our trip together would end, in Crete, where the Minoan mother cultures made their last stand.

My mother pulls out her manuscript from her purse, and instantly her mood begins to improve. The exhaustion of the flight evaporates. She runs her finger over her notes, over her beautiful, almost musical handwriting. Wondering out loud, she says, "I keep asking myself, why did we let them? That's what I'm trying to figure out in my book."

"What do you mean?"

"We must have seen the patriarchal hordes coming," my mother continues. "Why didn't we fight?"

"Maybe we loved too much," I say. "They were our lovers, our husbands, our children. Maybe we didn't want to fight them."

"Well, actually, we did fight," she says, going on to remind me of our favorite stories, of the Amazons of Libya and Phrygia, clans of female warriors, archers who fought on horseback from the virgin woods and desert wilderness.

"But the patriarchy still won," I say. "They had bigger weapons." The stewardess comes to take away our plastic cups, water bottles, and empty pretzel bags, telling us to prepare to land. Below us, Athens clamors for our attention, white and dense, industrial warehouses and shipping yards; I can see the Parthenon off in the distance.

Everyone is smoking at the Athens airport. Pink oleanders line the highway into the city, just like they do in L.A. "The Latin name for those is *nerium*," my mother tells me. "They're known as one of the baneful herbs in witchcraft. Poisonous."

Our Brazilian travel agent picks us up in a van. "Tell them about the coffee here!" she commands the driver.

"We love coffee in Greece," the driver tells us, describing one varietal with an aftertaste like chocolate.

Mom can't hear him. "What? What?" She asks me, "It's like a mocha?"

"No, Mom," I tell her. "It tastes like chocolate. It's not a mocha." I want to be less sharp, less temperamental. More Oracle, less Amanda. I remind myself how I would feel if someone was patronizing and impatient with me in a foreign country where I was trying to impress my only daughter. I would feel like shit. It would only make me more stressed. Still, I find myself being impatient with her when she seems confused or has difficulty walking. As if her body is an augur of my own future.

Throughout my childhood, my mother was never able to stay in her body, never had much interest in taking care of it. I watched her disassociate from it, simultaneously tethered to the body's pleasures and seeing it as a site of torment and rejection. I remember asking her questions while we were cooking or driving. She would answer five minutes later, as if the question had to travel a great distance to reach her. She was drifting past Pluto, communicating to me on earth through a series of satellites.

Our first morning in Athens, we sit having breakfast on the hotel balcony, looking out over the rooftops colliding against the Acropolis, the tallest point in the city, built on a hill, surrounded by fortifications of golden stones. My mother is questioning me about how I intend to get milk for our coffee. She's concerned that we aren't supposed to bring our coffee cups to the milk at the buffet, but instead are supposed to fill the little jugs with milk and bring them to the tables. "I've been on this planet for decades," I snapped. "I think I can manage to get milk in our coffee without supervision."

"I'm just worried that we'll look like rubes," she tells me. That word again. *Rubes.* She said it at the airport too. Later I look up the word *rube* on the Internet. I know what it means, but I want to see the precise definition since she uses it so much, describing how she fears people might see her, might see us. *Rube: an awkward, unsophisticated person. RUSTIC. A naïve or inexperienced person.* She's worried in Greece everyone knows how to get milk in their coffee but us; everyone will know we're hicks from an unsophisticated country with a smug white supremacist for a president.

Later in the day, as we're walking up the slippery marble steps to the Parthenon, the temple to the goddess Athena, my mother labors to find footing with her cane. "I can do this!" my mother incants, clearly believing the opposite as she hobbles up the path through the olive trees to the ancient temple of the Goddess of Wisdom and War.

"Of course you can!" I tell her. "Focus on the part that doesn't hurt. Old dancer's trick. Focus on your shoulders."

"Are those not supposed to hurt?" she puffs. In the end she can only make it halfway. She stops just short of the entrance. We've traveled halfway around the world to get here, but she doesn't get to see the temples with all their golden stones, the caryatids rising somberly above the olive tree. She sits on a bench near the buses and when it gets too hot, she gets a strawberry lemonade.

Human frailty is on my mother's mind. Her very close friend, Ginny, is in hospice in California, her right side paralyzed, her eyes glued shut because they no longer produce the fluids necessary to keep them wet, her body riddled with cancer. Ginny, co-leader of my mother's Moon Circle and a mentor of mine who took me to care for abused horses and gave me books by Ursula K. Le Guin. She had two boys about my age and raised them on her own (her husband killed himself without warning, or even leaving a note, when her children were young. She walked in holding their hands at Christmas and found him hanging in the garage). When her parents grew old, she took care of them, moved in order to be closer to them, wiped their brows and their bums; but now, facing death, finding someone to care for her was proving difficult. Ginny insisted that we go on the trip, despite the fact that she might die while we were away. My mother thinks of her constantly. She brings a little goddess figurine they used to keep on the altar during their Moon Circles to every site we visit. She pulls out the little goddess and holds her up in front of the friezes, at the Café Diogenes, in front of the columns lining temple of Zeus

301

across the street from our hotel, so she can send Ginny the pictures on her cell phone, and show them to her when she gets home and say, "You were with us in spirit!"

In the museum of the Parthenon, on a stone tablet on the first floor, a citizen thanks a priestess by name for taking such good care while presenting his offerings to the goddess Athena. Upstairs are dozens of statues of the Korai, women dressed in priestess's robes, presenting offerings of apples, pomegranates, and libations of wine to Athena and other deities who had smaller chapels all over the Acropolis. But according to the wall text, the Korai are not priestesses; they are "female figures." When the Parthenon was in active use, there were thousands of these women, these statues, standing with wide, unblinking black eyes all over its grounds, amidst the groves of herbs and olive trees, their marble eyes painted in kohl, their linen robes bright with ochre paint, smiling as they presented their offerings. But still, the wall text informs us that no one knows who or what they were. When, however infrequently, male statuary appear, they are of course identified as heroes or priests. The presence of so many women in a sacred space is totally mysterious. Why on earth were they there? "Perhaps," the wall text wonders, "the gods found the female figure *pleasing*?"

"We're going to get this," my mother says, her voice rising as she pleads with the buttons of the cramped antique elevator of our hotel. It resists our demands. "We're going to figure this out." She squints again at the sign, half English, half Greek, warning us not to take the elevator during an earthquake.

302

"Mom." I place a gentle hand on her shoulder. "You say that as if you have some doubt it might be true. The elevator is old and temperamental; it's not our fault it's not working." My mother always seems to think that everything that goes wrong can be attributed to a failure on our part.

At the temple of Asclepius, a statue of Athena lunges forward, her arm raised; she wears a cape fringed in hissing snakes. Snakes are symbols of the goddess of the earth. Snakes travel underground, shed their skins, and are reborn; they are symbols of immortality. Even when statues are found decapitated, or with arms missing, leaving only the bust, scholars can always tell it's Athena because of the snakes. Reading me Greek myths as a child, my mother always reminded me, "Athena was born fully grown from her father's head, because in fact, as a goddess, she preceded him." When she first appeared in northern Africa, Athena was called Neith, "the terrifying one," mother of the universe. As creator of the universe, Neith gave birth to herself. On her temple were carved the words:

I am the things that are, that will be, and that have been. No one has ever laid open the garment by which I am concealed. The fruit which I brought forth was the sun.

But the learned men of ancient Greece revised the story of Athena's birth as follows: Zeus, the king of the gods, rapes Athena's mother, Metis, goddess of wisdom, a bunch of times, then eats her alive while she's pregnant. Eating Metis, Zeus thus

303

becomes "wise" himself and eventually "gives birth" to Athena from a crack in his skull in a migraine-oriented form of rapey parthenogenesis. It's in that version of the story that Athena becomes the patriarchy's darling. Now she's the goddess of wisdom *and* the goddess of war. But wherever Athena appears, so too does the serpent, coiling up her feet, circling her arms, writhing on the head of Medusa, who always appears on the goddess's breastplate. Medusa is Athena's shadow self, her underworld reflection, her anger, her history, which she always carries with her. It is by the snakes of Medusa that Athena shall be known.

In the fifth century BC, the Persian army of King Xerxes invaded Greece because the Greeks refused to pay their taxes. After the Persian invasion, the Greek women and children reappeared from hiding to find Athena's temple smoldering in ashes. Her columns fallen. The goddess's yellow dress, embroidered by the tiny hands of young girls, ripped from her body. Her temple looted. Its reliefs stolen. The smell of burnt olives still lingering in the air. The Athenians never fully recovered after the Persians destroyed the Parthenon.

They rebuilt the temple as best they could. But then the Turks invaded and stored their gunpowder in it; when the Venetians attacked with their flaming arrows, the rebuilt Parthenon exploded. What remained was later vandalized by Christians, turned into a church, then a mosque, then raided by an English lord. Marbles and reliefs that once graced Athena's temple are now the pride of the British Museum. Yet, Athena still guards the city. The Parthenon has been reconstructed once again. Now it's a tourist attraction with a fancy museum and gift shop. My mother and I admire it from the balcony of our hotel where we enjoy a dry red and eat spanakopita with flaky filo crust.

Seeing us marveling, the waiter asks us, "First time here?"

We nod. "It's so beautiful," my mother says.

The waiter bows. "When you live here, you feel proud but defeated. You know your best days ended two thousand years ago."

The Greeks were not innocent when the Persians invaded; they were not rubes. Their conversion to patriarchy had happened long before. Slaves did most of the labor and women were hardly allowed to participate in public life. Still, from the balcony I imagined that feeling of seeing your most sacred site, which evolved over thousands of years of building and refinement, celebration and ceremony, destroyed over and over again; it could create a bloodlust that would turn your people into hungry vampires for generations. Considering how most civilizations on earth have seen that kind of destruction, it's no wonder there's so much bloodlust, so many vampires.

My mother and I are both excited to go to Delphi, home of the ancient Oracle. It takes us three hours to get there from Athens by bus, winding up double-lane roads, stopping at a café that sells iced Café Alfredo, olive oil soap, Parthenon magnets, and Zeus snow globes. When we finally arrive at Delphi, our matronly tour guide tells us we will only get forty-five minutes to linger at the site. My mother squeezes my arm and gives me a sorry look. I want to be there, still and quiet, but tour groups jostle around, crowds spuming like ants across golden stones crumbled like croutons. Couples smile with selfie sticks; a tourist in yoga pants performs Dancing Warrior Pose on a scenic overlook. Offended, the sky gods thunder. Rain advances down the mountain. Grasshoppers shiver red-legged in the wild oats as I stand looking toward the sea. I imagine pilgrims as they made their way from their ships, leaving offerings at each temple while they trekked up through the valley, until they finally reached the temple of the Oracle; Delphi was once considered "the navel of the world." From all the most distant lands, for thousands of years, pilgrims, leaders, mothers, warriors, and politicians would travel to seek the Oracle's wisdom.

I hear rhythmic incantations and a drum; I look around to see if anyone else hears it. They don't. I can feel the Pythian crones flocking, landing on the columns, winking at me with sharp, black eyes. I don't feel like I was the Oracle in a past life, but I could've been at her service, a dancer maybe, or a mentee. Standing in her ruins, I ask the Oracle to show me how to bring her wisdom back into the world, to call the snakes back into the garden, to resurrect the Goddess of the earth. *To receive my words,* I heard her say, *open up your womb. You hear the voice of the goddess in your body, not your mind. Let your womb expand and be receptive. Spirit enters through the womb, as it did even for the Virgin Mary, as it does for all humans. Focus on listening. Spirit speaks through conception. Conceive in your body, then bring forth into the world.*

I didn't understand her to mean I needed to have a child, or even that I needed an actual womb. Women without wombs, transgender and nonbinary folks, and even men can still hear the Oracle speaking. She meant that through tuning in to our bodies,

306

to our organs of regeneration, we connect to the life force, and that by tapping into that energy, we can know the nature of reality, far beyond what we can experience through our limited ego-mind.

Delphi pushes out from between the legs of two mountains, crowning like a newborn, named after the dolphins that used to frolic in the bay below. Before the Olympian gods took over, the people of Attica worshipped the earth, the animals, the plants. The Oracle stood outside on a big black rock shaped like an anvil, called the Rock of the Sibyl. Her voice hammered across the valley, over olive groves, laurel, cypress, and pine, sailing out across the sea. Hers was a voice that echoed around the world. When the Byzantine Christians came, they chopped down the laurel and the pine groves; they had no use for them. But they kept the olive trees for their merchants; olives were useful. They could sell the oil.

My mother and I stood together surveying this once lavish and sacred place. "Can you imagine all of this set up for oracles now?" my mother asks me. I think of my appearance on *Tucker Carlson Tonight*; it's hard for me to imagine him kneeling and presenting me with a goat and a bushel of grain.

The ancient Oracle was skilled in poetics and had a flair for drama. "Know Thyself" was the epitaph inscribed above the entrance to her chambers. Chosen from the eldest and wisest women of the village, she would emerge from a crevice in the rock into a central temple, standing before a bronze cauldron decorated with sirens, griffins, and eagles' heads. She'd step into bellowing vapors of burning laurel leaves and say things like, "O holy Salamis, you will be the death of many a woman's son between the seedtime and the harvest of the grain." I appreciate how she says Salamis will cause the deaths not of soldiers but of women's sons. In Greece there is a saying that when a general looks at an army, he sees soldiers, whereas a woman sees only sons. Obviously, seeing sons instead of soldiers gives one a different perspective in relation to whether or not war is a good idea.

I can feel that the Pythia is old even before I go into the museum and learn from the guide that most of the Pythia were elderly. The image of an old woman, wizened, gaunt, eyes lined in kohl, stands in sharp contrast to the paintings of the oracle from the neo-Classical and Romantic periods, or even in recent films like the animated movie *300*. The patriarchy always depicts the Oracle at Delphi as a roofied nymphet draped in a transparent negligee, nipples pink, vibrating with desire to whisper her swoony maxims: *With silver spears you may conquer the world*. The perfect title for a classically Greek-themed porno.

Originally, the Oracles at Delphi were priestesses of the Snake Goddess, the divine essence of nature; Her serpents guarded groves of sacred trees throughout the Mediterranean, where she went by many names: Astarte, Ashtoreth, Ariadne, Neith, Wadjet, Isis, Ishtar, Inanna, Tiamat…But then the Olympian god Apollo arrived in the Oracle's temple.

As *his* historians tell it, Apollo, god of music and order, arrived in Delphi only to find the locals complaining about a hideous snake monster named Python. This she-monster lived in a sulfurous cave that just happened to be where the priestesses of the snake goddess gave their prophecies. Apollo plunged his golden arrow into the heart of the Python and smiled as she twisted and

308

bled upon the black rocks. When Apollo got back to the local tavern, bragging about his heroism, the locals cheered. Kind of like when the United States Army invaded Iraq and the Iraqi people were "dancing in the streets."

Apollo commanded the people to build his temple on top of the old one. There he would have *his own* prophetic priestesses. Worshipping in nature wouldn't do for Apollo; even glamping was too rustic for that blond beauty. Apollo liked nice things. Throughout his tenure at Delphi, it grew into a palace of world renown: columned courtyards rich with statues, a sphinx on a plinth donated by the wealthy Nazians, a five-thousand-seat amphitheater made of marble, treasuries filled with luxuries from around the world. Being a generous god, in honor of the slain Python, Apollo decreed that his priestesses would be named Pythia. That was the official title of the oracles at Delphi: Pythia, after the Python Apollo killed. The maw of the monstrous snake goddess would still hiss her wisdom, but now she would speak with the voice of Apollo.

Snakes in the ancient world kept the pests out of the grain storage; most of them weren't poisonous. But in mythology, the killing of snakes is almost always a dog whistle for the destruction of the goddess religions. As a child, on Saint Patrick's Day, my mother would make me green four-leaf-clover pancakes with mint chocolate chips and as I ate them she'd tell me about how Saint Patrick drove the snakes out of Ireland. What the myth really meant was that he drove the goddess-worshipping pagans out of Ireland. When the bards of patriarchy say *snake*, what they really mean is *goddess*. As when Saint George killed the dragon. Or when, in Mesopotamia, the hero Marduk killed the dragon goddess Tiamat.

She was creator of the universe; she held the Tablet of Destinies that allowed her to know all things. Marduk the hero came and took care of all that:

> *And the lord stood upon Tiamat's hinder parts,*
> *And with his merciless club he smashed her skull.*
> *He cut through the channels of her blood,*
> *And he made the North wind bear it away into secret places.*

Of course, if you invade a territory, take over its temples, and impose a new god, the conquered people won't just suddenly stop fighting and do as you tell them. In order for your new ideology to succeed, you have to either vilify the old gods (Snake Goddess becomes Satan, evildoer responsible for the downfall of humankind), or you allow people to follow their old traditions but tell them your new god is speaking through their old gods' mouth (Apollo speaks through the mouth of the Pythia).

After the Apollonian invasion, priests were assigned to "interpret" the Pythia's words. She still spoke her oracles, but the priests would follow up by saying, "What she really means is…" One time, the Oracle told Emperor Nero that, because he'd murdered his own mother, his presence at Delphi was an offense to the gods. Furthermore, she continued, his own days were numbered. "Seventy-three is going to kill you," she said. A prophecy I'm sure the priests found difficult to spin in Nero's favor. But it was also true. Eventually, a seventy-three-year-old man slayed the emperor. In the meantime, furious at her impertinence, Nero had the Oracle burned alive.

* * *

On the ferry to Crete, I splash myself in lavender oil and obsess about female pattern baldness. Does everything in a woman's life come in a female pattern? I didn't have a pastry at breakfast because I don't want to get female pattern diabetes. Over a chocolate croissant, my mother insists sweets and fat and food *do not* cause diabetes. It disturbs me when she makes assertions like these, because then I feel that I must cast into doubt all the other things she says that I trust and believe in. Her ideas about spirituality, her ideas about feminism and history, which I love and admire. "Either you have diabetes or you don't; there's nothing you can do about it," she says as she gobbles a piece of baklava as big as one of Aphrodite's golden doves. I don't believe her. Everyone in my family has diabetes. Before my grandmother died, she had her legs amputated because of it, but I tell myself I can stop it. Corkscrews of neuropathy twist through my mother's feet as if she were an accused witch of the medieval period. In Athens I'd watched her hobble over the cobblestone streets with her cane, protesting the distance between things in that ancient walkable city built before anyone had even thought of cars, when they still had to carry ceramic urns of water up the hills on their heads. It hurt to watch, but I consoled myself with the fact that the last time I'd tested my blood sugar about a year before, it was a satisfyingly low 73.

We arrive in Heraklion and convene on the rooftop of the Olympic Hotel for the opening ceremony of our Goddess Pilgrimage through Minoan Crete, led by Yale scholar Carol P. Christ. My mother is a fan of her work, so she arranged the tour for us.

Twenty women sit in a circle: lawyers, herbalists, college professors, social workers, artists, writers, PhD students, folk singers, seminary students, all ranging in age from twenty-five to seventy-five, with the bulk, not surprisingly, being in the later end of the age spectrum.

While we make introductions, I watch the swifts swooping in endless silhouette over the Mediterranean. Don't the swifts get tired? They never rest. They live to fly. Swifts are like swallows, only they never land; they even sleep midair, and they twirl in endless spirals above the white spires of this ancient city named after the conquering hero, Heracles.

We state our lineage. "I am Amanda, daughter of Lucinda, daughter of Patricia, daughter of Lila, daughter of Marianna, daughter of Emma...I come from a long line of women, some whose names are known, many unknown, going all the way back to the primordial Eve in Africa."

Our tour host, Carol, a blond septuagenarian, tall as an Amazon, wearing a purple straw hat and dripping with snaky gold jewelry, explains to us that on the island of Crete, before the age of heroes and war, there may have been a golden age where priestesses governed from sacred sanctuaries like the one at Knossos, which we will visit the following day. She tells us that women invented agriculture, weaving, pottery, and poetry. In Neolithic times, women were valued for their intelligence and so they had a lot of power. Crete was the last flowering of that culture because they were far away from the patriarchal hordes of the Indo-European invaders.

The next day we visit the sacred center of Knossos, an ancient complex of shrines, courtyards, and divination chambers. I inspect what remains of the frescos: Minoan priestesses dance in tiered skirts made of linen, stained as red as berries, as blood, serpents coiling up between their breasts and around their wrists, whispering secrets of the earth. In the frescos and figurines of Knossos, the people and animals are always smiling. The smiling priestesses dance, their long black hair arcing up toward the sun. They stand holding instruments, a lyre, a lute, or with their arms raised in joyful celebration. Even the men dance and leap, jumping over the smiling bulls, bringing offerings of fish to the Goddess and urns of wine.

At the museum, we see gold coins, rings, and other objects all depicting "the epiphany of the Goddess," the moment when the Goddess emanated from the earth. Bees roll in ecstasy inside juicy golden flowers. Like the bees, the Goddess appears hovering above her sacred tree; its fruits engorge and grow succulent. Below, her priestesses dance their exultant rites. Throughout the ancient world, the Goddess is often associated with groves of trees. In Sumer, priestesses of the goddess Asherah wore long woolen cloaks inlaid with white spiral shells and lapis lazuli. In groves of trees they worshipped her. In fact, in Greek, Asherah is translated as *grove*. When the Christians came, they cut down Asherah's trees and told her worshippers that their sacred grove was a thing of the past, a Garden of Eden that was no more. Besides, the garden was haunted by an evil snake.

Carol is careful to call the ancient sites we visit "sacred centers," rather than "palaces" as they are traditionally called. There is no evidence that these sacred centers were ruled by kings, no

313

evidence that there was the concept of "rule" or a segregated class-based society as we know it at all. In the Minoan sacred centers, half the village was dedicated to the storage of grain, wine, and olive oil, collections from the surrounding community to be shared with all those in need.

Wherever you find kings, you find warriors, their great deeds recorded and sung by bards, painted in fresco or carved into obelisks. After all, kings need someone to defend their treasure. But the Minoans have no art celebrating warriors, just dancing priestesses, women playing lutes, men joyfully leaping over bulls, and happy animals squawking and smiling. After the Mycenaeans invaded from the north, they brought their warrior ethic to Crete. They destroyed the temples of the Goddess and used the stones to build shrines to their own gods. Brutality seeped into Cretan art: men wrestling, stabbing each other with swords, stabbing lions as they grimace and roar. Warriors appear, raping women, pillaging villages, plundering wealth. With the Mycenaeans, warrior graves appear at the Cretan archeological sites. The Indo-European raiders rode down from the north, the sky god's thunderbolts igniting their torches. The warriors had no art, but they had very inventive weapons. Shiny swords inlaid with lapis, given names, like we do to corporations: Monsanto the destroyer, Nestle the drought-bringer. The priestess's sacred centers became the palaces of warrior kings, walled cities guarding treasures, women, and slaves.

We sit in our tour bus looking out across the sea as we're leaving Heraklion. The water is choppy and fierce, a tangle of swirls, like the designs on the ceramics shattered by the Mycenaeans. I'm sitting next to Sharon, a queer English professor from the Midwest with a passion for the work of Audre Lorde. She's always looking out for everyone, always asking after my mother. "Think how dangerous it must have been for the first Cretans arriving from Anatolia, rowing into that water on a small boat carved from a cypress tree," she says. I gaze at the choppy water and think of all the children, the Syrians, the Congolese, the Libyans, whose bodies wash up on these shores even now. If we could see with forensic goggles, the waters of the Mediterranean would be red with blood.

It's halfway through the tour. We check into a hotel high up in the mountains surrounded by citrus groves. A freshwater spring fills a pond at the local taverna where they breed the trout they serve at dinner. The full moon in Sagittarius hangs low over the cypress trees and I can hear locals playing their three-stringed lyra, practicing the songs for this evening when they'll teach us the steps of their folk dances. My mother rests in our room while I grab my things. The rooms are so cheap here, I decided to get my own room for the night. I know she's feeling hurt, even though she doesn't say anything, but I can tell by how withdrawn she is, how short her answers are.

"It's not your fault," I tell her. "Everybody snores. I'm just a sensitive sleeper."

"Of course. It's fine," she says, rolling over and putting on her eye mask.

"This way you won't have to worry about keeping me up and you can just relax."

315

She nods but says nothing. As I grab my bags, I notice her blood sugar test kit on the nightstand. "Hey, can I test my blood sugar?" I ask.

"Do you know how?"

"I think so."

"Well, don't use too many. I need them for the rest of the trip."

"I only need one," I say. "What was yours this morning?"

"Eighty-five," she tells me, and I feel relieved. Only a year before I'd nearly clobbered her when I found out she'd stopped taking her meds and her blood sugar had gone up to 300. "You could have gone into a coma!" I'd yelled. "You could have gone blind. You could have DIED. Can you PLEASE just take CARE of yourself?" She said she knew, that I didn't need to worry. But her answers were vague and unconvincing. It was like she had a shield up. Nothing I said penetrated.

I prick my finger and let the machine have a taste of my blood. "Beep," says the machine. The numbers come up: my blood sugar is at 95. Prediabetes starts at 100.

"My blood sugar is ten points higher than yours," I say, and feel a little like I'm sinking into the floor.

Lifting off her eye mask, my mother looks at me. "It might be because we're traveling. Maybe with the time change your body is confused..."

In the Sacred Center of Malia, Asha and I stand together in a circle of stones paved with chalky red clay the color of garden pots. Asha, a forty-eight-year-old herbalist from Montana with a serene smile and hair down to her thighs, is telling me how she was cast out by her biological white family at age fifteen for getting pregnant by a Native American man. "They called me a spiteful renegade hedge witch," she says, laughing bitterly, shaking her head. Her new partner's family took her in, the Shoshone women of the Rocky Mountains. They were kind to her and taught her their rituals, which is how she came to be interested in herbs. The Shoshone helped her with the birth of her child. Now she has six children.

As she's speaking, I feel a gripping in my womb and then a release. I tell Asha, "I just got my period five days early." Most of the women on our tour are past menopause, but still their bodies pulled my cycle toward our collective center.

"I know," she says. "I haven't had my period for eight months. Thought I was done. I had a croning ceremony and everything. But yesterday in the cave, I began to gush blood."

"It's so amazing how just traveling together for a few weeks can affect us... biologically," I marvel.

"Women naturally come into sync," she says, "It's like Wi-Fi. We get together and immediately we start to come in sync with each other. Our bodies, minds, and spirits connect."

As we speak, two snakes rise from between the smooth red rocks, coiled together in an ecstatic dance, the same black and white snakes that writhed around the wrists of the Cretan snake priestesses three thousand years ago. Asha and I stop and watch them, breathless, until the snakes part ways and hum back into their holes.

In the seaside town of Mochlos, I am befriended by Milena, a Bulgarian woman in her early thirties, tall with sharp cheekbones and dark almond eyes; when she smiles, she reveals a mouthful of beautifully crooked, smoke-stained teeth. A waitress at a seafood restaurant, she takes breaks from her service to dance Cretan folk dances with her boyfriend, a Greek man in his late seventies. She kneels on the ground, clapping while he performs a dance called the *robetiko*, a dance just for men, created by displaced people shunting the liminal lands between Turkey and Greece. Though aged and at least ten inches shorter than his Bulgarian girlfriend, he's proud and dances with all the passion and vitality of a god, stomping and kicking his feet, a cigarette dangling from between his fingertips.

"How did you two get together?" I ask my new friend.

She lights one of her filterless cigarettes and inhales, holds it. "I used to take care of his mother," she says, exhaling. "He was so kind to me. He arranged my papers. That's when we fell in love."

The owner of the restaurant comes to our table and apropos of nothing tells me the Bulgarian "works like an ox." She sends money home to her mother. He claps her on the shoulder and leaves.

"Everyone I know is in poverty," she tells me.

Milena gestures to an ancient Minoan site that sits atop a rocky island a hundred meters off the coast. Milena barely speaks any English; it's hard for me to understand her. "Vasilisa, Vasilisa," she tells me, urgently pointing to the island where there is a temple ruin and a cave full of bones. I recognize the word *Vasilisa* from the Russian fairy tale by the same name. But I don't understand what she means. Another waiter comes up and translates, "She's telling you that thousands of years ago, a powerful queen once ruled this

318

island." Milena looks at me proudly and nods, beaming, flashing her crooked teeth.

The "queen" she was referring to was probably Ariadne, the goddess worshipped all throughout Minoan Crete. The suffix -*ne* is not part of the Greek language, and so linguists suspect that it is a pre-Greek term from the Neolithic Cretan language. Ariadne was the Snake Goddess celebrated by the priestesses of Knossos. When the patriarchal hordes arrived, once again they changed the narrative. Whereas once Ariadne was a life-giving *goddess*, in the new version of the myth, she became a *princess*, daughter of King Minos. In the new version, when the Greek hero Theseus arrived on the island of Crete, the princess Ariadne fell helplessly in love with him. Wanting to conquer the land, Theseus convinced her to betray her people. "Help me slay the Minotaur," he begged her, offering her roses and rings and candy and all the other things girls like. The Minotaur was a bull that lived at the center of the labyrinth, sacred to the goddess; bull horns appear everywhere in Minoan art. Once Theseus killed their beloved beast, the people of Crete were understandably furious. They turned against Ariadne for helping him. By cover of night, the couple escaped together by boat, pushing out over the cold sand. But almost as soon as they left, Theseus got sick of hearing his new girlfriend crying, yammering on about all she'd lost. He left Ariadne on the shores of a deserted island and ran off with her sister. Devastated, Ariadne waited on a cliff for a week and then, realizing Theseus would never return, she hanged herself from a tree. Once a goddess, now a lovesick suicide.

* * *

In the afternoon, my mother is tired. We keep trying to connect but can't seem to do it. Slowly, we make our way back to the hotel from the restaurant where we had our lunch, eggplant moussaka and wild greens with capers, lemon, local olive oil, goat cheese, and oregano. I'm going to drop her off, and then, before we meet back up with our group, I want to swim out to the island with the ancient temple. I feel a sense of urgency as I walk next to my mother; I only have an hour and a half. She navigates the rocky terrain with her cane, fussing with the floppy hat the wind keeps blowing off her head, tangling the cord around her neck. "Let me hold your purse," I say. She hands it to me but doesn't look my way. Again, she's being short with me; I can feel something simmering beneath the surface but she won't tell me what it is. "What's wrong?" I ask her.

She shakes her head and says nothing. I worry that maybe she's sick. She left her diabetes medication in the refrigerator of the hotel in another town. "Were you able to find a pharmacy?"

"Yes, yes. That's all being handled."

We arrive at our hotel. The lock is tricky, but we make it into the room. With some difficulty, she lowers herself onto the bed. I want to leave, to grab my suit and go swimming, as today will be my last chance, but it doesn't feel like it's the right time. We sit in the dark room, curtains drawn, my mother having flung her arm over her face, listening to the incongruous sound of our neighbors next door, a bunch of college kids belting out Beyoncé, "All the single ladies," as they pound shots of raki.

Finally, my mother says, "You don't seem to want to be near me. Here we are together on this trip, who knows when we will get to

320

do something like this again, or if we ever will, and you don't even want to be around me."

I feel a flash of anger, as I always do, much to my own frustration, whenever my mother admits a vulnerability. Her woundedness is a shot fired, launching my chariot race. The words leap out of my mouth before I can even think: "It just feels like we can't have a conversation without you warning me or trying to modify my behavior. Asking me if I said thank you, telling me to pick up my purse. When you ask me about my book, you don't seem excited; you're just anxious I won't get it done in time. I'm on vacation. I don't want to be monitored all the time."

Stung, she responds quietly, "I'm your mother. I'm just doing that because I want to protect you. I want you to be happy."

"I'd be happy if we could have *one* interaction where you didn't criticize me."

"I'm just trying to protect you," she repeats.

I imagine most kids have arguments with their parents like this one, but for me, whenever my mother and I argue, there's always this rage hovering just beneath the surface. Our arguments quickly escalate. We're not here, in the hotel room in Crete; we're flying on broomsticks over my childhood, looking down on all the fires. All the ways we both went wrong.

We keep going, a few more back-and-forth exchanges, small accusations and defenses, excavating minor wounds, and then suddenly the fires leap up to lick us, catching our clothes. We leap, from the present moment, back three decades into the past in a single instant.

"You can't protect me. You never protected me. You were too

wounded, too broke, too broken. Every time I suffered, you just let it happen. You let yourself suffer, and you let me suffer with you. You were valedictorian of your high school, you could have done anything you wanted, and then you lingered on in these shit jobs, dependent on men who didn't love you, didn't care about you, never taking care of yourself, and we both paid the price for it. But *I'm* the difficult one. I was hard to raise. I'm the rebellious one that makes everything hard for you."

She sighs. Her sigh is a key that opens the door on one of our most familiar rooms and we both step in. The room is dark, heavy and hot, too close. It's a place my mother can really get comfortable; it's her territory. The room of her failures, my fury. The room that appeared in every house throughout my childhood, no matter which town or neighborhood. She doesn't get mad in this room. She takes everything on.

"I *knew* that you were angry. You've always been angry. I thought if I could just absorb it, just absorb it and absorb it, whatever anger that came my way, we'd be okay."

I see her absorbing like a swamp absorbs toxic chemicals. I didn't want her to absorb; I wanted her to make pollution unthinkable. "I didn't want you to absorb it. I wanted you to set limits. To set boundaries, to protect yourself and protect me."

"You *didn't* want me to set boundaries. You wouldn't accept them. I tried. You just plowed through and did whatever you wanted to do."

"I was a child."

"Nothing I did was ever good enough. You would run around; you wouldn't mind anyone."

322

"I hate that story. I was a child. I wasn't in control of anything. And you just gave in. You didn't fight for us." My heart is racing, my blood boiling, totally out of proportion to what is happening.

"I tried, Amanda. But I was doing it alone, and it wasn't easy. I was tired. I did my best…" She sinks back heavy into the bed. "But clearly it wasn't good enough."

I can never tell what's real when we get to this place. Am I mad because I'm truly mad, or am I just feeling defensive, worried that I'm making her life more difficult once again? Is she saying she wasn't good enough because she wants to make me feel guilty, or because she genuinely believes it?

"You've always wanted me to single-handedly fight the patriarchy and win. And I couldn't do it, Amanda. I'm sorry."

As she says it, I know it is true. I wanted her to protect herself. To keep us safe in a world where it was impossible *to be* safe. But the fact that she couldn't was not her fault. My anger was misdirected. I was angry at a larger system of injustice, not angry that my mother, with her library of goddess books and her apothecary of garden herbs, was not able to overthrow our entire patriarchal civilization by herself. I know that as a child I often directed my anger at my mother because she was the only person around who was ever willing to take any responsibility. In fact, she took *all* the responsibility. Absorbing it whether it was hers to take or not.

As we argue, I rearrange my things, unpacking and repacking my bags, shuffling for my bathing suit. As I did so, a little brown treasure rolls to the floor and under her bed, where my mother stares bleakly at the ceiling. Scrounging on my knees on the cold tiles, I fish it out.

323

"What's that?" my mother asks me.

I hold it up, a fibrous little brown locket. "It's a seed from that fruit that fell at my feet at Knossos." A few days before, when our pilgrimage had visited the sacred center of Knossos, Carol had been giving a lecture on the history of the goddess cultures, of Ariadne and Persephone and Demeter, while we pilgrims rested in the shade. And as she was speaking, a fat, fuzzy fruit fell from the apricot tree and rolled to a stop, just touching my sandaled foot.

"Oh yes!" my mother says, excited. "I remember seeing that. What a gift." She smiles at me and pats my hand.

"I'm sorry," I tell her, pushing up to sit next to her on the bed, clutching the seed in my palm. "You may not have been perfect; neither was I. But you brought me here. Not just here, to Crete, but here to my life. Everything I hold most dear and most sacred in my life is in it because of you." Like the tiny seed in my palm, that sacredness was both vulnerable and resilient at the same time.

"I love you," she tells me, the historic room of failure and fury dissipating around us as if it were a mirage. Using the arm of a nearby chair, she pushes herself to standing, ruffles my hair. "I'm just glad we get to be here together." She walks over to the window and pushes back the blue curtains. From where I sit, I can see the peeling white walls of the cantina across the street. A skinny black cat, blinking in the midday sun, nurses her kittens on the roof. "What are you going to do with the seed?" she asks.

"Bring it home. Put it on my altar. Try to make it grow."

She smiles, but I see a flash of nervousness. "How are you going to get it through customs? I don't think you're supposed to…"

"I guess we'll find out, won't we?" I say, wrapping the seed in a scarf and hiding it in my bag.

I know she wants to question me again. To make sure I won't get in trouble. But in keeping with her character, she also chooses peace. "To get it to grow, crack the pit open and soak the seed in water overnight. Then you can plant it and it will sprout."

That evening, we pilgrims perform a labyrinth ritual on the hillsides of Mochlos, gulls flying low in the pink sky as we walk the serpentine stone path in a procession through the town, then sing a revision of a Reclaiming chant:

> *She goes down and we go down*
> *We follow her underground*
> *Hail Ariadne, who dies and is reborn*
> *And deep calls to deep, and deep calls to deep . . .*

Jenny, an artist with quiet, watchful eyes, proceeds through the labyrinth first, performing the role of the Priestess of Ariadne. The only way to resurrect Ariadne is to practice her rites. She recites a poem to the ancient one, Minoan goddess of the labyrinth. "You have found center," our priestess tells each of us as we reach her. "Return to the world with joy."

A big part of our Goddess Pilgrimage involves descending into caves, into the underworld, literally. We go to so many caves, I lose track of which one is which. The mouth of Skoteino cave is wide, hidden in muffs of olive trees, dripping with bat guano and the green lace of ferns. *Skoteino* is the modern Greek word for darkness. Stones breathe and bleed in layered drips of rust, lichen green, and bone. Water drips to the floor along stalactites formed over a million years, their inner marrow gelled in deep time. Inside the cave is a dark cathedral, flying buttresses twisting organically through the shadows. We bring a ladder with us, to help us descend into the second chamber, a smaller and closer place, lit only by the sweet-smelling beeswax candles we carry. We lower the ladder and feel our way down the cool, stone curves.

Three thousand years ago, the Minoans left offerings in this underworld shrine, on an altar formed of a natural outcrop, talismans and other things to be cast into the abyss, a black gash exhaling digestive gases that smell of wet walls and damp earth. We must be careful not to fall into it ourselves. We set up our own menagerie of goddess figurines here, one for each of us pilgrims, showering them with flowers and libations of milk, honey, and wine.

Before we left for Crete, Carol had directed us to bring a stone from home that represented something we wanted to banish. I brought a black obsidian knife that I had collected at a geological shop while visiting my father in the north, a replica of a Native American tool. But Native American culture is not what I wanted to banish. I wanted to banish the bloodlust in my own culture that had enacted genocide on the Native Americans and then sold their culture at a gift shop. I wanted to banish the arrows that had killed the Python, that had lodged in my own heart, and that I had then directed against myself and others. I wanted to banish the weapons of trauma and abuse that had been used against the

326

women in my family for generations. I wanted to let go of any weapons I had picked up, like some scared fugitive backed into a corner, that I used to defend myself. I wanted to feel safe in the world without my weapons. I wanted to feel confident I could navigate the world without wounding others. I wanted all weapons to disappear.

One by one, with the pilgrims and goddess figurines as our witnesses, we stand in front of the abyss and present our objects. As each pilgrim stands before the chorus of candlelit faces, she chants:

Guide me Ariadne, guide me Skoteino, as I enter the darkness
I am stripped naked. I am letting go.

Finally, it's my turn. I walk, trembling, to the mouth of the fissure. To throw the stone into the void is a symbolic gesture, but because of the context, there in the dark, with our chanting echoing off the cool, wet stones, it feels real, real as the blade of the obsidian knife cutting into my clenched fist. I step up before the other women and try to speak but can't. I don't know why this is so hard. I hold up the knife, its sharp edges glinting in the candlelight. Without my weapons I'd be defenseless. Regardless of my desire for it to be otherwise, it's still a dangerous world. If I lay down my weapons, how will I protect myself? But the problem with weapons is as much as we turn them against the world, we turn them against ourselves: *Live by the sword, die by the sword.* To let go of my weapons means committing myself to finding healthier ways of dealing with conflict. Even if I don't always know what

327

those are, I know I need to be willing to fumble around in the dark until I can figure it out. "I'm sick of fighting against the dominator culture, of playing by its terms of engagement," I say. The women around me nod; they are not strangers to these battles themselves. "I want to find a new way of living. I want to use wands, not weapons." I hold the knife above my head and bellow: "I cast my weapons into the abyss!" With a grunt, I cast down the knife, listening to it clink against the cave walls and then disappear into the deep black void.

When each of our stones is gone, we extinguish our candles and sit in the pregnant darkness. It only takes a few moments before I lose my sense of direction. I can hear the scrape of the women's feet against the stone, the sound of their breath, I can feel them near me, but I cannot see them. I can feel them living, but the stones also feel alive, as does the earth itself. Each of us is anonymous. The dark is boundless; we reenter the womb, a time before we were even conceived. What were we then but earth? Wheat, minerals, insects, water sloshing against rocks, gurgling in pipelines, coursing down our mother's gullet to form our new bodies.

In our contemporary world, we build structures to take us as high into the sky as we can go. We want the penthouse apartment; we want to shout our dominion from the mountaintops. But we rarely go underground anymore. We go on subways sometimes, but they are brightly lit, packed with people, places where we wait impatiently to be taken from place to place while we read a book or listen to a podcast. We don't make it a regular practice any longer of being humbled inside the earth.

But what if we honored the underworld and its messages? If

we honored our trips into the unknowing and weren't always trying to rush back to productivity? What if, as a culture, when we visited the underworld, instead of trying to escape, we listened? Caves take us inward, to a place where civilization's rules and laws and authorities can't harm or defend us. In myth, the underworld holds gems, gold, and wealth. Only through the earth is wealth created. All wealth comes from the land. Our food, our work, our homes, our friends, our bodies; without the earth we live on, none of it exists. In our culture we don't remember what true wealth is. True wealth is our connection to the earth, our community, our ancestors, to the life force itself.

Our group sits meditating in the underworld of the cave until one of the women says, "Let there be light." We relight our candles and make our way back up to the surface. Unable to make the climb down, my mother is waiting at the mouth of the cave with Rebecca, a redheaded video artist from Canada with dark-rimmed glasses and a sassy bowl haircut. Rebecca had adventured around the world to make her art but felt queasy at the idea of descending into the cave. As each of us emerged into the light, my mother and Rebecca threw their arms up and rejoiced, embracing each one of us they exclaimed, "Oh, good! Another girl!" The feeling of being embraced like that for being a girl was surprisingly moving, like a bird flapping in my chest, a sense of lightness and motion. So many of us had faced disappointment from our fathers at not being boys. Ann, a Canadian folk singer in her seventies, tells us the story of how when her father came home from the hospital after the birth of the youngest sister in her family of four daughters, he'd locked himself in his study for two days and would not speak.

As we leave, we descend down the mountain through a field of wild grapevines and goat pellets, the tolling of sheep bells and bee hum. My mother points out the long soft ears of the mullein plant. I remember the sweet herbal taste of mullein because my mother used it to make my asthma medication when I was a child. Now the plant is healing her, inspiring her with its joyfully protruding stalks of yellow blossoms. She walks with the help of three women from our group as they sing to her:

Heal Lucinda, heal Lucinda, oh Goddess heal Lucinda, heal her with your love.

This is what magic is: singing in caves, lighting candles, meditating in groves of trees, taking care of each other. Rituals heal us because they honor our experiences; they help us to remember that the earth, and our lives, are sacred. And in fact, by doing these rituals, we *make* them sacred. We consecrate them. Ceremony can seem like a pain, climbing to the tops of mountains, lugging statues of goddesses and bottles of wine down the slippery inclines of a remote cave, singing, frequently off-key in the darkness after an exhausting day. But somehow, we do it and life takes on new meaning; we feel encouraged to keep going. But *our* healing alone is not the purpose. We must then go out and take that healing to the world, to whichever corners of the world we live in: doing spiritual work means creating justice for all beings.

We are exhausted, but still, later in the day we visit the Eilitheia cave, "the cave of the pregnant rock," hidden in a hillside fragrant

330

with purple thyme. Down the hill the sea sparkles, sapphire streaked with aquamarine, blinking bright as a peacock. At the entrance to the cave, a fig tree grows, bursting with fruit, humming with bees. As we step inside, we reach out to touch the stalagmites, round and smooth. Fat, naturally occurring fertility goddesses congregating at the center of the cave. When Minoan women wanted to conceive, they would rub their bellies up against these rock formations, a practice that continued well into Mycenaean times. Over thousands of years of caresses and supplications, the women wore the limestone figures smooth. But the heads of the goddess rocks are missing, their necks broken and raw. Women went to this cave for millennia to celebrate love and life, and when the Byzantine soldiers arrived, they hacked off the heads of the sacred stones with an ax. Everything the Goddess worshippers loved was destroyed. Their assailants wanted to make sure no stone was left undefiled.

The forces of patriarchal authority have destroyed our stones, our caves, our temples, our cathedrals. Turned our Goddesses into scorned women, whores. Controlled our wombs. Taken our bodies. Ignored our words. Burned us at the stake. But we are still here. Throughout history, in secret, witches have kept the fires of the divine feminine burning. Small coals, tended secretly in our caves. Our initiations are the pains of our labor. The Goddess is being reborn.

On the final day of our trip, we climb down the mountain from Kato Symi, an archaeological site where an ancient plane tree grows, hollowed out into a fold. The tree grows above a sacred

331

spring at the site of a Minoan shrine, which evolved over the millennia into a temple of Aphrodite and Hermes of the Tree. We follow the water down the hill to a family-run taverna where the spring flows freely for all weary travelers to drink from a marble spigot plugged into the mountain wall. All around the taverna, the creek flows into a series of pools holding schools of curious orange, white, and gold koi. We stand in a grove of cherry trees, the fat red orbs glowing in the leaves. Around the corner a braying donkey wants to eat our skirts, and a gaggle of chickens cluck. We set up an altar to Sappho, strung with flowers and jewels, incense smoking, just as she would have done it, with the poet's guardian, Aphrodite, goddess of love, at the center. Once the most famous poet in all of Greece, most of Sappho's work has now been lost to history and appears only in fragments, sometimes just a single word. But even in just that word, you can feel her longing for beauty, for love, to share its qualities with the women by her side. Each pilgrim chooses a poem to read out loud. Mine is a fragment about a young woman whom the poet loves, who has to leave the beautiful idyll in which they live, to return to her home town where she must be married, and according to Greek custom at the time, lose her freedom. Sappho says:

I have not had one word from her

Frankly I wish I were dead.
When she left, she wept

332

a great deal; she said to
me, "This parting must be
endured, Sappho. I go unwillingly."

I said, "Go, and be happy
but remember (you know
well) whom you leave shackled by love

If you forget me, think
of our gifts to Aphrodite
and all the loveliness that we shared

all the violet tiaras,
braided rosebuds, dill and
crocus twined around your young neck

myrrh poured on your head
and on soft mats girls with
all that they most wished for beside them

while no voices chanted
choruses without ours,
no woodlot bloomed in spring without song..."

I love to think of her, with the girls in the fields, and the oasis of beauty she created in a land clamoring with the swords of heroes and great men. After reading Sappho and pouring our libations, we honor the poets, activists, artists, and scientists who still influence us, to whom we are grateful: Dolores Huerta, Nina Simone, Remedios Varo, Hildegard Von Bingen, Marie Curie, Harriet Tubman, Sei Shōnagon, Emily Dickinson, Hypatia, Artemisia, Boudicca, Simone Weil, Toypurina, Ada Lovelace, Sojourner Truth, Enheduanna...we say their names and for each one we give an offering.

As our ceremony ends and our pilgrimage concludes, we ascend a stone staircase leading out of the grove. At the top stands Chloe, Carol's assistant, a PhD student of anthropology with a gift for making everyone's needs, no matter how impractical, seem worthy of being met. Beneath a bower of grapevines, she anoints each of our foreheads with oil of myrrh, her jade-green eyes meeting each of ours in turn. "Welcome to the Ariadne Sisterhood," she whispers.

My first initiations brought me into the underworld. Persephone playing in a field of flowers, taken to Hades by force, initiated into the ways of patriarchy, humbled there in the dark. But Persephone didn't just *eat* the seeds of the underworld...she WAS the seed. The seed of Demeter, goddess of the earth. The goddess within us goes underground, and in that dark, she grows and changes, until she bursts forth and becomes the tree that bears her own fruit. Our initiations are not the end. Our initiations mark a beginning. In the story of our species, and the story of our lives, our initiations come again and again, like waves. Our sorrows initiate us into the cult of the mysteries. They humble us before the power of the life force, the Goddess herself. However they find us, our initiations lead us into the underworld, where we witches, priestxsses,

334

and magical beings are keepers of the seeds. In winter the gardens die, but in the spring they are reborn.

We are the trees in Her sacred grove. We are Her seeds that grow. And now, we rise. Now we sing our songs, we pour our libations, we dance our dances, we make love in the fields, we link our arms, we stand together, we refuse to be dragged from the protest, we storm the prisons, we jam the phone lines, we tie ourselves to the trees of knowledge, we protect those trees, we eat their fruit, we plant their seeds, we march in the streets, we love, we resist, we re-enchant the world.

Gratitude
ɔ ɔ ɔ

Even for a project such as this one, which has required countless hours spent alone, there have been a thousand hands supporting me, without whom I'd have never been able to accomplish this work. First of all, thank you to everyone at Grand Central for all of your work, but especially Maddie Caldwell, my editor. Maddie, you were knight, page, and fairy godmother all in one. Thank you so much for holding the thread for me as I went down and fumbled around in the dark. You gave me courage. Thanks for your sensitivity and rigor and patience. And thank you so much to my agent, Adriann Ranta Zurhellen at Foundry. Thank you for finding me, for being such a hungry huntress, and for always knowing just what to do and how to do it. Your steadiness and professionalism have made the process of publishing so much easier than I ever imagined it could be. Thanks so much to you and the entire Foundry team.

For my more personal thanks, I have to begin of course with my mother, the first witch in my life. Mom, thank you for your endurance, your brilliance, your kindness, your unfailing belief in me, and your nuanced application of witchcraft. Thank you for encouraging me, not censoring me, and for being a constant source of knowledge and inspiration. And thank you, Will, for being such a great consort to my mother, for teaching me what it means to work in service, for all your kindness and humor. I don't know what our family would do without you. Thank you to my father and Linda, for your generosity and love, and your desire to bring us together as a family. Thank you, Dad, for wanting family, even when we don't always know how to do it perfectly; thank you for trying to create it with me. I think we're getting there in the end. Thank you to Conor for your joyful spirit, intelligence, and love. Thank you, Nick, for your curiosity and your calm. I feel so grateful to have you both in my life. Thank you, Steven and Vanessa, for coming in. Thank you, Gram, for the orange rolls and the brownies and the stories, and Pop for the chocolate milk and tigers. Thank you both for all your care; I never would have made it through my childhood without you. Thank you, Aunt Sandy, for always stepping in to help. Thank you, Steve, Larry, and Lance. Thank you, Aunt Tammy and Uncle Larry. Thank you, Jennifer. Thank you to all my family, who have given me endless support and certainly lots to talk about.

Thank you to my teachers: Nancy Yokabaitus, for putting me in G.A.T.E. I might not have made it if it wasn't for you. Jan Clouse, for getting me interested in language and craft. Val Rimmer, for holding me to a higher standard. Thanks to Nancy Buchanan, Bruce Bauman, Jon Wagner, and Berenice Reynaud, and all my other teachers at CalArts, especially Janet Sarbanes, Dodie Bellamy, John D'Agata, James Benning, Sam Durant, Thom Andersen, Steve Erikson, Gary Mairs, and Rebecca Baron. Ryuishin, Hojin, Hogun, and Daido at ZMM, thank you.

Thanks, Dr. Marion North, for giving me a chance. Francesca Lia Block, thank you for the inspiration, the wisdom, and cracking open the door for us literary witches. Thank you, Amanda Foulger, for the spirits, and Robert Allen, for the technique. Thanks for the reading, Lon Milo Duquette. And thanks, Jenn Witte, for your bookselling heroics.

Thank you to my friends, colleagues, and coven: Jade Chang, for always being my bridge over troubled water, let's sail on silver, forever. Margaret Wappler, so glad to be in this life with your bright spirit. Lauren Strasnick, for your loyalty and endless love. Milly Sanders, because I could just talk and talk and TALK with you, about everything. Nancy Stella Soto, we're *hacer-ing* it! Love you so much. And thank you, Max Maslansky, for being hilarious and brilliant. Thank you forever to Carolyn Pennypacker Riggs, for your love of magic, and for bringing the *Strange Magic* clan together. Thank you, Sarah Faith Gottesdiener. What would I do without you in my life? Thank you so much to all our *Strange Magic* listeners and to our worldwide coven; your support was essential in my garnering the strength to write this book. Thank you to Mary Lowry, for always promoting the project of witchcraft in the world. Thank you to Michael Massman, Stuart Krimko, Danielle Waldman, Joanne Wilmott, Kira Riikonen, Nikki Darling, Akina Cox, Brian Getnick, Christie Roberts Berkowitz, Deb Klowden Mann, Edgar Fabian Frias, Vera Brunner Sung, Brigid McCaffery, Jessica Ceballos, Salima Allen, Asher Hartman, Carol Che, Carrie Cook, Adrienne Walser, Reneice Charles for the biscuits, Leah Garza for the Zapatista quote, Michelle Garcia, Sophia Lyons, the WCCW,

Sophia Louisa Lee, Claire Anderson, Paradox Pollack, John Precour (thanks for breaking down '90s SF with me), Alexandra Grant, Zoe Crosher, Jillian Speer, Ginny Harper, Nancy Self, Kiran Mahto, Benjamin Sealey, Scott Jeffress, Bill Langworthy, Jordan Press, Carolyn Elliot (you made me go big or go home). Thank you, Niki Ford, for all the nourishment. Beth Pickens— OMG!! I couldn't have done this without your support. Thank you, Priscilla Frank, Agatha French, Lucianna Bellini, David Elliott, Kerry McLaughlin. Thank you to the witches of the Commons and Johanna Hedva. Melanie Griffin for the brilliant herb workshop. Michelle Tea for creating my first public reading experiences. Thank you to Michael M. Hughes, for all you've done for magic in the world. Thank you to Leslie, for traveling between the worlds with me. Thank you, Gabriel Garcia; our chapter together here had to be cut, but it would have needed volumes anyway; thank you for all your encouragement and support. Thank you, Matthew Houck; I see you across the snow and smile. Thank you, Benjamin Russell; you had to listen to me cry and stress, refuse the sunset, and nearly snap so many times, but you always showed up with kindness, generosity, and the best lentil soup under the sun. Thank you for sharing your genius with me. A huge thank you to my clients from whom I learn so much; it's such a privilege to be allowed into your worlds. Every day I thank the Goddess that we get to make our magic together. Thank you to Carol P. Christ and the women of the Ariadne Sisterhood; you're the source of the happy ending. Thank you to my ancestors, those who lived well and with love. Thank you to the Chumash and the Tongva people, on whose land I grew up. Thank you to all the unsung laborers who have made my life possible. Thank you, Pythia. Thank you, Boudicca. Thank you, Sappho. Thank you, Muses. Thank you, Medusa. Thank you to Mercury, Venus, and Jupiter. Thank you, Hecate; thank you, Ariadne; thank you, Persephone. Thank you, Demeter. Thank you, Earth. Thank you, magic. Thank you, witchcraft. Victory to the Goddess! Thank you to all my spirits, for showing up every day with humor and grace. Thank you to all the witches throughout time who made this work possible. I may not know all your names, but I have not forgotten you.